Japanese Gardens

Japanese Gardens

An Illustrated Guide to
Their Design and History

Josiah Conder, F. R. I. B. A.

With the SUPPLEMENT of Forty Plates & a New Preface by
Clay Lancaster

DOVER PUBLICATIONS, INC.
Mineola, New York

Bibliographical Note

Japanese Gardens: An Illustrated Guide to Their Design and History was first published by Dover Publications, Inc., in 1964, as *Landscape Gardening in Japan.* This volume is an unabridged and corrected republication of the second, revised (1912) edition of *Landscape Gardening in Japan,* and the *Supplement to Landscape Gardening in Japan,* both originally published by Messrs. Kelly & Walsh Limited in 1893. The Preface was specially prepared for Dover Publications, Inc., by Clay Lancaster.

Library of Congress Cataloging-in-Publication Data

Conder, J. (Josiah), 1852–1920.
    [Landscape gardening in Japan]
    Japanese gardens : an illustrated guide to their design and history ; with the supplement of forty plates & a new preface by Clay Lancaster / Josiah Conder.
        p. cm.
    Originally published: Landscape gardening in Japan. New York : Dover Publications, 1964.
    ISBN 0-486-41995-9 (pbk.)
    1. Gardens, Japanese—History. 2. Gardens—Japan—Design—History. I. Title.

SB458 .C66 2001
712'.0952—dc21

                                  2001028872

Manufactured in the United States of America
Dover Publications, Inc., 31 East 2nd Street, Mineola, N.Y. 11501

PREFACE TO THE DOVER EDITION

Josiah Conder, a promising English architect of twenty-five, went to Japan in 1877 at the invitation of the Japanese government to become the first Instructor of Architecture in the Engineering Department of the Imperial University. He is credited with having introduced the Western style into the island empire, and designed and built some seventy buildings, including the Imperial Museum, headquarters for the Navy Department, the Tokyo Club, the Austrian Embassy, the Russian Orthodox Church, the Yokohama Union Club, and mansions for Prince Arisugawa and Baron Iwaseki. He served as adviser to the Department of Public Works, the Department of the Interior, and the Department of Agriculture and Commerce, and held a special post on the Imperial Palace Construction Bureau. Conder was elected first President of the Institute of Japanese Architects, which was organized in 1886.

In addition to these activities that have to do with the propagation of Western architecture, Josiah Conder took a deep interest in certain native Japanese art forms. The publication of several books resulted from this interest. The first was *The Flowers of Japan and the Art of Floral Arrangement,* issued in 1891. It was illustrated with line cuts and color woodblock prints. The second, of greater concern to us because it was the original edition of the present work, was *Landscape Gardening in Japan.* It was published in 1893, a second, revised edition appearing in 1912. The book gives an historical sketch of the development of the Japanese garden and discusses such elements as garden stones, lanterns, pagodas, water basins, enclosures, wells, bridges, arbors, the use of water, vegetation, and the five species of gardens: hill and water gardens, flat gardens, ceremonial tea house gardens, passage gardens (in narrow approaches), and fancy gardens. Among the illustrations are lithographs by a Japanese artist, Mr. E. Koshima, some of them modeled on traditional woodcuts contained in the early nineteenth century book, *Tsukiyama Teizō-den,* one of which is reproduced here (Figure A). The cut depicts a *shin* style of *hira-niwa,* or flat garden, the prototype of Plate XXVIII in the present volume. One notes that the gate in the wall to the left and the edge of the porch floor in the foreground have been omitted from the later lithograph, and the garden space seems more constricted. In addition to the illustrations in the original volume, a supplement was prepared in 1893 composed of forty collotype plates of photographic views of famous gardens and natural settings. The photographs, taken in large part by Mr. K. Ogawa, constitute a valuable record of Japanese landscape art at the end of the nineteenth century. This supplement is reproduced in its entirety at the end of the present volume.

FIGURE A

FIGURE B

Floral Arrangement and *Landscape Gardening* were among the earliest books to acquaint the West with the fundamental principles of these exotic arts. As such they exerted considerable influence, both directly and indirectly. For instance, an article in the July 1908 issue of *House & Garden* bore the same title as the second Conder work. The text incorporated material from the book, illustrated by six of the lithographs—the legends were set below the prints rather than in the side margins. The frontispiece for the article depicted a *sansui* (hill and water) garden, designated a favorite among the Japanese because it is a small-scale version of the mountains where they love to vacation. The American rock garden seems to have originated from this source, in reaction to the then-prevalent Western garden based on a two-dimensional symmetric layout featuring geometric beds of perishable flowers.

A number of Americans learned Japanese gardening through personal contact with Josiah Conder. One of the most talented was John Scott Bradstreet, a New Englander who settled in Minneapolis, Minnesota, in 1874, and for the next forty years contributed to the cultural development of that city. He opened a small shop which expanded into the nationally-known Bradstreet Crafthouse, an establishment employing skilled artists and artisans dedicated to creating beautiful interiors. The Crafthouse included Japanese on its staff after John Bradstreet made his first trip to Nippon in 1886. Afterwards he made biennial journeys to the East, alternating these with visits to Europe. About 1900 the Bradstreet Crafthouse moved into its permanent home, a remodeled Italianate villa on Fourth Avenue at Seventh Street. The renovation embodied oriental touches. One entered the grounds through a Japanese gateway, and temple carvings adorned the front door. A Japanese garden was laid out next to a side porch, with gravel paving, ornamental boulders, an artificial mountain of stones, imported planting, and screen fences (Figure B). Bradstreet created other Japanese gardens for his own home and for clients. His most ambitious landscape project involved converting a series of lakes and streams bounding Minneapolis on the west and south into a reproduction of Japan's Inland Sea, with Japanese *torii,* stone lanterns, bronze cranes, pagodas, open pavilions and arched bridges lending authentic atmosphere. However, the dream was not realized as Bradstreet envisaged it.

Josiah Conder's influence in bringing Western art forms to Japan and Japanese forms to the West challenges estimation. He dealt in the two styles without synthesis. His own home in Tokyo, begun in 1903, bears out this fact. He married a Japanese, the former Miss Kameko Mayeba, and half of their house was in the indigenous manner for Mrs. Conder, while the other half was in the Old English style.

Josiah Conder was honored by the Japanese Court with the Third Class Order of the Sacred Treasure and the Fourth Class Order of the Rising Sun, and was awarded a Doctorate of Engineering by the Tokyo Imperial University. Following his decease in 1920, his memory was perpetuated by a life-size bronze portrait statue erected in front of the College of Engineering at the University, where he had been Professor of Architecture for eleven years.

CLAY LANCASTER

Brooklyn Heights, New York, January, 1964

PREFACE TO THE FIRST EDITION.

The favourable reception accorded to his work on the " Flowers of Japan, and the Art of Floral Arrangement," has encouraged the author to issue another volume on the more comprehensive but kindred Art of Landscape Gardening. His researches into the subject date from several years prior to their present publication in book form. In May, 1886, he contributed to the " Journal of the Asiatic Society of Japan" a paper in which the theory of Japanese garden composition was first laid before European readers. Prof. E. S. MORSE published in the same year a popular work on " Japanese Homes and their Surroundings," in which were described and illustrated some of the picturesque features of the city garden. Mr. F. T. PIGGOTT'S recent artistic publication, entitled " Garden of Japan," is a diary of the seasons, with running comments in that writer's own attractive style. In July, 1892, Mr. LAFCADIO HEARN contributed to the *Atlantic Monthly* several charmingly written chapters treating of the ethical side of gardening as practised in this country.

The present work is an exposition of the rules and theories of the Art of Landscape Gardening in Japan, as followed from ancient to modern times, so far as they can be gathered from a thorough study of native authorities, added to personal observation of the best remaining examples. A treatise of the kind, aiming at some degree of completeness, must necessarily include much that is rudimentary and by no means exclusively peculiar to Japanese design; but the writer's task is partly accomplished if he succeeds in showing that beneath the quaint and unfamiliar aspect of these Eastern compositions, there lie universally accepted Art truths.

To those desirous of reproducing elsewhere a model garden after the correct Japanese fashion, this copiously illustrated volume should afford some aid, and at the same time impart a meaning to methods which, unexplained, possess merely the empty charm of novelty. Some may, however, hold that landscape gardening should be typical of the scenery of the soil, and regard the servile imitation of a foreign style as unnatural and purposeless. To this class the abstract principles of the Art may prove not totally unworthy of attention, and may even supply suggestion for a modified form of Western gardening. Robbed of its local garb and mannerisms, the Japanese method reveals æsthetic principles applicable to the gardens of any country, teaching, as it does, how to convert into a poem or picture a composition, which, with all its variety of detail, otherwise lacks unity and intent.

The following Japanese publications have been consulted in the preparation of this work :—

Tsukiyama Teisaku Den, by Hishigawa Kichibei.	1633.
Tsukiyama Teizo Den, Part 1, by Kitamura Enkin.	1736.
Miyako Rinsen Meisho Zuye, by Akisato Ritoken.	1800.
Somoku Sodate-gusa, by Abe Rekisai.	1815.
Tsukiyama Teizo Den, Part 2, by Akisato Ritoken.	1829.
Ishigumi Sono-U Yayegaki Den, by Akisato Ritoken.	1829.
Kinsei Zu-Fu, by Choseisha	1832.
Tsukiyama Sansui Den.	1838.
Sakutei-no-Ki (Manuscript), by Gokiogoku Kakuo.	1838.
Engei-Ko, by Yokoi Tokifuyu.	1891.
Zukai Teizo-Ho, by Honda Kinkichiro.	1891.
Fuzoku Gwa-ho (Magazine).	1891 and 1892.
Tsuikiyama Sansui Teizo-hiden, by Takatsu Chugoro.	1892.

The author has freely borrowed from these books to illustrate his subject. In the recent work by Mr. K. HONDA, the diagrams of gardens from KITAMURA's " Tsu-kiyama Teizo Den" are represented in a modern style of drawing by lithography, and some of these plates have been reproduced for the present work by Mr. E. KOSHIMA, the lithographer associated with Mr. HONDA.* Full acknowledgments are tendered to both of these gentlemen. The help afforded by Mr. UDAKA SANZO in procuring matter, and by Mr. MAYEDA RENJIRO, in revising Japanese names, calls for thankful mention. The writer also desires to record his grateful indebtedness to Mr. W. B. MASON for considerable aid and many useful suggestions, and to Mr. J. E. BEALE for valuable technical advice and generous assistance in bringing out the work.

Tokio, June, 1893.

*In this Dover edition, these plates are reproduced as black-and-white halftones.

CONTENTS.

LIST OF ILLUSTRATIONS.

PLATES.

XIV

FIGURES PRINTED WITH THE TEXT.

FIGURE.

LANDSCAPE GARDENING IN JAPAN.

INTRODUCTION.

A garden in Japan is a representation of the scenery of the country, though it is essentially a Japanese representation. Favourite rural spots and famous views serve as models for its composition and arrangement. The laws of natural growth and distribution are closely studied and punctiliously applied in the management of even the smallest detail. The artificial hills, rocks, lakes, torrent beds, and cascades of gardens are copied from striking features in the varied landscape of the country.

To one acquainted with the peculiar characteristics of Japanese scenery, even the grotesquely shaped trees and shrubs of gardens lose much of their weirdness. But a familiarity with the type of landscape prevailing in Japan is not sufficient to remove entirely the impression of fantastic unreality which the designs of the landscape gardener produce on the minds of Westerners.

In these compositions, as in the pictorial works of painters of the old school, there is an absence of that perfect realism which we are accustomed to look for in a naturalistic art. The same subjection to conventional cannons noticeable in the works of the Japanese landscape painter, is paramount in the compositions of the landscape gardener. A representation of nature is, in neither case, intended to be a completely realistic reproduction. The limits imposed by art in Japan require that all imitation should be subject to careful selection and modification. It is this habit of selection which tends, though perhaps unconsciously, to an exaggerated accentuation of leading characteristics. Lovers of Western art, with its more comprehensive and self-effacing methods, will doubtless find in the results of such restricted mannerisms something of the sensual and grotesque. On the other hand, the more subtle and emotional representations of European artists appear to the Japanese, in a similar degree, weak and insipid.

Though the people of this country, both high and low, are unrivalled in their genuine love of nature, their manner of observation and enjoyment is one peculiar to themselves. It is a taste educated through the medium of their traditional customs, arts, and cults. The national interpretation of nature, stereotyped into motives for their numerous liberal arts, has been continually before the humblest classes, in decorative designs applied to the simplest as well as to the most costly industrial object, and has thus made them familiar with the accepted rendering of every form and combination derived from natural life. Such conventional representations have become the standard by which nature herself is viewed and judged. As with the Greeks, so with the Japanese, even female beauty has its established ideal type. In a similar manner, the pine tree, the plum tree, mountain, lake, and water-fall, possess their ideal standard of comparison.

Japanese landscape gardening may therefore be described as a representation of the natural scenery of the country as it appears to and impresses the Japanese themselves, in a manner consistent with the limitations of their arts. Transferred to a foreign clime where landscape presents itself in a different garb, and regarded by a people who interpret nature in another manner, these lovely gardens can hardly fail to appear as examples of a quaint and fanciful conceit.

It is almost a matter of surprise that history affords so few examples of a style of gardening truly representative of natural landscape. In England, at the close of the eighteenth century, garden compositions first assumed a character of freedom which was called the *Natural Style*. The noted gardens of the ancients prove to have been formal orchards and plantations of the most artificial kind. The famous hanging gardens of Babylon were simply elevated terraces of evergreens enriched with formal architectural constructions. The Roman style was distinguished by similar regularity and restraint. External nature was excluded by a square enclosure containing terraces, canals, fountains, balustrades, and monuments in strictly geometrical arrangement. Even the trees and shrubs were planted in rows and squares, and their foliage cut into formal and unnatural shapes. Elegant symmetry and methodical order were the chief characteristics of this style. The romances of the middle ages have lent to the gardens of that period a charm which is, however, chiefly one of enchanting words. "Fair Rosamond's Bower" was a square hedged enclosure of regularly planted trees; the *labyrinth* of mediæval verse was a thick plantation or shrubbery crossed by narrow tortuous paths.

The Renaissance led to the re-introduction of all the stately architectural grandeur of the Roman gardens. In the grounds of the principal French palaces this uniformity was followed to an extraordinary degree. Trees, shrubs, flower beds, walks, and earthworks were disposed in stiff lines and geometrical combinations. Stretches of refreshing water became straight canals and circular or oblong basins, adorned with artifical fountains and edged with ashlar work. For the rest, the grounds were crowded with stately ornaments in the form of statues, vases, balustrades, and steps. Yet it was the garden of Versailles, a noted example of this unnatural style, which, a contemporary author asserted, was to him a foretaste of Paradise!

England, following the fashion of the Continent, was not long in adopting the same formal treatment for the pleasure grounds of mansions and palaces. It was the Dutch influence that introduced into the English style a further abuse of nature, in the clipping of trees and shrubs to resemble the outlines of statues, animals, and even such trivial objects as vases and tea-cups. Perhaps these extreme absurdities were the ultimate cause of a change of taste resulting in the development of a more natural style. The park, a peculiarly English feature, had long presented a refreshing contrast to the formality of orthodox garden arrangements. Semi-cultivated reaches of forest land, mead, and water, these English parks were kept for the enjoyment of primeval nature little altered by the hand of man. The national taste for rural pursuits that distinguishes the English people, may have assisted in rendering popular a new style of natural gardening in which all the most cherished classical precedents were discarded.

Horace Walpole, in his well-known treatise upon landscape gardening, has attributed to Milton the first conception of a garden designed in all the freedom and variety of natural scenery. In the poet's description of Eden, he says:—

—from that sapphire fount the crisped brooks
Rolling on orient pearl and sands of gold,
With mazy error under pendent shades,
Ran nectar, visiting each plant, and fed
Flow'rs worthy of Paradise, which not nice art
In beds and curious knots, but Nature born
Pour'd forth profuse on hill, and dale, and plain,
Both where the morning sun first warmly smote
The open field, and where the unpierced shade
Embrowned the noontide bowers : thus was this place
A happy rural seat of various view.

Kent and Bridgman were the first artists who applied to practical gardening the modern principles for which writers and others had prepared the public taste. How novel and original this new departure was considered at the time, may be seen from the following panegyric on the designer Kent:—"Painter enough to taste the charms of landscape, bold and opinionated enough to dare to dictate, and born with a genius to strike out a great system from the twilight of imperfect essays, he leaped the fence and saw that all nature was a garden. He felt the delicious contrast of hill and valley changing imperceptibly into each other, tasted the beauty of the gentle swell or concave scoop, and remarked how loose groves crowned an easy eminence with happy ornament, and while they called in the distant view between the graceful stems removed and extended the perspective of delusive comparison. Thus the pencil of his imagination bestowed the art of landscape on the scenes he handled." The new style thus inaugurated under the name of *Landscape Gardening* could, however, only be applied to a portion of the grounds. Whilst the distant parts of the garden were laid out according to the novel principle of picturesque irregularity, the areas adjoining the mansion were required to accord with the formality of the adjacent architectural constructions. Thus the parterre, terrace, avenue, and other strictly geometrical arrangements were retained in the foreground. Symmetrical design and accidental irregularity were blended in the same compositions, one enclosure containing both the formal garden and the natural landscape. It was not long before this taste for imitation of indigenous scenery, and for freedom of design, began to degenerate into license and extravagance. Fictitious and imaginary scenes were selected in preference to a faithful representation of nature. A fancy for distant and less familiar landscape, clothed by literature in fascinating imagery,—which inspired the early painters of this century,—was displayed also in the garden compositions.

Poetical associations connected with monuments and ruins of antiquity caused them to be considered desirable adjuncts to picturesque landscape gardening. No structure seems to have been thought too foreign or incongruous to administer to this new fancy. Greek temples, ruined Roman aqueducts, Italian bagnios, Turkish kiosks, Chinese bridges and pagodas, were capriciously scattered in the same design. Extravagant, not to say mendacious, descriptions of Oriental splendour assisted to excite this passion for fantastic luxury. Sir William Chambers, a famous architect and scientific writer of the middle of the last century, has left a most marvellous picture of Chinese gardening derived, as he says, from his own observations in China, from conversations with Chinese artists, and from remarks transmitted to him at different times by travellers. After a long dissertation on Oriental gardening in general, he continues;—
" The Chinese, in their large gardens contrive different scenes for different times of the day, disposing at the points of view buildings which from their use point out the

proper hour for enjoying the view in its perfections. * * * They have besides scenes for every season of the year : some for winter, generally exposed to the southern sun, and composed of pines, firs, cedars, evergreen oaks, phillyreas, hollies, yews, and many other evergreens, being enriched with laurels of various sorts, laurestinus, arbutus, and other plants ; and to give variety and gaiety to these gloomy productions, they plant among them in regular forms, divided by walks, all the rare shrubs, flowers, and trees of the torrid zone, which they cover during the winter with frames of glass disposed in the form of temples and other elegant buildings. * * * Their scenes of spring likewise abound with evergreens, intermixed with lilacs of all sorts, laburnums, limes, larixes, double-blossomed thorn, almond, and peach trees ; with sweet brier, early rose, and honeysuckle. The ground and verges of the thickets and shrubberies are adorned with wild hyacinths, wall-flowers, daffodils, violets, primroses, polianthus, crocuses, daisies, snowdrops, and various species of the iris ; * * * and as these scenes are also scanty in their natural productions, they intersperse amongst their plantations menageries for all sorts of tame and ferocious animals and birds of prey ; aviaries and groves, decorated dairies, and buildings for the exercise of wrestling, box-ing, quail fighting, and other games known in China. * * * Their summer scenes compose the richest and most studied parts of their gardens. They abound with lakes, rivers, and water-works of every contrivance, and with vessels of every construction, calculated for the uses of sailing, rowing, fishing, fowling, and fighting. The woods consist of oak, beech, Indian chestnut, elm, ash, plane, sycamore, maple, arbutus, and several other species of the poplar, with many other trees peculiar to China. The thickets are composed of every deciduous plant that grows in that climate, and every flower or shrub that flourishes during the summer months ; all uniting to form the finest verdure, and most brilliant harmonious colouring imaginable. The buildings are spacious, splendid, and numerous, every fence being marked by one or more ; some of them contrived for banquets, balls, concerts, learned disputations, plays, rope dancing, and feats of activity ; others again for bathing, swimming, reading, sleeping, or medita-tion. In the centre of these summer plantations there is generally a large tract of ground set aside which is laid out in a great number of close walks, colonnades, and passages, turned with many intricate windings, so as to confuse and lead the passenger astray, being sometimes divided by thickets of underwood, intermixed with straggling large trees, and at other times by higher plantations or by clumps of rose trees and other lofty towering shrubs. The whole is a wilderness of sweets, adorned with all sorts of fragrant and gaudy productions ; gold and silver pheasants, peafowls, partridges, bantam hens, quails, and game of every kind swarm in the woods,—doves, nightin-gales, and a thousand melodious birds perch upon the branches ; deer, antelope, spotted buffaloes, sheep, and Tartar horses frisk upon the plains ; every walk leads to some delightful object, to groves of orange and myrtle, to rivulets whose banks are clad with roses, woodbine, and jessamine ; to murmuring fountains, with statues of sleeping nymphs and water gods, to cabinets of verdure, with beds of aromatic herbs and flowers, to grottoes cut in rocks, adorned with incrustations of coral shells, ores, gems, and crystalisations ; refreshed with rills of sweet scented water and cooled by fragrant artificial breezes."

To such imaginary descriptions as the above may partly be attributed the extravagant taste for grotesque garden structures of Eastern form, and for a confused variety of fanciful scenes, which gradually destroyed the naturalness of English landscape gardens.   A demand for every kind of exotic plant and tree accompanied this fashion for the imitation of foreign and antique constructions.   Gardening had its scientific as well as its artistic side, and advances in horticultural science led to the collection of botanical specimens from all parts of the globe.   Tropical vegetation, which refused to flourish in a temperate climate, was enclosed in conservatories and reared by artificial heat, and the winter-garden became an essential adjunct of every gentleman's grounds.

This short reference to the history of English gardening has seemed necessary in order to form some comparison with the style of composition practised in Japan, the manner of treatment followed in the two countries each claiming to be considered a *Natural Style*.   While to a great extent the same æsthetic principles control both methods, wide differences exist in many points.   And here it may be advisable to disclaim any intention of depreciating the numerous attractions of European gardens, or the unsurpassed progress which horticultural art has attained in Western countries. It is the *artistic* aspect of Japanese gardens, as shown in the methods of design employed, which will be mainly considered in the present treatise.

An examination of landscape gardening, as taught and practised by the Japanese, reveals an art of considerable refinement, built upon a charming system of ethics. Following, with but rare exceptions, the model of the scenery around him, the designer is not tempted to represent nature in combinations with which he is unfamiliar.   It being contrary to his principles to admit into compositions exotic productions, with the conditions and surroundings of which he is imperfectly acquainted, he invariably selects as his material the vegetation and natural products of his own country.   The resulting arrangements have always the merit of consistency, and are rarely disfigured by hybrid and incongruous elements.   Even the structural ornaments introduced, partake of the character of national constructions and monuments, and are therefore suggestive of the real landscape of Japan, or of the kindred type of China. Garden bridges, pagodas, shrines, and arbours, are but miniature representations of the larger rustic structures which occur as a part of every rural view.

The art, however, is not entirely free from unnatural eccentricities. To a limited extent the clipping and carving of trees and bushes into such shapes as mountains, water-falls, boats, and buildings, may be noticed in ancient and even modern gardens ; but such vagaries are kept within the bounds of moderation. For the most part the artificial contours thus imparted to certain trees and shrubs, are a more or less conventional imitation of favourite types of growth observed in nature. The force of character displayed in less frequent rather than in commonplace types is to the Japanese mind one of nature's chief charms.

The gardener's model pine tree is not the ordinary pine tree of the forest, but the abnormal specimen which age and tempest have moulded into quaint and unusual shapes. (See Fig. 1.)

But whether or not the Japanese conception be the ideal art-expression of nature, it is undoubtedly governed in its execution by a scrupulous attention to æsthetic rules. Considerations of scale, proportion, unity, balance, congruity, and all that tends to produce artistic repose and harmony, are carefully preserved throughout the designs.

FIG. 1.

It has been customary among this people to divide most of their liberal arts into three degrees of elaboration,—one distinguished by the roughest and sketchiest treatment, another by the highest finish and minutest detail, and the third by an intermediate character. Whichever of these three manners is adopted in a work of art, it must be consistently followed throughout, and by this means is avoided the conflicting combination of coarse and delicate treatment in one and the same design. Arbitrary and confining as such restrictions may appear, they are actually conducive to the simple harmony pervading Japanese compositions, which, whatever may be their other defects, are seldom wanting in congruity and unity.

A landscape garden in Japan is more than a simple representation of natural views, it is at the same time, a poetical conception. As tersely put by another writer, it expresses "a mood of nature and also a mood of man." It is intended to have a character distinct from that of rough or delicate execution—though one to which the degree of elaboration partly contributes. According to this theory, a garden should be designed to suggest a suitable idea and arouse definite pleasurable associations. In some cases, a rural scene of historic interest may be presented to the fancy; in others, a purely abstract sentiment may be expressed.

The æsthetic principles governing the art are hardly separable from the ethics which inspire them. The sage, the poet, and the philosopher, have been in Japan the chief patrons and practitioners of the accomplished arts. The art of painting, the tea cult, the floral art, and also the art of landscape gardening, are alike enveloped in an atmoshere of quaint philosophy. It is customary to invest with the mystery and sanctity of philosophical import, rules and theories of design which might be easily explained by mere considerations of artistic taste. An appeal to superstitious reverence seems to have been thought necessary in order to preserve the arts in their purity, and prevent them from degenerating into license. Thus, that which offended the taste of the cultured was forbidden to the vulgar, as being inauspicious. Combinations in design, destructive of æsthetic harmony, were placed under the ban of ill-luck; and others productive of artistic repose were classed as specially propitious.

The early philosophy of Japan taught that the inanimate objects of the universe were endowed with male or female attributes, and that the beauties of the physical world were created by a mysterious blending of the sexual essences. Ideas derived from these ancient axioms were applied to the composition of landscape gardens. Obedience to laws of balance, contrast, and continuity in line, form, mass, and colour, applied to the component parts of gardens, was enforced through the medium of such precepts. Rocks, trees, stones, and even water-falls were endowed with imaginary sex, determined according to their correlative æsthetic value in artificial compositions. Strong, erect, and stately forms were classed as male in character, and paired or balanced with forms of opposite or *female* quality. Beliefs as to fortuity in connection with different aspects exercised considerable influence upon the laying out of grounds. The cardinal points governed and restricted the gardener, not for climatic reasons alone, but on account of particular occult virtues attributed to directions. The flow of lakes and streams through grounds, the points for their inlets and outlets, the position of gates, and the disposition of buildings, were partly controlled by rules founded on such superstitions.

Great care seems to have been taken by teachers of the craft to preserve purity of style. Japanese writers denounce the tendency to make the garden a display of wealth and luxury by over-crowding it with collections of rare plants and rocks. The vulgar ostentation of such methods is condemned as being detrimental to the highest aims of the art, which should be inspired by a genuine love of nature, with the object of enjoying, within a narrow compass, some of the varied beauties of natural scenery. Gardens should be so arranged that the different seasons may contribute in rotation to their artistic excellence. They should form refreshing retreats for hours of leisure and idleness,—or, as oddly expressed by a native writer, " places to stroll in when aroused from sleep,"—rather than resorts for the pleasures of society.

The ideal Japanese garden being therefore, before all, a retreat for secluded ease and meditation, it should be in accord with the temperament, sentiments, and occupation of the owner. The garden of the priest or poet may be designed to express a character of dignified solitude, virtue, and self denial; that of the *samurai* should be of bold, martial character. Other sentiments, such as peaceful retirement, modesty, prosperity, old age, and connubial felicity, have been attributed to famous historical examples. Fanciful as such theories at first thought appear, they can be shown to be not incapable of practical application. Nature in her changing moods,—placid, gay, savage, or solitary,—arouses in the soul of man emotions of varied shades, according to his temperament and culture. Traditional and historical associations also assist in conveying such impressions. Like the symbols of mediæval art, many of the motives of Japanese decoration have become in themselves expressive of moral virtues. In the horticultural art, the Elysian Isle, the lotus-covered lake, the pine tree, the plum tree, the bamboo, the suggested shapes of tortoise and crane, and even the antique well, have all an art-language of their own helping to convey some familiar sentiment.

The subjection of a garden to the lines and disposition of the adjoining buildings is by no means disregarded. It is, however, a subordination entirely different from that followed in Western styles, and in its own manner far more complete. The plans of domestic buildings in Japan differ in two important particulars from those of European constructions. These peculiarities,—namely, the absence of symmetry and lack of compactness,—render them far more consistent with freedom of design in the surrounding gardens. The aspect most desirable for the dwelling rooms, and the external prospect which they are intended to command, govern the whole arrangement of plan, to which any irregularity may be given, so long as it assists in providing important chambers with a desirable outlook. These objects, aided by the light, low character of the buildings, lead to the habit of dividing different parts of the same establishment into separate blocks connected by covered passages of sometimes very intricate design. Such irregularity of distribution renders consistent a variation in character for the different parts of the garden, according to the purpose and importance of the nearest adjacent chambers. In a single and continuous enclosure, this variation will not be allowed to interfere too visibly with the prevailing character and unity of the whole composition. It is, however, an important rule in laying out grounds that the class of building or of chambers adjoining must control their style and character.

An elaborately finished garden, full of delicate details, is suitable for being laid out in front of the state apartments of a nobleman, whereas one rough and sketchy in style, is fitted to face a tea-room or a rustic retreat. The particular aspect of the garden, as seen from the important rooms, is carefully considered in designing, and the composition is elaborated so as to present pleasing combinations from other points of view. Like the modeller who works alternately in front and profile to produce a model perfect from all points of view, so the gardener tests his masses, groups, and contours from the different situations of the spectator. Such situations are, principally, the rooms of the over-looking residence, and, in a secondary degree, points in the garden marked by important stones, bridges, arbours, and summer-houses. It is true that such principles are by no means neglected in Western landscape gardening; but the more formal and compact character of our buildings renders less essential the careful consideration of so many different aspects.

The perfection of a large and elaborate garden in Japan will often consist in the number and diversity of these views, contrived so as to preserve unbroken the unity of the whole composition. Such scenes include not only the contours and features of the grounds themselves, but in many cases, the external prospects. Wherever possible they are made suggestive of famous natural views celebrated in poetry and romance. And in this connection, a charm attaches to the mere employment of certain numbers. Eight is a favourite number for garden prospects, in allusion to the *Hak-kei*, or Eight Views, for which certain favoured landscapes in Japan are famed.

Besides the relations preserved between the garden and adjacent buildings,— namely, harmony in character and perfection of prospect,—there is to some extent observable the influence of architectural regularity upon the immediately surrounding areas. Formal and geometrical arrangements of trees, shrubs, and parterres, as common in European gardens, are indeed rarely admitted, but certain rectilineal objects, such as oblong slabs of hewn stone, straight flower-beds, and short screen-fences, are introduced near to the building. In addition, the grouping before the dwelling, of stone lanterns, water basins, and inscribed tablets, as well as the use of broad stretches of raked sand or beaten earth, adorned with formal stepping-stones leading to the verandahs, gives a conventional regularity to such areas. The more artificial ornaments of a Japanese garden are not however entirely confined to the immediate foreground. There is no perceptible division or sharp change in character between the building grounds and the landscape. Stone lanterns of different shapes, miniature pagodas and shrines, are scattered here and there throughout the compositions. Also a variety of garden bridges, rustic arbours, and tea-rooms are employed. Even peasants' cottages or farm-houses with suitable surroundings are often introduced into large grounds to impart a specially rural character to certain portions. All these architectural objects, though placed with due consideration and design, are devised so as to look as accidental and natural as the landscape itself.

The important artificial features in a Japanese landscape garden have descriptive names suggestive of historical or romantic connections, and their accessories and surroundings are such as to contribute to the fancy expressed. A river bridge will have its neighbouring maple trees or iris beds to convey a hint of the river scenery at Tatsuta * or Yatsuhashi †; and a clump of pine or cryptomeria trees close to a garden monument or shrine, will suggest some sacred temple grove familiar to the people. The figurative names applied both to structures and to natural objects impart a further charm, making the garden at once a picture and a poem.

In the distribution of vegetation the laws and precedents of natural production are rarely violated. Plants from the valleys or river beds,—trees and shrubs from

---

* Tatsuta,—a rural spot in Japan famous for its maple trees lining the river banks.
† Yatsuhashi,—a place in the province of Mikawa noted for its beds of iris flowers crossed by a curious bridge.

the rocks and hills,—are always appropriately placed in corresponding situations. Implicit obedience to these natural laws assists the designer in depicting impressions of actual scenes. Thus, the idea of the river Tamagawa * may be conveyed by *kerria* and *lespedeza* flowers near a shallow stream, or that of the mountain of Arashiyama † by garden hills planted with wild cherry trees and maples. This treatment of a landscape garden, not merely as an artistic medley of pretty contours and choice vegetation, but as a single composition, abounding in suggestions of natural spots and favourite fancies, is one which seems to give to the Japanese art a rank and importance unsurpassed by any other style.

---

* Tamagawa,—the name given to six different rivers in Japan, each noted for some special flower growing on its banks.

† Arashiyama,—a spot near Kioto famous for its wild cherry trees in the spring, and for its reddening maples in the autumn.

CHAPTER I.

HISTORY.

BEFORE proceeding to describe in detail the various rules and theories which guide the landscape gardener in Japan, some reference to the history of his craft will not be out of place. Japanese writers point to India as the original source from whence ideas of garden composition were derived. This opinion may possibly be traced to descriptions of the scenery and arts of India as related by those Chinese pilgrims, who, near the commencement of the first century, studied Buddhism and philosophy in the famous Vihara of Nalanda. Even up to quite modern times, the historical mountains, lakes, and rivers, associated with the life and religion of Shakya Muni, served as ideal models for artificial landscape in the gardens of Japanese temples and monasteries. But the influence which India has exercised upon the gardening art as practised in this country has been one of religion and sentiment rather than of method and arrangement. If outward forms have been thereby modified or directed, the modification has been the result of fanciful conceptions of Indian scenery derived at second-hand, and is in no way traceable to the direct influence of the artificial and formal art of horticulture as we know it to have been practised by the Aryan people.

To China, undoubtedly, Japan owes her first practical lessons in this as well as other arts. In the 6th century, when religion and its attendant cults were brought from the neighbouring continent, the first mentioned gardens were constructed in connection with the early monasteries of Biodo-In at Uji, and Todaiji and Kofukuji at Nara. The Chinese attribute the invention of the art to one Yohan Koan Han, who constructed artificial hills or rockeries one hundred feet high, and conducted running water from a distance of many miles for ornamental purposes. In the time of Shoan Ho of the Son dynasty it is recorded that an artist of the name of Chumen Tonkwan arranged flowering plants and trees in the garden of the reigning Emperor, building immense rockeries about two hundred feet in height. The stones employed on this occasion are said to have been specially selected for their interesting shapes, becoming for the first time of individual importance in the design; whereas, hitherto such material had been employed without selection, merely as an aggregate for irregular rockeries. The period of the Son dynasty would appear to have been distinguished for its large and luxurious gardens, even allowing for considerable historical exaggeration. It is recorded that the capital alone boasted a thousand pleasure grounds of enormous size. The paramount influence of China upon the style of artificial landscape developed in Japan may still be traced in the names of lakes, mountains, and water-falls of the Celestial Empire as represented in numerous designs. Fig. 2 exemplifies a famous lake, with hills, rocks, and water-falls, taken from the scenery of the Middle Kingdom, and applied in a modified manner to the gardens of this country.

FIG. 2

Japanese authors, in classifying the different styles of gardening practised in their country, refer to an ancient method of arrangement followed, prior to the influence which Chinese culture exerted in the sixth century. And, indeed, it seems only reasonable to suppose that, simultaneously with the construction of palaces and buildings of importance, however primitive in style, some kind of distribution and display of vegetation would be adopted to impart order and attractiveness to the surrounding grounds. The early style referred to is called the *Shinden-Shiki,* or *Imperial Audience Hall Style,* being the arrangement adopted for the area immediately in front of the detached palace intended for Imperial receptions. The large, oblong hall, with extensive corridors forming wings, occupied the South side of a quadrangle, on the East and West sides of which were secondary buildings for the Court attendants. The North side was bounded by the large entrance gate and principal enclosing wall. In the middle of the quadrangle is said to have existed a large lake of irregular shape containing a central islet reached from the banks by a picturesque bridge. Reference is also made to a plum tree and orange tree planted one on either side of the area immediately in front of the audience hall. Though this is all that is known of the earliest style of garden arrangement, it is sufficient to show that some fancy for natural variety, and for a suggestion of real landscape, existed even in the most primitive and formal designs.

The second historical style belongs to the *Kamakura Period*,—that is from the middle of the twelfth to the beginning of the fourteenth century, during which time Kamakura was the seat of the Regency. The art of gardening, together with architecture and other attendant arts, seems then to have received a great impulse at the hands of the Bulddhist priests. Considerable attention was bestowed on the selection and grouping of *standing*-stones, which were given imaginary religious and moral attributes, and disposed so as to represent the members of the Buddhist pantheon (see Fig. 10). As will be afterwards explained, many of these fancies still survive even in connection with buildings having no religious purpose. In the larger gardens of this period a lake was deemed an essential feature. Many names remain recorded for islets placed in lakes and rivers. Such are :—" Hill Island," " Wooded Island," " Rocky Island," " Wild-moor Island," " Cloud-shaped Island," " Misty Island," " Dry-beach Island," and " Pine-bark Island." A variety of cascades are also mentioned such as :—" Front Fall," " Side Fall," " Stepped Fall," " Spouting Fall," " Thread Fall," " Woolly Fall," " Right-and-left Fall," and " Folding Fall," these terms alluding to the character of the torrent displayed. The direction of the flow of garden streams was, as fixed by rule, from East to West, the opposite arrangement being pronounced left-handed and unlucky. References are made to the technical methods followed in arranging ornamental sheets of water. First, the general outline of the lake and islands were designed and excavated, due attention being paid to the nature of the site. A few of the most important rocks were then placed in position, and finally, the stream or water-fall forming the inlet, and also the outlet of the lake, were carefully arranged.

The construction of *Kare-sansui*, or Dried-up Water Scenery, was first adopted at this time. Designs of this kind consisted in representing lakes and rivers by means of hollowed-out beds and courses strewn with sand, pebbles, and boulders ; the position and direction of the supposed inlet and outlet being always carefully indicated. Such imaginary water was spread out widely, and deep channels were avoided, in order to approach reality as much as possible by suggesting those broad shallow water-courses which are often parched up by drought. The *Kare-sansui* garden generally represented a wild natural scene amid mountains.

Artificial hills were also introduced, the level portions below presenting the appearance of valleys. Stones and winding pathways added to the general effect. Besides the standing-stones, to which a religious import was attached, other large groups of rocks were introduced to suggest features of natural scenery. These were distinguished by such names as,—"Ocean Rock," "Large River Rock," "Offing Rock," "Mountain Torrent Stone," "Hill-side Rock," *et cetera*. The *Nōhara*, or Wild Moor, formed a favourite design for parts of many gardens, and was used notably in combination with the *Kare-sansui*.

The foregoing description of the *Kamakura Style* would tend to show that the art of gardening, as subsequently practised, was already considerably developed. But it remained chiefly in the hands of priests, who applied it principally to the grounds of temples and monasteries, and enveloped it in sacred mysteries; and it was not yet reduced to rule as in later times.

The great era for popularising the art of landscape gardening was called the *Muromachi Period*, corresponding with the ascendency of the later Ashikawa Regents, in the fifteenth century. At the commencement of this epoch, it is said that a famous priest called Soseki gave considerable study to the subject and established many rules; but no written work of his remains. Another priest named Muso-Kokushi became renowned for his garden compositions, and the temples of Tenriuji, Riusenji, and Saihoji in Kioto, all possessed noted landscapes attributed to him. The same tranquil and prosperous times which helped so much to advance the sister arts of poetry and calligraphy; and which first stimulated the cultivation of the tea ceremonial, also brought patronage to the art of the landscape gardener. The arrangement of grounds became one of the important accessories of the refinement of the *Cha-no-yu*, or Tea Ceremonies, and henceforth the professors of this cult became the principal designers of gardens. They reduced to rule and theory the art which had hitherto been practised by the Buddhist priests, adding important modifications with special reference to the peculiar ethics of tea-drinking. Sho-ami, sometime called So-ami—a famous Tea Professor and Painter patronized by Yoshimasa—gave particular attention to the art of gardening which he greatly changed, introducing among other novelties the practise of clipping trees into various fanciful shapes. Examples of his work remain, though much broken and neglected, in the gardens of the Toji-In—a portion of the temple of Saihonji,—of the temple of Riuanji, of the monastery of Kiyomizu, and of parts of Maruyama, all situated in the city of Kioto. Fig. 3, from the grounds of a monastery called the Banto-In, in Kioto, exhibits an example of this treatment. The garden at Riuanji was considered the most remarkable in the northern part of the city, being a striking example of Sho-ami's fondness for austerity in style. His saintly patron who resided in the temple precincts having expressed a desire that no tree should screen his view of the distant shrine on the Yawata mountain, Sho-ami therefore selected an ocean prospect as the subject of his design. Abstaining from employing even a single tree, he combined clipped shrubs and bushes with rocks of fantastic shapes to represent the forms of ocean islands. To Sho-ami is also attributed the design of the garden of the

FIG. 3.

Ginkakuji, or Silver Pavilion, built for Ashikaga Yoshimasa after his retirement from public affairs. See Plate XXXVI.

Other notable *Chajin*, or Tea Professors, of the Ashikaga period were :—Shuko,

a teacher of Yoshimasa, Showo, No-ami, and Gei-ami.   These were followed by Sen-no-Rikiu, Furuta Oribe, Ota, Hosokawa, Fujimura Yoken, Kuwabara, Enshiu, and Oguri Sotan, all famous names associated both with the tea ceremonial and the laying out of gardens.   Of the latter, Sen-no-Rikiu, Furuta Oribe, and Enshiu were perhaps the most erudite.   Sen-no-Rikiu, a youth from Sakai, who studied under Showo from the age of seventeen, showed unusual talent, and was employed by Nobunaga who gave him the title of *Sosho*, or Professor of Elegant Arts.   He became afterwards the favourite teacher of Hideyoshi whom be accompanied in his campaigns, and from whom he received exalted rank as Abbot of Daitokuji.   He, however, fell into disfavour with his imperious patron, and was compelled to commit *hara-kiri* at the advanced age of seventy-one.   Rikiu was the originator of many changes in the tea ceremonies, in the design of the buildings called *Chaseki* or *Suki-ya*, used for their observance, and in the composition of the surrounding gardens.

Enshiu, whose real name was Kobori Totomi-no-Kami, was a retainer of the Shogun Iyeyasu, and he became teacher of accomplished arts to the Regent's son. His most famous work in gardening was the garden of the Katsura Rikiu, a detached palace near Kioto, formerly a villa of the Imperial Prince of Hachijo.   The site had the one natural advantage of the river Katsura running through it, but for the rest, the beauties of the landscape design were entirely due to artificial contrivance. This garden still remains, though now much neglected, and it is said that for more than a hundred and fifty years after the death of Enshiu, not a single stone had been removed.   Other designs of the same artist are :—the gardens of the Konchi-In, in the temple of Nanzenji, of Shoden-In in the temple of Kenninji, of the temple of Kodaiji, and of Koho-An in the temple of Daitokuji.   The Konchi-In garden is celebrated for its arrangements of stones and rocks which are said to form the Chinese ideograph 心 "heart."   That of Kodaiji is described as one of the most beautiful scenes in the eastern part of Kioto, being intended to suggest a miniature of the fabuluous Garden of Paradise.   It is noted for the profusion of its cherry blossoms in spring, for its irises in summer, its lespedeza flowers in autumn, and its snow scenes in winter.

Fujimura Yoken built the garden of the Seiho-In in the temple of Kurodani at Kioto.   At the end of the sixteenth century Katagiri Katsumoto, by the command of Hideyoshi, constructed the garden of Chikubushima and that of Eizan-no-Sato-no-Bo in the temple of Jizoji.   Also belonging to this period was the small but artistically arranged temple garden called Tokusui-In which surrounds the Hiun-Kaku,—a pavilion in the grounds of the temple of Nishi Hongwanji at Kioto.

From the close of the fourteenth to the end of the sixteenth century most of the famous compositions were of the "Tea-Garden" class, and were governed in their arrangements by the severe rules of design and ethics that distinguished this cult. The principal Tea Professors have each recorded his ideal conception of the sentiment that a perfect Tea-Garden should express. Rikiu's fancy was that of the "lonely precincts of a secluded mountain shrine, with the red leaves of autumn scattered around." Enshiu is reported to have said that his ideal garden should express "the sweet solitude of a landscape in clouded moonlight, with a half gloom between the trees." Another designer named Oguri Sotan considered that the best conception was that of a "grassy wilderness in autumn with plenty of wild flowers." Different as were these conceits, they all agree in ascribing to the Tea-Garden a character of wildness and sequestered solitude.

The more modern style of gardening, of less severe type, may be said to have been introduced by Asagori Shimanosuke of Fushimi, who arranged the grounds of the Kiaku-Do of the temple of Hongwanji in Kioto, and restored and altered many other compositions made by the priests and *Chajin* of the preceding period. A great number of the ancient gardens of the western capital bear the impress of his skilful reconstruction. This brings us down to the Tokugawa times when the city of Yedo, during a great portion of the year, became the residence of the feudal lords. Between the Kwansei and Bunsei epochs (1789-1830) numerous palaces were built in this capital, and were adorned, in most cases, with magnificent gardens. Of these, a number have been destroyed, some have been converted, and one or two only remain in anything approaching their former beauty. A list is here appended of the principal specimens :—

The garden of the Daimio of Mito, at Koishikawa, called Koraku-En.
The garden of the Daimio of Owari, at Ushigome, called Toyama-En.
The garden of the Daimio Matsu-ura, at Shitaya, called Horai-En.
The garden of the Daimio of Nagato, at Hatchobori, called Chinkai-En.
The garden of the Daimio of Koriyama, at Komagome, called Mukusa-no-Sono.
The garden of the Daimio of Iida, at Takata, called Kiraku-En.
The garden of the Daimio of Kuwana, at Tsukiji, called Yoku-on-En.
The garden of the Daimio Mizoguchi, at Kobikicho, called Kairaku-En.
The garden of the Daimio of Izumo, at Osaki, called Osaki-no-Tei-En.
The garden of the Daimio of Kishiu, at Akasaka, called Tei-En.
The garden of the Daimio of Bizen, at Mukojima.

There remain to be mentioned the garden of the Shogun in Yedo Castle, properly called Kin-En, but generally known as the Fukiage garden, and those of his detached palaces in the same city, namely,—the Hama Rikiu at Shiodome, and the Shiba Rikiu in Shiba. These have all become Imperial gardens, as also the Tei-En of the old Kishiu Yashiki, which, after the Restoration, was converted into a temporary palace and occupied by the Emperor until the present new palace was completed. The Imperial garden parties to view the cherry blossoms are held in the Hama Rikiu, and the chrysanthemum shows in the Tei-En.

Of the Daimios' gardens above enumerated, the Koraku-En,—now a part of the enclosure of the Koishikawa Arsenal,—is the best preserved. The Mukusa-no-Sono forms a portion of the extensive park belonging to Baron Iwasaki, at Komagome, but it is much changed and extended, covering at present an area of about a hundred acres. A fine entrance gate, with lodge in the old Japanese style, opens on to a wide gravelled drive leading up to the residence, past a grove of cherry trees and evergreens. The garden proper is divided from the outer approach by a rustic fence and gateway. The area immediately facing the principal rooms is partly occupied by a large lake of irregular, serpentine shape, having a picturesque island adorned with fine trees and a handsome rockery. This is reached by a rustic bridge built of faggots and covered with earth. Another similar bridge crosses the narrower end of the lake, close to which a magnificent leaning pine tree spreads its branches over the water. Some gigantic old pines of rare and picturesque shapes, with their extended branches supported on props, adorn the lawn around the lake. A handsome granite standard-lantern about fifteen feet high, having a shaft about thirty inches in diameter, forms a striking feature of the foreground. Scattered here and there on the edge of the water are a few fine rocks and stones with bushes and evergreen shrubs. On the further side, opposite the house, is an eminence planted with azaleas, pine trees, camellia bushes, and variegated bamboos, having a stepped pathway leading to the plateau which forms the summit, and from which an extensive view of the garden can be had. Here is placed a stone said to have been used in ancient times by one of the Shoguns. Other parts of these extensive grounds are laid out with plantations of cryptomeria, spruce, and pine, and groves of blossoming trees and shrubs, such as plum, cherry, peach, quince, pyrus, lespedeza, and kerria. In one spot may be seen a rustic tea-house fitted up in exact imitation of the hostelry of a country road. Another picturesque summer-house is placed on the side of the lake. Forming an important feature of these grounds, in common with the parks of most Japanese gentlemen, is a large decoy pond entirely surrounded by thick trees.

This garden also boasts the modern additions of a model farm, and orchards of native and foreign fruit trees.

Other comparatively modern gardens in Tokio which can still be visited, or are rendered familiar by photographs, may be mentioned. The "Satake-no-Niwa," near Asakusa was built about sixty years ago by Ito Monzaburo of Mikawashima. It was originally presented by the Shogun to one of his Ministers, Mizuno Dewa-no-Kami, but afterwards given to the Princess Asa-Hime as an occasional resort. Still later, about fifty years ago, it became the property of Matsudaira, Daimio of Echizen, by whom, ten years afterwards, it was again transferred to the Daimio Satake whose name it still bears. The fine rocks and stones, for which this garden is famous, were arranged by the first owner, Dewa-no-Kami, being brought at great expense from his own province of Suruga. The garden has a lake encircled by hills, rounded shrubs, and bushes, with some fine old granite lanterns interspersed, and the whole backed by high shady trees. It is still quite worthy of a visit though disfigured by certain modern barbarities.

Until quite recently there existed at Fukagawa a beautiful garden belonging to Hotta, the lord of Sakura in Shimosa, and popularly called "Hotta-no-Niwa," noted for its large lake with numerous monolithic bridges, curious rocks, and fine stone lanterns, the background consisting of hills planted with clipped bushes and rare trees. This garden has unfortunately been broken up, but has been reproduced so often by the camera that some reference to it seems called for. The public garden of the Shokonsha at Kudan, laid out by the gardener Suzuki Magohachi, has a small sheet of water, and is, on a limited scale, a good example of Japanese landscape design. The grounds at Fukagawa, belonging to Baron Iwasaki, are beautifully laid out after the native method, with a large lake, islands, hills, river beds, water-fall, and other characteristics of the *Hill-garden Style*. The distant view opposite the mansion represents the mountain Fujisan with the river Fujikawa below running into the lake. The river, as well as the cascade, is waterless, and represented only by stones cleverly arranged. This garden is remarkable for the enormous number of its rare rocks, brought, regardless of cost, from all parts of the country. A portion of the grounds in the rear is laid out as a lovely little Tea-Garden, in imitation of a mountain dell, a dry torrent-bed running through it, shaded with trees and bushes.

The palace of H.I.H. Prince Arisugawa, at Urakasumi-ga-seki, has a picturesque garden designed by a pupil of Ito Shichirobei.

The numerous religious establishments of the western capital, Kioto, possess the remains of what were once magnificent gardens, now sadly out of repair, and in many cases robbed of some of their most valuable features. Woodcuts scattered through the text show portions of some of these gardens. Fig. 4 illustrates a part of the grounds of the Hoshun-In of the temple of Daitokuji, with a lake and a curious roofed bridge. Fig. 5 shows a portion of the entrance court to the priests' residence in the same temple enclosure.

FIG. 4.

The garden of Kinkakuji, or the Golden Pavilion, in Kioto, is well-known on account of its interesting historical associations. Long neglect has converted what was once an elaborate artificial landscape into a wild natural scene of great beauty. The plantations of coniferous trees have the appearance of uncultivated woods, and the pine-clad islets have become island wildernesses. A few references to the principal features of this garden, as first arranged for the Regent Yoshimitsu, will give some idea of its original design. The lake, called Kioko, or the Mirror Ocean, represented the Sea of Japan, and contained three islands adorned with rare rocks and pine trees intended to suggest the land of Nippon. The name of the "Thousand Dragons' Gate" was given to the waterfall supplying the lake, which was backed by a high natural hill fancifully called "Silken Canopy Mountain." In one spot was a mossy nook from which welled up a natural spring of the purest water, described as the "Silver Spring." In addition to the principal three-storied pavilion,—

internally loaded with the richest gilding,—there existed other garden structures, such as the "Lake View Arbour," and the "House of the Sound of the Sea Shore."

The grounds of Ginkakuji, or the Silver Pavilion were laid out by the artist Sho-ami, in about the year 1480. It was to this spot that Yoshimasa retired after transferring the reins of active government to his successor. Kinkakuji, as designed for his predecessor Yoshimitsu, was copied to some extent in the arrangement of the buildings and landscape. Though much out of repair, this garden forms even now one of the noted sights of the old capital. It contains an extensive lake, thickly planted with lotuses, and backed by a magnificently wooded hill. A cascade, several islands, and numerous granite bridges adorn the grounds. Considerable care was bestowed by Sho-ami on the selection and arrangement of the garden stones, which are of rare and curious shapes, distinguished by characteristic

FIG. 5.

fancy names. The foreground was originally spread with white sand ornamentally raked in patterns, and there existed a circular sanded plateau, called the Kogetsu-Dai, used for viewing the effect of the moonlight upon the landscape. A bubbling spring of the purest water gushes out in one portion of the grounds. The surrounding hills and islands are adorned with pine trees and other evergreens of interesting shapes, and a mound towards the West is thickly planted with azaleas and reddening maples.

Plate XXXVI. gives some idea of the arrangement of this garden as originally planned, though the drawing is lacking in correctness of detail. Here also age and neglect have combined to change convention into nature, and almost obliterate the aid of art and artifice.

Some reference must be made to the grounds of the Imperial Palace at Kioto, principally those parts known as the Ike-no-Niwa, or Lake Garden, and the Tsune-goten-Niwa, or Garden of the Tsune-goten.* The former has a fine lake ornamented with fancy bridges of wood and stone and picturesque water-worn rocks; the banks are adorned with rounded bushes and dwarf pine trees, and higher trees occupy the background. Also worthy of notice are the gardens of the Nijo Castle in Kioto, and the Momoyama-goten in Fushimi near to the Osaka Citadel.

Many of the old castle-towns of the interior possess fine gardens which adorned the Daimios' provincial palaces, but which are now converted into public parks. Among these may be mentioned the public garden at Kumamoto, and that at Oka-yama in the province of Bizen, to be afterwards described. The garden of a part of Prince Shimazu's residence at Kagoshima,—well-known from photographs,—is interest-ing as a characteristic example of the severe and aristocratic style of composition, in which a stately simplicity dominates. A serpentine lake, crossed in one place by a fine slab of hewn granite, supported in the middle on stone trestles, is edged with numerous water-worn boulders, schists, and rocks, between which are planted azaleas and other bushes, water plants, and evergreens, having their foliage cut into spherical shapes. A graceful stone lantern, with umbrella-shaped top, placed in conjunction with a few fine rocks and a trained pine tree, forms a prominent feature on the lake side, just in front of the rooms. The cascade,—an indispensable feature of lake gardens,—is, in this example, divided from the principal sheet of water by a sanded space, and has its own separate basin, which, together with a handsome rockery and mound backed by enormous rounded evergreens and other hills, makes a handsome composition at the side of the dwelling. One or two quaintly trimmed pollards near the verandah, and some fine pines in the extreme background, are the only large trees in the design.

A pretty garden at Niigata, in the province of Echigo, belonging to a certain Mr. Shirase, is a very fine example. It has a small lake, the banks of which are

---

* Tsune-goten,—the name given to the Mikado's private chambers in the Kioto palace.

crowded with rocks, having round bushes and grasses planted between them. On the surrounding areas are pine trees of rare shape, with their foliage conventionally cut into discs in what is called the *Tamatsukuri Style.* In the background, is a hill with a cascade and rockery, backed by large clumps of spherical bushes.

Fuller descriptions follow of some of the more important of the large gardens included in the preceding list, the information being partly taken from a publication called the "Fuzoku Gaho." In some cases the gardens described remain in a state approaching their former splendour, and have been personally visited by the present writer; but the majority have been so broken up that to mention them as existing examples would seriously mislead and disappoint any one wishing to visit them. Their detailed notice, therefore, belongs properly to the historical section of this work.

FUKIAGE GARDEN.

The area of these Imperial grounds is nearly eighty-five acres. Situated within the northern circuit of the Shogun's Castle, they consisted originally of a large park of wild flowers containing a detached pavilion called Hana-batake Goten, or the Palace of the Field of Flowers. The Shogun Tsunayoshi, at the end of the seventeenth century, made extensive changes in this part of the Citadel, excavating new moats, constructing a palatial villa and garden, with arbours, tea-houses, summer-houses, and shrines, and at the same time levelling a large portion of the site to be used for equestrian sports. The garden structures bore such names as "Maple Arbour," "Cascade-viewing Arbour," "Country House," "Pine-tree Tea-house," and "Shrine of the Water-fall."

Iyetsugu, a later Shogun, built here a small palace for his mother, together with numerous detached structures for the recreations of her Court, such as a study, painting room, observatory, dancing room, embroidery room, and dyeing establishment. Small factories for the manufacture of *saké,** cakes, and sugar, and a dispensary for herbs and drugs were also arranged. The open spaces were at this time planted with cherry trees, pine trees, maples, chestnut trees, bamboos, and autumn plants. At a later date the Shogun Yoshimune broke up many of the buildings, leaving intact only

---

* *Saké,*—Japanese wine brewed from rice.

a few arbours and garden pavilions. Other buildings were again erected by a later Regent, the names of the principal being :—" Grove Tea-house," " Wistaria-trellis Arbour," " Suwa* Tea-house," and " Herb-field Arbour."

In the Meiji Period, about the year 1868, the whole of the grounds and those portions of the constructions within the Shogun's Castle which had escaped conflagration, became an Imperial estate, and prior to the completion of the new Palace it was occasionally permitted to a privileged few to visit what remained of the Fukiage Garden. As it stood a few years ago this was divided into three parts: that near the Fukiage gate called the New Enclosure, laid out as a grassy moor with clumps of pine trees and stone lanterns ; the circular horse-ride, used for equestrian sports in the old style ; and a hilly portion, containing rare rocks and a picturesque cascade and arbour. Garden structures still intact from ancient times were : the " Cascade-viewing Arbour,"—near the water-fall,—the " Maple Arbour," and the " Country House." The " Cascade-viewing Arbour " afforded a fine prospect across Tokio Bay, as well as a view of the water-fall, and looked down upon a bed of irises and other flowering plants spanned by a fantastic bridge of planks. The " Country House " was constructed in imitation of a farmer's house, with a cattle-shed, containing the model of a sleeping ox, and was furnished with various peasants' utensils. Few large gardens in Japan are without some such suggestion of the simplicity and picturesqueness of rural life. The portions of this garden best known are the water-fall and surrounding rockeries, which form a fine example of artificial cascade design.

HAMA RIKIU GARDEN.

This is another of the Imperial gardens of the capital taken over from the Shogunate at the time of the Restoration. It occupies a site which, until the middle of the seventeenth century, was merely a marshy level, fifty acres in area, overgrown with reeds and rushes, and used as a hawking ground by the Shogun. Iyetsuna presented the land to one of his relatives, who converted it into a garden, and furnished it with suitable buildings. It became an occasional summer resort for the Regent and his Court, its position, on the shore of Tokio Bay, rendering it a cool and refreshing retreat, and obtaining for it the name of Hama Goten, or the Palace on the Coast. Records dating from the year 1708 mention the following

* Suwa,—a spot in Japan celebrated for its beautiful sea view.

garden structures: " Island Tea-house," " Ocean Tea-house," " Bubbling-spring Tea-house," " Shrine of Kwannon," " Shrine of Koshin,* " and " Bridge of the Front Gate."

An extensive conflagration in the year 1725 destroyed the buildings and damaged the grounds, which were remodelled under the Shogun Iyenari, at the end of the eighteenth century. The principal detached pavilions then erected were: the " Swallow Tea-house," " Pine-tree Tea-house," " Thatched Tea-house," " Pine-grove Arbour," " Hut of the Salt-coast," " Arbour of the Royal Mountain," " Arbour of the Fifth Moat," and " Azuma Arbour"—Azuma being an ancient name for Japan. Just before the Restoration, in 1867, the estate passed into the hands of the Ministry of Marine, and in the following year was transferred to the Ministry of Foreign Affairs and used for entertaining foreign visitors of distinction. Eventually the Imperial Household Department took possession of the site, when the name was slightly changed to Hama Rikiu, or Detached Palace of the Coast, the term *Rikiu* being applied to all the secondary palaces or Imperial villas. Meanwhile, the garden had become much out of repair, only a few of the ornamental arbours remaining.

An old book, published in 1843 by Oyamada Yosei-O, a retainer of Prince Kwacho, gives the following account of the chief attractions of these grounds :—An elevated hillock called the " Mountain of Eight Views" afforded an extensive prospect of the sea and distant hills. Near its base was a small lagoon containing irises and other water-plants. " Ocean View Hill" was the name of another eminence over-looking the Bay planted with mountain grasses and pine trees. In the western quarter of the garden, and providing an uninterrupted prospect of Fujisan, was another hill called " Fuji-viewing Hill." Close to a rocky mound, covered with azalea bushes, was a beach arranged with artificial salt-making beds and kilns, designed in imitation of the primitive salt factories abounding on the Japanese coast. A few peasants' huts embowered in high grasses and wild flowers, and a picturesque cottage, called the " Sea-shore Tea-house,"—from which a sea view, including the cliffs of the opposite coast could be enjoyed,—imparted a charming rural character to this spot.

Another feature of the garden was the " Embroidery Hall," a detached building used for the manufacture of the beautiful *Aya-nishiki*, the working of which was formerly a favourite pastime of the Court ladies. A grove of pine trees, in which was buried a little arbour called the " Pine-grove Tea-house," lined the approach to

---

* Kwannon and Koshin are both popular deities, shrines dedicated to whom exist all over Japan.

this hall.   The " Thatched-hut Tea-house," already mentioned, was constructed to resemble the hostelry of a country road, fitted up with the simple implements and furniture peculiar to country life.   It is said to have been used by the Shogun as a hunting-box for hawking.   A miniature structure, built in delicate taste, and called the " Swallow-Tea-house," was furnished with several valuable Chinese pictures and other antique treasures of the So period.   At the side of a winding pathway leading to the garden lake was a pretty bower, called the " Trellised Arbour," overlooking a large bed of chrysanthemums.

Other buildings referred to were : the " Orchid House," containing Chinese orchids and other rare plants arranged in flower-pots ; a closed summer-house called Azuma-Ya ; and a little fane to Azuma Inari, the Fox God, half hidden in a small plantation of trees suggestive of a temple grove.   A hill, called Reijisan, gave a good prospect of the neighbouring garden of the Shiba Rikiu, to the south-west.   It was rocky and precipitious on one side and adorned with crooked, overhanging pine trees, in imitation of the wild scenery of the Japanese coast.   From still another eminence, more than twenty feet in height, and named Kembanzan, the large trees of the distant Fukiage Garden could be seen.   The cascade at the head of the lake, the water for which was brought from the river Tamagawa, was picturesquely designed.   A striking feature of this garden is a long winding bridge crossing the lake, covered in parts with wistaria trellises, which are loaded with immense racemes of purple flowers in the season.   The Hama Rikiu is now chiefly known for its unrivalled show of double cherry blossoms in spring, forming an attraction honoured yearly by an Imperial visit and reception.

SHIBA RIKIU GARDEN.

This is a comparatively small garden, covering only twelve acres, now oc-cupied by a modern villa belonging to H.I.H. Prince Arisugawa.   Anciently, the site was given to Kato Yoshiakira by one of the Shoguns, and about the year 1755 his grandson joined a branch of the Shogun's family called the Shimizu-Ke, or the House of Shimizu.   In 1847 the property passed into the hands of the Daimio of Kishiu, the original owner of the Akasaka Rikiu, by whom it was held until the time of the Restoration, when it received its name of Shiba Rikiu, or Detached Palace of Shiba. Unlike most other noted landscape gardens, no special description of the Shiba Rikiu garden appears to have been published.   In character it is not unlike the garden of the Hama Rikiu, having inlets from the sea, supplying a small lake dotted with pine-clad islets, and surrounding hills and mounds adorned with arbours from which sea views across the Tokio Bay are obtained.

AKASAKA RIKIU GARDEN.

This extensive garden, now a part of the Imperial Palace at Akasaka, was originally the property of the lords of Kishiu, by whom it was known as the Tei-En. Designed on a scale of almost natural grandeur, high wooded hills and wide shady valleys take the place of the shrub-clad hillocks and depressions of ordinary landscape gardens. The Shogun Iyenari was an enthusiastic admirer of its splendid scenery, and honoured it with frequent visits in the summer season. In those day, aviaries of peacocks, golden pheasants, storks, and other rare birds lined the approach leading to the reception hall. In front of this building were arranged beds containing many varieties of chrysanthemums, and the displays of this autumn flower still continue to be one of the chief sights of these Imperial grounds. Near the hall is a two-storied building the upper galleries of which afford, in one direction, a fine prospect of the green and red foliage of the majestic pine and maple trees of the garden, and in the other an uninterrupted view of the blue bay of Shinagawa, dotted with white sails.

As one advances inwards a winding stream is seen, overhung with trellises of wistaria creepers which, in May, reflect their purple blossoms in the water. At this point a pretty bamboo fence and thatch-roofed gateway mark the boundary of the inner garden. Entering, past a clump of giant pines and native oaks, the path leads to a *Torii** called Ko-Saga, after the noted shrine of Saga in Kioto, and here in a shady spot stands an old stone well of clear spring water. Adjoining, is one of those fancy arbours constructed of bamboo, reeds, and plaited rushes, in the primitive and fragile style so characteristically Japanese. On a neighbouring hill another small building boasts a treasure in the shape of an antique bronze bell suspended from its eaves, which is said to have been reclaimed from the sea on the Kishiu Coast, in the thirteenth century. Groves of bamboo and pine plantations line the pathway, leading to a picturesque valley which is watered by a winding river, crossed in several places by stone bridges. Here and there the crooked branches of stunted pine trees overhang the stream. The name of Sen-Shin-Tei, or Heart-cleansing Arbour, is given to

---

* *Torii,*—a trabeated framework used as an archway in front of temples.

a small resting house on the river bank. The whole prospect of this charming vale is obtained from another fancy building occupying an elevated wooded spot to the south. Crossing the surrounding heights, a winding road of rugged steps descends upon a small lagoon called Tojaku-Su, or the Iris Marsh, thickly planted with flags, and spanned by a winding plank-bridge, in imitation of the Yatsuhashi landscape. The name of "Flying-geese Bridge" is given to this structure, in reference to the zigzag order taken by a flock of birds in flight.

To the south of this bed of irises is a deep clear lake, poetically called Seki-sui-Chi, or the Cerulean Lake. Surrounding hills of evergreens and trees that redden in the autumn reflect their foliage into the mirror below. It may here be mentioned that the Japanese have a single expressive word *Koyo* which is applied to the crimson and golden foliage of certain trees in autumn. Sycamores, maples, oaks, ashes, and certain varieties of the *Rhus, Eunonymus, Edgeworthia,* and *Ginkgo,* are the principal trees of mellowing leaf. Certain rural spots are yearly visited to enjoy the sight of the rich colouring assumed by the wooded hills and glades in October, and no garden of importance is complete without some copy in miniature of such autumnal scenery. Two parallel arched bridges, bearing the name of "Rainbow Bridges," span the lake, and on the further side a plantation of cryptomeria and pine trees have been planted so as to suggest scenery on the road to Kamakura. Winding paths of rough stone steps lead up the neighbouring eminences to other objects of interest, in the shape of an antique mossy well, named after the poet Saigio, and a building called Gi-Shun-Kwan, or the Hall of the Lovely Spring-time. From this commanding spot the greater portion of the garden can be seen,—a prospect at all times charming, but specially so in spring and early summer. To the west appears the flower garden Rokwa-En, to the south the garden lake flanked by wooded hills, and in other quarters, according to the season, may be seen groves of blossoming plum and cherry trees, beds of irises and flowering water-plants, and banks of blazing azalea bushes and maples.

In one spot an area is laid out after the manner of a gardener's nursery with numerous potted plants, peonies, dwarf plum and wistaria trees, orange trees, and specimens of *Nuphar japonicum, Nandina domestica, Acorus gramineus,* and *Psilotum triquetrium.* Here are also a small summer-house called Koyo-no-Tei, or Arbour of Reddening Foliage, and several lithic curiosities such as a slim stone column, and an anchor-shaped stone, said to have been brought up from the sea-bottom on the Kishiu coast.

Another garden valley, designed for an autumn scene, contains a rivulet whose banks are thickly planted with reeds, rushes, and bushes of kerria. The rich yellow of those flowers reflected in the water, together with the glow of maples and other reddening trees behind, have procured for this spot the name of Ogon-Kei, or the Golden Dell.

KORAKU-EN GARDEN, TOKIO.

The Koraku-En, at Koishikawa in the northern part of Tokio, is one of the most famous and best preserved gardens of the city. It was originally laid out in the beginning of the seventeenth century, by Mitsukuni, Daimio of Mito, who, amongst other æsthetic pursuits, was passionately fond of landscape gardening. It is stated that the Shogun Iyemitsu himself gave advice as to its arrangement, and lent the assistance of a famous Chinese artist, called Shunsui, who was the real practical designer. This would account for many Chinese characteristics in the garden, which is a combination of Japanese and Chinese scenery. It has a large lake with a central island, formerly connected with the shore by a long wooden bridge which has been since destroyed. The bridge was in fact never an orthodox feature of this particular island, which was called the "Elysian Isle" and represented one of the sea islands of the Chinese classics on which mysterious genii were supposed to dwell. On the island is a shrine called Benzai-Ten-no-Miya. On the east side of the lake are high shady trees and a hill clad with Chinese palms, pine trees, cryptomerias, firs, and bushes of *Olea fragrans*. On the south is a level portion designated the Kiso Valley, with a stream called the Tatsuta River entering the lake, both of these names having reference to places in Japan renowned for their beauty. The river of Tatsuta or Tatta is, in imitation of its natural model, planted with maples and other reddening trees, forming a beautiful spot in the autumn. Near here is a little shrine called the Saigio-Do, after the noted traveller and poet Saigio, whose name is connected with so many spots and natural objects in rural Japan and close by is a horse-ride called the Sakura-Baba, planted with cherry trees. On the west, a fine giant pine spreads its branches over the Oi-gawa, another stream boasting a river-side tea-house, called the "Glass House," built at a time when glass was a great rarity in Japan. The name Oi-gawa, meaning Rapid-river, belongs to a noted stream in the province of Yamashiro which is rendered picturesque by a wide pebble-strewn bed with bamboo baskets of stones piled as breakwaters on the banks: similar scenery may be observed on the river Tamagawa near Tokio. An expanse of water planted with white lotuses, and called the Seiko-tsutsumi, after a famous Chinese lotus lake, forms an important feature, and is spanned by a semi-circular stone bridge of Chinese design called Togetsu-kio, or Full Moon Bridge, made by Komahashi Kaihei.   A hill called Shorozan, after a mountain in China, overlooks the lake.   In the vicinity are a shrine to dedicated Kwannon, a small tea-house, some hills called "Loochoo Mountains," thickly planted with white azaleas from Loochoo, and a cascade named Otowa-no-taki, after a famous Japanese water-fall. On the north side of the garden stands a large hill supposed to represent a distant mountain, and a pine grove to suggest a forest, and formerly there existed a fane to the household god Fukurokuju, used in the landscape as a mountain shrine.   This building, which was altogether in Chinese style and paved with tiles, was destroyed in the great earthquake of the Ansei period, some fifty years ago.   A marshy area, planted with irises and spanned by a zigzag plank bridge in imitation of the scenery of Yatsu-hashi, occupies another portion of the grounds, near which is a shrine to the Fox God, Inari.   In the same quarter is an antique stone monument named after Ono-no-Komachi, a famous beauty of Japanese romance, the locality of its production being a place called Ono, in the province of Hitachi.   Such plays upon words are common in Japanese poetry and other arts.

Not far from here is a suite of reception rooms, called Kawara-Shoin, with a dancing stage attached.   In the north-west corner of the grounds a small boundary fence with a neat thatched gateway encloses a rustic water-mill of two storeys, with the miller's cottage adjoining.   The water-wheel serves for raising water to the upper storey, from whence a conduit, carried to the hill Shorozan, supplies the cascade of the lake.   In another part of the garden is a conical hill, called Fuji-no-yama, and crown-ed, with white azaleas, the white flowers suggesting the snowy cap of mount Fuji; and not far from this runs a stream called "Water of Eternal Youth," remarkable for the clearness of its water.   The cascade at the head of the lake, described as Kiyo-mizu-no-taki, falls near a shrine to Kwannon, built in imitation of the Kiyomizu-dera at Kioto.   The garden contains numerous monolithic stone bridges and lanterns, rare rocks, boulders, and trees, and other interesting details.

HORAI-EN GARDEN.

The Horai-En, in the Shitaya district of Tokio, is a small garden of a little over two acres in extent, originally laid out as a Tea-Garden in the beginning of the seventeenth century, by the famous Tea Professor, Kobori Enshiu, associated with the priest Kogetsu.   Its owner was the Daimio Matsu-ura.   Water from the river Sumida was brought by aqueduct from Samisen-bori, to supply the lake, which was also connected with the canals leading into the bay. The lake scenery of the garden, therefore, reaches perfection at high tide. A picturesque island of double form, called the "Twin Islands," is the principal lake feature, and is adorned with a fine old pine tree, a miniature stone pagoda, and a curiously shaped rock called the "Triplet Rock"; also with other rare stones placed at the edge of the water. A meandering pathway, consisting in some places of rugged stone steps, leads round the lake, affording varied views of the promontories, islands, bridges, and opposite banks. The surrounding areas are variously designed with hills, tree clumps, and open spaces.

In one spot is an aged moss-covered monument surrounded by pine trees, with kerria bushes near by. A little further on, a grove of rare trees receives the name of Tamuke-no-Mori, or Forest of Bountiful Gift; and from this spot, extending to the lake island, is a causeway, on the sides of which grow some large pine trees with their crooked trunks picturesquely reaching over the water. At one place a small inlet flows amidst a clump of foliage, crossed by a light bridge, called the Ukikusa-no-Hashi, or Floating Sea-weed Bridge. Under the shadow of the leafage a small shrine, named Ono-no-Yashiro, nestles beside a moss-covered well-border, and an inscribed stone tablet. The outlet of the aqueduct which supplies the lake resembles a natural spring issuing from the rocks, while a stone lantern stands in the bed of the stream below. This arrangement is copied from Enshiu's famous design in the garden of the Katsura Rikiu. On the south side of the garden spreads a moor of high grass, on which is found a sequestered looking tea-house. From here to the right, a narrow pathway between trees leads to an antique granite lantern, named after Shizuka-Gozen, the beautiful favourite of the warrior Yoshitsune. It is said to have come from a spot near the temple of Hachiman at Kamakura, whither this unhappy lady went nightly to pray.

At one place the banks of the lake expand into a wide pebble and boulder-covered beach, adorned with a shrine, a stone lantern, and a curious hollowed rock serving as a water basin. Numerous cherry trees border another inlet issuing from the lake, in representation of the scenery of Yoshino.* An open area called Matoniwa-Hara, used as an archery range, surrounded by bushes of pyrus and lespedeza, suggests the landscape of Miyagi, in the province Oshiu; and close by blossoms a grove of plum trees. Further on, a trellis entwined with wistaria creepers flanks an eminence called Irokazan, or Mount of Colour and Fragrance, planted with wild cherry trees.

---

* Yoshino—a pretty spot in the province of Yamato noted for its wild cherry trees.

A rustic fence, with a gate made of plaited rushes, leads to an enclosure containing a summer-house and a tiny tea-room, not far from which may be observed a high bank cut out of closely planted box-trees, near to a small waiting-room used in connection with the tea-room. Here are many maple trees, and further on is a grove of bamboos, called Hatsune-Hayashi, or Glade of the First Note, in allusion to the early song of birds. An elevated spot, named Shimoteru-Oka, or the Mound o'erlooking Brilliant (Foliage), contains some fine old maple trees, and in another part of the garden are several beautiful weeping willows. This garden is particularly noted for its variety of scenery arranged within a very small compass.

TOYAMA-EN GARDEN.

The site of the Toyama-En originally covered seventy acres, which was afterwards increased by more than fifty acres, making it the largest landscape garden in Tokio. As first laid out by Mitsusada-Kio, in the year 1665, it had twenty-five remarkable features, besides many other objects of special interest, bearing different fancy appellations. Within recent years the garden has been partly demolished, and the site applied to the purposes of a military school. A central lake, having inlets, rivulets, promontories, and islands, occupied the centre of the design; the surrounding areas abounded in scenery, consisting of groves, moors, hills, marshes, and rice fields, with numerous summer-houses, monuments, and bridges. The palace was situated in the north-east corner of the grounds. The whole arrangement may be seen from the plan (Plate XXXVII), in which many of the principal features are numbered as follows :—

1, The Palace, with inner garden and ornamental enclosures. 2, The Magician's Dell. 3, Garden Tea-room. 4, Hill of Embroidery,—so named from its numerous coloured azaleas and maples. 5, Farmer's House. 6, Water God Shrine. 7, Double-view House. 8, Hermit's Shrine. 9, Jewel-shaped Peak. 10, Gate of Rare Bamboo. 11, Horse Ride, about 150 yards long. 12, Farmer's House, and small Farm. 13, Race Stand. 14, Mirror Well. 15, Stone Image. 16, *Seigwanji** Shrine. 17, Carriage Gate. 18, Shrine of *Kwannon.** 19, Shrine-attendants Dwelling. 20, Plum-grove. 21, Five-storied Pagoda. 22, Pine Forest. 23, Shrine of *Dainichi.** 24, Waiting House. 25, Shrine of *Hitomaru.*† 26, Clear Spring. 27, Dragon-dwelling Valley. 28, Wide Moor. 29, Cherry-forest. 30. Sword-point Peak. 31, Horse-archery Ride. 32, Moor-viewing Arbour. 33, Shrine. 34, Store for Herbs. 35, Shrine of *Shaka.** 36,

---

* Budhist deities.　　　　　† Shinto deities.

Jewel Bridge. 37, Flower-hidden Bridge. 38, Bridge of Cool Breezes. 39, Pine Plantation. 40, Shrine of *Monju.** 41, The Six Shrines. 42, Royal-entrance Gate. 43, Shrine of *Shimmei.*† 44, Landscape-viewing Plateau. 45, Shrine of *Amida.** 46, Willow-side Arbour. 47, Phœnix-dwelling Valley. 48, Distant View Arbour. 49, Porcelain Kiln. 50, View Stand. 51, Shrine of *Benten.** 52, Road. 53, Three Huts. 54, River-side Hut. 55, *Kamakura*§ Road. 56, Mountain Village Tea-house. 57, Bubbling Spring. 58, *Kawagoye*§ Road. 59, Distant-view House. 60, Shrine of *Giogi.** 61, Shrine of *Oji-Gongen.*† 62, Bamboo Gate. Although the above translations can convey but little idea of the significance of the vernacular names given to the views and objects of this garden, they are sufficient to show what special interest and meaning is attached to every artificial detail.

The numerous garden shrines all bear the names of protecting deities, of historical temples, or of country fanes. Descriptive terms applied to hills, valleys, and other spots, allude either to their purpose in the landscape, to their peculiarity of shape or colour, or to some mysterious charm which they are supposed to possess. As examples of each method of nomenclature may be mentioned:—Shusui-Dai, or Fine View Plateau; Kenzan, or Sword-point Peak; Himmeizan, or Embroidered Mountain; and Meiho-kei, or Phœnix-dwelling Valley. Some of the references are classical, requiring for their elucidation and appreciation some familiarity with ancient Japanese or Chinese history and legend. Such, for instance, are:—Shusen-koku, or Valley of Magicians; Takuei-sen, or Spring for Washing the Cap Strings,—a Chinese idea suggestive of extreme purity; and Kohaku-bashi, or Jewel Bridge,—the term jewel implying great ethereal beauty. The plan of this garden may be taken as a characteristic example of the arrangements followed in most of the larger landscape gardens of Japan. The sixty-two descriptive names refer only to special spots of interest in the scenery, and to garden buildings. In addition, the important rocks, stones, tree-clumps, lanterns, water basins, and garden fences have also their distinguishing terms, applied in accordance with the rules of gardening which will be afterwards explained.

YOKU-ON-EN GARDEN.

The Yoku-on-En, forming until recent years one of the attractions of the capital, occupied a site presented by the Shogun, in 1793, to Shirakawa Shosho, the

---

* Buddhist deities.　　†Shinto deities.　　§ Places of interest.

Daimio of Kuwana.   Much skill and creative fancy appear to have been bestowed upon its elaborate design.   It is said to have contained fifty-two noted *views*, under which head are included several rare garden structures in the Chinese style,—for it must be understood that the *views* of a Japanese landscape garden include not only scenes and prospects, but special objects of beauty, or of romantic and historical interest.   They may be enumerated as follows,—the poetical Japanese names being in this case given as well as their approximate translations :—*Chitose-no-hama* (Beach of a Thousand Years) ; *Chiyo-no-iwa-hashi* (Eternal Bridge of Rock) ; *Kinugasa-yanagi* (Silken Canopy Willow) ; *Iroka-no-sono* (Garden of Colour and Fragrance) ; *Ariyake-no-ura* (Coast of Ariyake),—a famous sea view in Harima ; *Yakoe-no-hashi* (Sunset Bridge)—or literally,

Karasaki Pine-tree, Lake Biwa.
FIG. 6.

"the Bridge of the Eight Crow-cries," a poetical allusion to the cawing of the crows at sunset ; *Ni-O-no-kayoiji* (Road of the Two Deva Kings); *Nishiki-ga-shima* (Island of Rich Embroidery) ; *Nagori-no-shima* (Island of Leave-taking) ; *Harukaze-no-ike* (Lake of the Spring Breezes); *Sazanami-no-tani* (Wavelet Valley),—referring to the waving grasses ; *Utsugi-no-seki* (Boundary of *Deutzia* Trees) ; *Tsukimatsu-ura* (Coast for Awaiting the Moon-rise) ; *Hayama-no-seki* (Boundary of Thick Foliage) ; *Hana-no-shita-michi* (Path beneath the Flowers) ; *Sakura-ga-fuchi* (Cherry-tree Pool); *Hana-no-kakehashi* (Bridge amid Flowers)—meaning ; a light mountain bridge with surrounding wild flowers ; *Take-no-hosomichi* (Narrow Path through Bamboos) ; *Takaoka-yama* (High Plateau Mountain) ; *Tsuki-to-sato* (Moonlight View Hamlet)—meaning literally, "the hamlet for communing with the moon;" *Shinonome-no-ura* (Coast of the Early Dawn) ; *Yukari-no-ya* (House of Fond Attachment)—an expressive word is here used which implies home-sickness ; *Shirasagi-no-hashi* (Bridge of the White Crane) ; *Yamabuki-no-seki* (Boundary of the Kerria Flowers); *Irone-no-yamaji* (Flower-strewn Mountain-road) ; *Tamamo-no-ike* (Lake of Bounty)—the term used implies a gift from a superior ; *Tamamo-no-yama* (Hill of Bounty) ; *Chiyo-no-hosomichi* (Eternal Narrow Path) ; *Kazashi-no-yama* (Flower-clad Peak); or literally " the decorated mountain," *Misogi-zaka* (Steps of *Misogi*)—a famous shrine,

Hatsu-aki-no-mori (Forest of the Early Autumn); *Kuchinashi-yama* (Hill of *Gardenia florida*); *Kuchinashi-saki* (Cape of *Gardenia florida*); *Minato-da* (Harbour Rice-fields); *Funa-yama* (Boat-shaped Hill); *Matsu-no-kojima* (Pine-tree Islet); *Akikaze-no-ike* (Lake of the Autumn Winds); *Sennin-no-fuchi* (The Magicians' Pool); *Momiji-no-shita-michi* (Path beneath the Maple-trees); *Otome-ga-saki* (Angel's Cape); *Ajiro-ga-ura* (Plaited Coast)— in allusion to the appearance of the fishermen's nets spread out on the sandy beach; *Kuzurezu-no-kishi* (Overhanging Cliff)—literally, a cliff-head almost crumbling away; *Torii-ga-saki* (Cape of the *torii*); *Tokiwa-jima* (Evergreen Island); *Kakiwa-jima* (Dotted Islands); *Yanagi-ga-ura* (Coast of the Willow-trees); *Mahagi-ga-seki* (Boundary of Lespedeza flowers); *Obana-no-tsutsumi* (Bank of Flowering Grasses); *Chigusa-no-sono* (Garden of many Plants); *Harushiru-sato* (Spring-revealing Hamlet)—having reference to the surrounding view in spring-time; *Akikaze-no-hama* (Beach of Autumn Winds); and *Kazaori-yama* (Wind-dispersing Hill).

The garden contained an immense number of rare stones and trees, several quaint structures, plum groves, cherry groves, bamboo groves; besides chrysanthemums, peonies, and numerous specimens of the azalea, kerria, *Spiræa contoniensis*, *Senecio kœmpferi*, and *Hieracium umbellatum*, disposed in banks and beds in different parts of the grounds. A portion was laid out in the Chinese style, with numerous dwarf palms. The islets of the lake were planted with stunted pine trees, to typify the natural scenery of Matsushima.*

A steep road of rugged stone steps, in imitation of the Hakone Pass, led to a fine clump of waving bamboos. A horse-ride, about one hundred and eighty yards long, used for equestrian sports, and a shooting range, occupied other parts of the grounds. Lacquer trees and tea bushes lined the sides of these open areas. In other spots were a lotus lake and an iris marsh with a quaint bridge, and arbours for looking down upon the flowers. The "Beach of Autumn Winds" was planted with autumn plants and grasses, such as lespedezas, chrysanthemums, *Platycodons*, and *Eupatoria*. A small temple dedicated to Inari, and other shrines in honour of different Shinto and Buddhist deities, were situated in certain parts of the garden; and pear, apple, persimmon, and quince orchards occupied other portions. One of the most interesting objects in the landscape is said to have been a curious old pine tree, whose gnarled trunk and branches, supported on numerous props, extended forty-four feet in one direction and twenty-five feet in another, though its altitude did not exceed ten feet.

---

* Matsushima,—a group of rocky pine-clad islands near Sendai forming one of the most beautiful sea-views in Japan.

It resembled the *Karasaki-no-matsu,* or Pine-tree of Karasaki, one of the " Eight Sights of Lake Biwa." (See Fig. 6.)

KORAKU-EN GARDEN, OKAYAMA.

Among the many gardens for which the provincial towns of Japan are famous, the Koraku-En at Okayama, is a characteristic example.   It occupies the grounds formerly belonging to Ikeda, the Daimio of Bizen, but now taken over by the prefectural government.   Above it, still towers the picturesque

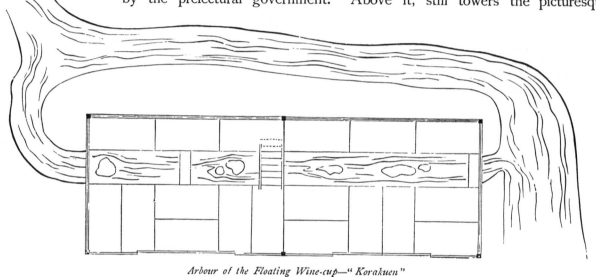

Arbour of the Floating Wine-cup—" Korakuen "
FIG. 7.

many-storied keep of the old feudal castle.   In the centre of the garden is a large lake of an irregular oval form, containing three islets, one of which, towards the south-west, is entirely cut off from all approach from the banks by either bridge or causeway. This is called the " Elysian Isle," a feature without which no lake scenery in Japanese gardening is complete.   It is intended to represent a sea island, and is, in this instance, of a flat conical shape, covered with turf, and embellished with a few rocks, a stone lantern, and a bent pine tree stretching out over the water.   The other two, called respectively the " Proprietor's Island," and the " Guest's Island," are situated in the shallower water on the opposite side of the lake.   Of these, the one more distant from the shore is approached by stepping stones, and a short plank bridge.   Its slopes are adorned with neatly trimmed evergreens and rare boulders.   An open pavilion partly overhangs the lake.   The nearer island is reached by an ornamental wooden bridge with a pretty balustrade, and it is furnished with a tiny tea-room set in a grove of miniature pine trees, and with a graceful stone lantern.   Flowing from the lake, a stream, with pebbled bed, meanders through different parts of the grounds, crossed in places by bridges formed of granite slabs or wooden planks. This winding rivulet is looped in the north-east quarter of the garden, in such a manner as to divert the flow into a channel carried right through a long pavilion, called Kioku-sui-En-no-Chin, or the Arbour of the Floating Wine-cup. This building, of which a plan is shown in Fig. 7, is copied from a similar structure in China : it is used for a pastime of Chinese origin, held on the third day of the third month, consisting of combined wine-drinking and sonnet-making. A sunken cemented channel, with natural rocks let into the bottom, runs longitudinally through the building, and, raised about eighteen inches on either side of this, are matted floors, respectively three feet and six feet wide, for accommodating the assembled guests ; movable boards being laid across in places to allow of passing from side to side. Over the lower end of the channel is a fixed plank upon which the superintendent of ceremonies is seated. The building has a steep staircase leading to an upper floor, forming a large banquet-room, the windows of which afford a fine view of the garden. The recreation consists in floating the shallow wine cups from one end to the other of the thirty feet channel, the period taken in transit being the measure of time allowed for the composition of a stanza upon some given subject. The stream is so arranged that it can be carried through the building or diverted around it at pleasure, by the opening or closing of a sluice. Beyond, it develops into a wide shallow pool or marsh, planted with irises and other water plants, and ornamented with a miniature island reached by a zigzag bridge of planks, in imitation of the scenery of Yatsuhashi. Towards the eastern side of the garden is a large hillock ascended by a winding pathway of rough stone steps, on the slope of which is a small summer-house of irregular plan, delicately constructed with attenuated posts and light low balustrades, the two sides towards the north being closed with plaited bamboo-work pierced with a crescent-shaped opening. The plan of this tiny building is shown in Fig. 8.

In another part of the garden may be observed some majestic pine trees forming a picturesque clump on a level expanse of beaten earth, and, close by, some enormous granite boulders measuring over twenty feet in length, which have been transported in sections and afterwards fitted together with lime and clay, the joints being partly hidden by moss and lichen. A small shrine with accompanying *torii* and fine stone standard-lanterns embellish another part of the grounds.

On the south-west side of the garden are one or two buildings,—remains of the old military palace,—and the grounds immediately in front of these are spread with neatly raked sand having raised footways formed of flat stepping stones, some being water-worn discs of irregular shape, and others monolithic slabs of squared granite.

Summer House—" Korakuen"
FIG. 8.

Just outside the verandah stands a fine natural rock hollowed out at the base, and supporting a water basin, provided with the ordinary pebbled pool and drain, and set off with several shrubs and a rush-work fence. Near here is found a group of evergreen bushes and trees sheltering a multi-storied garden-pagoda. To the rear of the building is another enormous granite boulder, surrounded with choice shrubs. The whole effect of the design is grand, simple, and placid; and there is here an absence of the minute and restless detail which distinguishes many other landscape gardens.

HONGWANJI GARDEN, KIOTO.

This is a somewhat rare example of what is called a *Sotetsu* garden, being thickly planted with dwarf palms of the *Cycas revoluta* species, called *Sotetsu*. It serves also to illustrate the arrangement of a *Kare sansui*, or Dried-up Water Scene, the central portions being arranged with pebbled and bouldered river-bed, stone bridges, and a rocky cascade-inlet, all intended to suggest the presence of water although none actually exists. In the background may be seen a few bushes trimmed into cubical and spherical forms. This garden, which is situated in front of the *Taimensho*, or Principle Reception Rooms, of the temple of the Western Hongwanji, in Kioto, is illustrated in Plate XXXV.

CHAPTER II.

GARDEN STONES.

BEFORE attempting to explain the method of composition adopted in landscape gardens of different kinds, a description of the various materials employed is necessary. A striking characteristic of Japanese gardening is the importance attached to the use of natural stones, rocks, and boulders. In a few of the most remarkable European gardens we find rock scenery of considerable grandeur introduced, perhaps the finest example of such treatment being the Buttes Chaumont in Paris. It is also a common practice, in comparatively small gardens of Western design, to arrange rockeries and fancy grottoes principally for the purpose of planting them with ferns and mosses. With rare exceptions, however, such rock-work consists of formless blocks of slag and broken stone held together with earth, and displaying but little regard to form or proportion.

In all styles of Japanese garden designs careful attention to the shapes and proportions of individual stones is of the first importance. Some teachers of the craft go so far as to maintain that stones constitute the skeleton of the garden, and that their proper selection and distribution should receive primary consideration, the vegetation being disposed in a manner entirely subsidiary to the stone-work. The sizes of the principal rocks and boulders give the scale for the trees, shrubs, fences, lanterns, basins, and other objects placed in proximity to them. Such being the case, great care must be taken to preserve due proportion between the size of stones selected and the area of the garden itself. Large stones would be unsuitable in a small garden, and those diminutive in scale would be out of place in an extensive one. In grounds of considerable area and elaborate design there may be as many as one hundred and thirty-eight principal rocks and stones having special names or functions, in addition to others of secondary importance; but in those of more limited scale and rougher style as few as five stones will often suffice.

The principal boulders of a landscape garden are supposed to suggest the mountains, hills, and rocks of natural scenery.   It is customary therefore to describe their altitude by fictitious measurements corresponding to the heights of their natural prototypes.   This not only helps to keep up the illusion of real landscape, but assists the designer to preserve a consistent character in the subsidiary features.

Another favourite conceit is that of attributing sex to stones of different form in landscape.   Thus is created an important æsthetic aid in maintaining fitting contrasts in compositions.   Rocks and stones are combined in pairs of contrast.   Generally speaking lofty masses are regarded as masculine when placed in apposition to lower masses, which are classed as feminine.   Some stones, in which the nature of both sexes is supposed to be united, are used singly.   There are, however, many rocks, such as those placed on the banks of garden streams or lakes, as well the smaller stones employed merely in an auxiliary manner, to which the idea of sex is not applied.

The secret of the art of arranging stones in an artificial landscape is to make them appear as if natural forces had placed them in position.   Extraordinary freaks of nature, as exhibited in certain lithic wonders, should not, however, be taken as models for imitation.   The enormous scale and prehistoric antiquity of the overhanging rocks and towering pinnacles in real landscape reconcile us to their threatening aspect, but if such phenomena were artificially reproduced on a smaller scale, a sense of instability and danger would be aroused in the beholder, inimical to that repose which is essential in artistic compositions.   A

FIG. 9.

general rule exists that no stone should be utilised which is larger at the top than at the base, and though it would not be difficult to find violations of this law, the exceptions usually present certain extenuating circumstances.   The object of such a rule being to create an impression of stability and repose, it no longer applies if the rock or boulder be flanked by a cliff or hill, or if its overhanging portion be supported by a companion stone. In using volcanic or water-worn rocks of irregular honeycombed shape, care must be taken to select forms such as are frequently seen in nature, so that the observer may be easily reconciled to their odd appearance.

From very ancient times it has been the custom, in the grounds of temples and monasteries, to apply a religious meaning to the principal stones, by giving them the names of different Buddhist deities, or the attributes of certain holy functions. Fig. 10 represents such an ideal arrangement of rocks and stones, which, even to the

Religious arrangement of garden stones.

FIG. 10.

present day, serves in a modified form as a model for the distribution of the principal lithic ornament of gardens. The illustration includes forty-eight rocks, each bearing the names of some Buddha or saint, as follows:—

1, Mida Butsu. 2, Kwannon. 3, Seishi. 4, Kokuzo. 5, Mio-on-ten. 6, Shitsu-bosatsu. 7, Ka-bosatsu. 8, Bu-bosatsu. 9, Fugen-Monju-bosatsu. 10, Chikei-bosatsu. 11, Taishakuten. 12, Waku-Fudo. 13, Fugen-bosatsu. 14, Waku-Gundari. 15, Ki-bosatsu, Yashajin, and Go-bosatsu. 16, Kwaten. 17, Waku-Daiitoku. 18, Bonden. 19, Kwaten. 20, Monju. 21, Futen. 22, Waku-kosanze. 23, Kwatsu-bosatsu. 24, Ri-bosatsu. 25, To-bosatsu. 26, Ho-bosatsu. 27, Satsu-bosatsu. 28, Ju-bosatsu. 29, Ga-bosatsu. 30, San-bosatsu. 31, Go-bosatsu. 32, Komoku-den. 33, Rasetsuten. 34, Tamonden. 35, Sho-bosatsu. 36, Ho-bosatsu. 37, Ki-bosatsu. 38, Kwa-bosatsu. 39, Enten-mon. 40, Jiten. 41, To-bosatsu. 42, Shiten-bosatsu. 43, Sho-bosatsu. 44, Jishi-bosatsu. 45, Ko-bosatsu. 46, Saki-bosatsu. 47, Isha-bosatsu. 48, Jikokuden. Some of the above, though phonetically alike, are written with different ideographs.

To a certain extent, this custom of applying a religious meaning to the principal rocks and stones of a landscape has been introduced into ordinary gardens, in which many of the important stones still preserve a sacred character. Formerly it was said that the principal boulders of a garden should represent the *Kuji*, or Nine Spirits of the Buddhist pantheon, five being of *standing*, and four of *recumbent* form; and it was supposed that misfortune was averted by observing this classification. Whatever the style of a landscape composition, the "Guardian Stone," "Stone of Worship," and "Stone of the Two Deities" must never be dispensed with, their absence being regarded as most inauspicious. On the same principle, there are certain lithic forms which are considered unlucky, and are therefore invariably avoided.

Numerous terms are applied to the stones employed in Japanese gardens. Some indicate merely their geological character or locality of production. *Mikage* stone is a kind of granite coming from a village of that name in the province of Settsu and *Sado* stone is a kind of jasper rock, of deep red colour, abundant in the island of Sado. Other kinds of granite produced in the neighbourhood of Osaka, from Hoki, Sanshiu, and Bingo, are much used for wrought slabs, steps, lanterns, and water basins. The irregular shaped blocks employed in the principal parts of a garden are generally limestones, which have been worn into interesting shapes by the action of water, or scoriaceous rocks due to igneous action. The blue and white limestones are brought principally from Mount Chichibu, in the province of Musashi, and from the river Yama-to-gawa in Kishiu; and the province of Iyo produces a rare specimen of yellowish hue. Some of these coloured limestones possess white veins of more compact forma-tion than the general mass, which, having better resisted the wearing action, stand up in ridges and produce a grain somewhat resembling that of weather-worn timber. Such curious and vermiculated effects are specially sought after. Large slabs, ragged on edge, are extensively employed, and these consist of slates and schists, generally of dark grey and green tints. Nebukawa, a village in the province of Soshiu, is the source of much of this kind of stone. A favourite species of volcanic rock containing numerous cavities comes from the mountains in the province of Idzu, and a honey-combed sea-rock of somewhat similar appearance is brought from the neighbourhood of Odawara. Such material should be used with a due regard to place of production, water-rocks for example, being only applicable to water scenery. Small round stones of dark red colour, taken from the beds of the Kamogawa in Kioto, and the Tenriugawa in the province of Enshiu, are much employed for the channels of drains, basins, and water-courses.

A rare kind of stone called *Shokwa-seki*, said to be petrified wood from India, and considered a great rarity, is occasionally to be seen. River pebbles of granite, sandstone, and flint, are in great demand for the beds of artificial streams.

The value set on stones of good shape, proportion, and colour, leads to the transport of such material from immense distances at the expenditure of much time and labour. It is recorded that in the Tempo period (1830-1844), the mania for rare and costly stones became so extravagant that an edict was issued fixing a limit to the amount permitted to be paid for a single specimen. For ordinary gardens, in which it is impossible to incur great expense for transportation, the stones introduced depend much on the locality. At Osaka and Kioto,—in the neighourhood of which cities granite boulders and river and sea rocks are easily obtainable,—the more common description of gardens will be found to possess them in profusion. Near Tokio and Yokohama the gardeners have recourse chiefly to the black volcanic rocks procurable in the vicinity of Hakone and Fuji-san, and the schists found at Nebukawa, near Idzu. The local experts also display much skill in constructing large artificial rocks of natural appearance with pieces of black mountain scoria.

For all gardens of large size, however, a certain number of immense blocks are essential, and these are often conveyed from remote localities with great mechanical ingenuity. In some exceptional cases such colossal masses are carefully split into pieces, marked, and after conveyance to their destination, cemented together with lime and clay. A fine example of such construction may be seen in the Koraku-En Garden at Okayama, previovsly described.

Stones sometimes receive names which refer to their position in the landscape, such as,—" Mountain-summit Stone," and in other cases they are described according to their real or supposed functions, such as,—" Torrent-breaking Stone." A number of the terms employed indicate the particular shapes of the stones, or some resemblance they are supposed to bear to other objects. The nomenclature has in some cases been bestowed by noted men and has only local significance.

There are five radical shapes recognized for stones employed in garden groups, as follows:—

A tall vertical stone, bulging out towards the middle and finishing conically at the top, called the *Taido-seki*,—the nearest intelligible translation of which is "Statue Stone,"—on account of its supposed resemblance in form to that of the human body.

A shorter vertical stone, rounded slightly at the base, finishing in an irregular blunted cone, and resembling the bud of a magnolia flower, the name applied to which is *Reiji-seki*, which may be rendered as "Low Vertical Stone." (See Fig. 9)

A low broad stone of irregular shape and horizontal character, with a flat top, rather higher than the ordinary stepping stone, and called the *Shintai-seki*, or "Flat Stone."

Another stone of medium height, with a broad flat top and bent over to one side in an arched manner; this is called the *Shigio-seki*, here freely translated as "Arching Stone."

The fifth is a long curved and bent boulder of horizontal character, rising higher at one end than the other, and somewhat resembling the trunk of a recumbent animal; it is called the *Kikiaku-seki*, or "Recumbent Ox Stone."

Of the above five shapes, the "Statue Stone," the "Low Vertical Stone," and the "Arching Stone," are vertical in character, or what henceforth will be termed *Standing Stones*, and the "Flat Stone" and "Recumbent Ox Stone," are of horizontal character, or what may be called *Reclining Stones*. They are variously arranged in combinations of two, three, and five, to form groups in the different parts of gardens, assisted by trees, shrubs, grasses, water-basins, and other ornamental objects. It is not to be supposed that such shapes are by any means exact; but natural rocks are chosen which approach as nearly as possible to the character indicated. These radical forms and their various combinations are shown in Plates I., and II. Certain groupings are considered suitable for particular situations.

The double arrangement of "Statue Stone" and "Flat Stone" is often used on the edge of a lake or stream; and the "Statue Stone" together with the "Low Vertical Stone" are placed near a clump of trees.

Of triple arrangements, the "Statue Stone," with the "Low Vertical Stone," and "Recumbent Ox Stone," are often disposed in juxtaposition at the mouth of a cascade or on the slope of a hill; the "Low Vertical Stone," "Arching Stone," and

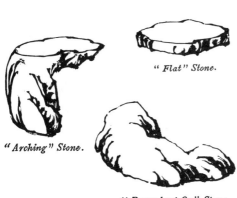

"Flat" Stone.

"Arching" Stone.

"Recumbent Ox" Stone.

"Low Vertical" Stone.

"Statue" Stone.

Combination of
"Low Vertical" Stone
and "Flat" Stone.

Combination of
"Low Vertical" Stone and
"Arched" Stone.

Combination of "Flat" Stone
and "Recumbent Ox" Stone.

Combination of "Statue" Stone
and "Recumbent Ox" Stone.

Combination of "Statue" Stone
and "Low Vertical" Stone.

Combination of "Arched" Stone
and "Recumbent Ox" Stone.

PLATE J.   RADICAL STONE SHAPES.

Triple Combinations.

Quintuple Combination of Radical Stones with Foliage.

PLATE II.   RADICAL STONE SHAPES.

" Flat Stone," are combined at the base of a water-fall; the " Statue Stone " " Low Vertical Stone," and " Flat Stone," form a suitable group for distant shady spots; the " Statue Stone," " Low Vertical Stone," and " Arching Stone," are employed in combination at the mouth of a cascade, so as partly to screen its outlet from view; the " Statue Stone" and " Arching Stone," united, and grouped with the " Flat Stone," are used at the foot of a hill or on an island; and the " Statue Stone," " Recumbent Ox Stone," and " Flat Stone," are arranged together near a garden entrance, occasionally replacing the " Stones of the Two Deities" (*Ni-O-seki*), to be mentioned later on.

In accordance with the principles of Japanese design previously explained, three distinct styles of elaboration are recognized for the above groupings, greater correctness of prescribed shape, and formality in method of combination, being followed in the gardens of more finished and detailed style. Especially is this noticeable when the stones are used in connection with trees and shrubs.

As already mentioned, these radical shapes are generally taken as a guide in the selection of natural stones for gardens; and it is interesting to note that the use of certain other natural shapes is studiously avoided. Stones, for example, with their tops bent or distorted, are technically called "*Diseased Stones*," and rarely admitted into artifical landscape. Other prohibitory terms are applied to rocks improperly employed in compositions. For instance, stones of vertical character, laid horizontally and liable to create the impression of having been overturned, are named "*Dead Stones*"; stones scattered at random in a garden, without any special function or connection in the landscape, are described as "*Poor Stones.*"

It is next necessary to enumerate and describe the different garden stones according to the position they hold and the functions they fulfil in different parts of the composition.

HILL STONES.

The raised parts of a Japanese garden are intended to represent the nearer eminences or distant mountains of natural scenery, and the stones which adorn them express either minor undulations and peaks, or rocks and boulders on their slopes. The principal hill-stones are as follows:—

" Mountain-summit Stone" (*Sancho-seki*),—placed on or near the summit of a hill.

" Mountain-base Stone" (*Reikiaku-seki*),—situated near the base of a hill.

" Mountain-side Stone" (*Sanyo-seki*), and " Mountain Path Stone" (*Hioin-seki*),—both arranged on the slope of a hill.

" Propitious Cloud Stone" (*Keiun seki*),—placed on a hill-top.

" Mist-enveloped Stone" (*Muin-seki*), " Clear Moon Stone" (*Seigetsu-seki*), " Moon Shadow Stone" (*Getsu-in-seki*), and " Cave Stone" (*Teito-seki*), or *Taido-seki*),—all occupying different positions on the sides of hills, the " Cave Stone" being always near the " *Kwannon* Stone."

" *Kwannon* Stone" (*Kwannon-seki*), is the name given to a stone symbolical of Kwannon, a deity worshipped on mountain heights, and often represented as seated in a cave; this is also placed on the side of a hill.

" Moss-grown Stone" (*Seitai-seki*),—placed near the base of a hill, but only employed when water is represented beneath. Of the above names, the first five refer to position and are self-explanatory; the remainder mostly allude to certain effects in mountain scenery which the stones are supposed to typify.

LAKE AND RIVER STONES.

Numerous ornamental stones are used in connection with the lakes, streams, cascades, and artificial torrents of gardens. The following appertain to garden rivers and lakes :—

" Mandarin-duck Stones" (*Fuwo-seki*),—a couple of boulders used upon the banks of a lake or stream, and intended to suggest a pair of these sleeping water-fowl, which are referred to in the Chinese classics as models of conjugal fidelity. These stones are also often placed on an island beach.

" Water-diverting Stone" (*Suigio-seki,*)—situated at the mouth of a river to divert the current and add interest and variety to the stream.

" Sentinel Stone" (*Metsuki-ishi*),—fixed on the extreme edge of a river or lake, and named after a class of feudal detectives, on account of its post of outlook.

" Angling Stone" (*Suicho-seki*),—a high stone with a flat top, overhanging a stream, and affording a suitable seat for anglers.

" Water-gate Stone" (*Suimon-seki*),—marking the outlet of a lake.

" Falling-water Stone" (*Rakusui-seki*),—placed in the pool at the bottom of a water-fall, to receive the torrent and break it into spray.

" Wave-receiving Stone" (*Roju-seki*),—laid in the current of a stream or lake to cause an eddy.

It must be remembered that garden lakes are often intended to represent sea views, hence the reason for some of the following names, which apply rather to ocean than to fresh water scenery :—

"Wild Wave Stone" (*Doto-seki*),—placed at the edge of a lake, to meet the ripple of the water.

"Flying Geese Stone" (*Suigan-seki*),—a stone which fancy has associated with the flight of wild geese.

"Sea-gull-resting Stone" (*Oshuku-seki*),—situated on the beach and supposed to form a favourite rest for sea-gulls.

"Water-tray Stone" (*Suibon-seki*),—a large flat stone placed in a lake so that at high tide its surface is just above the water level. It should be within an easy step from the bank. In deep lakes such stones are often supported from below by means of a platform built on wooden piles.

"Fish-diverting Stones" (*Yugio-seki*),—two stones on the brink of a stream or lake, hollowed out below so as to let the water flow underneath, and forming a passage for fish.

"Nameless Stone" (*Mumio-seki*),—placed in the bed of a river.

"*Tsuten* Stone" (*Tsuten-ishi*),—so called after a pretty river view near Kioto, noted for its fine maples. The same spot has a picturesque bridge, also imitated in landscape gardens, the *Tsuten* Stone being employed beside it.

"Planet Stone" (*Gesshuku-seki*),—placed in the middle of a wide river. The name seems altogether chimerical.

"Tortoise Stone" (*Kame-ishi* or *Ki-seki*),—fixed on the bank of a river, and resembling in shape a turtle or tortoise.

"Crane Stone" (*Tsuru-ishi*),—supposed to resemble a crane, and arranged to face the "Tortoise Stone." In Japan, both the crane and the tortoise are emblems of long life, and the presence of the above two stones on a beach or sandy bed is considered very auspicious. The resemblance to the objects suggested is, however, often very indistinct.

"Long Life Stones" (*Junio-seki*),—three stones placed together on the edge of a beach.

"Good Luck Stone" (*Fuku-ishi*), and "Life and Death Stone" (*Shobo-seki*), are two stones used on the banks of a lake.

"Green Moss Stone" (*Seitai-seki*),—mentioned also amongst hill stones,—may be included in this list, as it occupies an intermediary position between land and water.

The above are not only introduced into actual water scenery, but are sometimes employed in a Dry Garden (*Kare sansui*), in which water is merely indicated by a channel filled with white or black pebbles and sand. It is a rule that rocks and stones placed in lakes must have their foundations well prepared, and a specially firm support made for those having irregular bases, to provide for the contingency of the water being drawn off and the whole exposed to view. There are many instances in nature in which the large boulders of mountain streams, having fallen from the cliffs above, lie in topsy-turvy positions. For this reason certain top-heavy and abnormal shapes are often permitted for the large stones in garden rivers, provided that they are over-grown with moss and lichen, suggesting age and the action of natural forces.

CASCADE STONES.

The cascade is an almost indispensable feature of lake and river gardens, and even when water cannot be obtained, its position is indicated by means of rocks and stones. The following are the principal stones used in connection with real or imaginary falls :—

"Guardian Stone" (*Shugo-seki*),—a large rock of the "Statue Stone" shape, backed with earth, and forming the principal part of the rocky cliff over which the water falls. This is the most important of all garden stones, and, in some form or other, is always introduced as the central feature of the near distance ; it also often bears the alternative name of "Cascade-supporting Stone" (*Taki-soye-ishi*).

"Stone of *Fudo*" (*Fudo-seki*),—named after a Buddhist deity, who is represented holding a sword and surrounded with flames, and to whom cascades are specially dedicated. The outlets of many natural falls, such as that of Urami-no-taki at Nikko, have the image of this god carved on the cliff. Sometimes a stone statuette is erected instead. In connection with garden cascades a vertical stone of natural formation, and of the "Statue Stone" shape, is used, which is supposed to represent Fudo.

"Children Stones" (*Doji-seki*),—eight smaller stones often placed round the "Stone of Fudo," representing the spirits of children attendant upon the god.

"Double Step Stone" (*Nidan-seki*),—a stone with a stepped top sometimes used to give a double fall to a torrent.

"Cascade-embracing Stone" (*Taki-hasami-ishi*),—a rock, flanking the outlet of a water-fall, which may be appropriately called the "Cliff Stone." It is paired with the "Guardian Stone."

"Mirror Stone" (*Kagami-ishi*),—another name occasionally applied to the "Cliff Stone" on account of its wet polished surface.

" Cascade Basin Stone" (*Takitsubo-ishi*),—a flattish stone placed in the pool to receive the falling water.

" Current-dividing Stone" (*Namiwake-ishi*),—fixed in the torrent at the base of a cascade.

" Water-dividing Stone" (*Mizuwake-ishi*), and " Water-receiving Stone" (*Mizu-uke-ishi*), are other terms given to stones which are used in the torrent or secondary falls below a cascade.

ISLAND STONES.

Among the islands introduced into water gardening are three which require special stones for their adornment. The first of these is the " Elysian Isle" (*Horai-jima*), the idea of which is taken from Chinese legend (see page 32). It is represented in the form of a tortoise, and its ornamental rocks bear names typifying different members of this animal, as follows:—

" Tortoise Head Stone" (*Kito-seki*),—representing both in shape and position the head of the tortoise.

" Fore-legs Stones" (*Rioshu-seki*).

" Hind-legs Stones" (*Riokiaku-seki*).

" Tail Stone" (*Osaki-seki*).

The above are placed in position with great care, and a pine tree is planted in the centre of the island, as if it grew out of the back of the tortoise,—a common emblematical representation indicating the great strength and age of the shell of this animal. Sometimes a rock, having the form of a young tortoise, is used instead of the pine tree.

The other two islands alluded to, are called the " Master's Isle" (*Shujin-jima*), and the " Guests' Isle" (*Kiakujin-jima*); the principal stones placed upon them are mostly named according to the special pursuits or functions associated with these two islands. Those of the " Master's Isle" are as follows:—

" Stone of Easy Rest" (*Ankio-seki*),—supposed to form a favourite seat for the master of the house.

" Stone of Amusement" (*Yukio-seki*),—a suitable prominence for angling.

" Seat Stone" (*Yosoku-seki*),—of similar use to the " Stone of Easy Rest."

The principal stones of the " Guests' Isle" are :—

" Guest-honouring Stone" (*Kiakuhai-seki*),—intended as a resting place for an important visitor.

"Interviewing Stone" (*Taimen-seki*), also called the "Stone of Obeisance" (*Hai-seki*),—a flat stone located in front of the "Guest-honouring Stone," and on which the host stands to salute his visitors.

"Shoe-removing Stone" (*Ridatsu-seki*) or (*Kutsunugi-ishi*),—on which the clogs or sandals are placed.

"Sea-gull-resting Stone" (*Oshuku-seki*),—mentioned previously as being placed on the banks of lakes, but also introduced into the "Guests Isle."

"Water-fowl Rock" (*Suicho-seki*),—supposed to be for water-fowl to rest upon.

Another important stone placed on either the "Master's Isle," or "Guest's Isle," and which is sometimes introduced into other parts of the garden, is called the "Seat-of-honor Stone" (*Jaza-seki*). It takes the place of the "Guest-honouring Stone," and tradition avers that it represents a rock near a sacred tree in India, an idea which requires that a fine old tree should be planted close by.

Other island stones embody on a gigantic scale the different utensils used for writing. They are :—

"Hair Pencil Stone" (*Fude-ishi*),—a long cylindrical stone representing a Japanesewriting brush.

"Ink-slab Stone" (*Kenyo-seki*) or (*Kenteki-seki*),—a flat oblong or circular stone dished out in the centre, representing the palette on which writing-ink is prepared.

"Brush-rest Stone" (*Hikka-seki*),—a vertical rock supposed to resemble a Japanese brush-rest. The above are placed together in a group, after the manner of the objects represented.

VALLEY STONES.

The following stones are suitable for the low and level parts of gardens, such as valleys, plains, and pathways :—

"Stones of the Two Gods" (*Nijin-seki* or *Ni-O-seki*),—a pair of similar *Standing Stones* intended to represent the guardian deities of the site, and arranged in the flat portion of a garden, near the entrance, just as two statues of Buddhist Devas are placed in the entrance gates of temples. Formerly, the ceremony of erecting these stones in position constituted a sort of dedication of the garden. They were washed perfectly clean, and rice and wine were placed before them.

"Stones of the Three Gods" (*Sanjin-seki*),—three vertical rocks sometimes used in combination instead of the above.

"Stone of Worship" (*Reihai-seki* or *Hai-seki*),—generally placed near a sacred stone such as the " Stone of the Two Deities," and at some point in the front of a garden, to form a station from which the best view may be obtained.   It is a broad, flat stone upon which one stands in a posture of veneration.

"Waiting Stone" (*Hikae-seki*),—the name given to a *Standing Stone*, more or less conical in shape, placed in the foreground of the garden.

"View-receiving Stone" (*Shozo-seki*),—the meaning of which term is not quite clear.   It probably indicates a point from which the finest prospect of the garden can be had.

"View-completing Stone" (*Taito-seki*),—probably referring to the importance of this stone in the distant view.

"Distancing Rock" (*Mikoshi-iwa*),—a rock partly hidden behind a hill, or placed in some shady part of the background, and intended to increase the idea of distance in a garden.

"Peeping Stone" (*Nozoki-ishi*),—a stone screened partially from view by shrubs and trees.

"Wine Cup Stone" (*Sakazuki-ishi*),—so named from its supposed resemblance in shape to a Japanese wine cup.

"Way-side Stone" (*Dokio-seki*),—situated on the side of a real or imaginary pathway, and suitable for resting upon.

"Passing-on Stone" (*Koro-seki*),—placed at the side of a walk, like a milestone; it should be a vertical stone, unsuitable as a seat, and contrasting in character with the "Way-side Stone."

WATER BASIN STONES.

The water basins of a Japanese garden—fully described elsewhere—require certain natural stones for their surroundings and embellishment, and these are named according to their actual or supposed functions in connection with the basin.   They are as follows:—

"Base Stone" (*Dai-ishi*),—a natural rock, level on the top, and serving as a stand for certain water basins.

"Mirror Stone" (*Kagami-ishi*).   This name has occurred before as applied to one of the stones of a cascade.   The present "Mirror Stone" is a broad flat schist of polished surface and bluish colour, placed between the water basin and the verandah, and on which the waste water from the ladle is poured; when wetted it is supposed to reflect surrounding objects.

"Purifying Stone" (*Shojo-ishi* or *Kiyome-ishi*),—a stone of the "Low vertical" form placed beside the basin, and always kept scrupulously clean and wet. It is also sometimes called the "Peeping Stone" (*Nozoki-ishi*) because, by mounting it, one can look over the top of the basin, which, being generally used from the verandah floor, is some height from the ground.

"Water-filling Stone" (*Mizukumi-ishi*),—a long flat stone upon which the servant stands to fill the basin.

"Water-raising Stone" (*Mizuage-ishi*),—a higher stone than the former, also used for filling the basin from, and placed so as to be half concealed by shrubs.

"Water-drain Stones" (*Suikomi-ishi*),—the name given to several large pebbles placed to hide the drain hole. The drain beneath a water basin is a small shallow sink of irregular shape, either cemented or covered with round pebbles, and sometimes bordered by the heads of small piles of charred wood. The various stones of water basins may be seen illustrated in Plates IX., X., and XX. No vertical stones higher than three feet are allowed in the open space near the rooms of a house as they tend to interrupt the view.

TEA-GARDEN STONES.

The gardens attached to rooms for the Tea Drinking Ceremonies have special arrangements which will be described in referring to different classes of garden designs. The principal stones peculiar to them are named:—

"Kettle Stone" (*Yuto-seki*),—a flat stone suitable for placing the kettle upon.

"Candle-stick Stone" (*Teshoku-seki*),—intended to support the candle-stick or lantern when tea ceremonies take place after dark.

"Low Basin Stone" (*Tsukubai-chozubachi-ishi*),—a low hollowed stone holding water and used for washing the hands in. It is peculiar to Tea-Gardens, the ordinary basin being high and used by one in an erect attitude.

"Front Stone" (*Maye-ishi*),—placed in front of the "Low Basin Stone."

"Sword-hanging Stone" (*Katanakake-ishi*),—a double-stepped stone upon which one stands for the purpose of hanging the sword upon a sword-rest attached to the outer wall of the Tea Room.

As the Tea Ceremonies take place indoors it should not be supposed that the "Candle-stick Stone" and "Kettle Stone" are actually used for the purposes indicated;

they are merely intended to be suggestive of such uses. Some of these Tea Room Stones are illustrated in Plates III., XXXI., and XXXII.

Besides the above technical terms applied to stones common in most Japanese gardens, other special names, belonging to particular stones in the celebrated gardens of temples and palaces owe their origin to famous designers, patrons, or visitors. Such seem, in most cases, to have been suggested by the shapes, but sometimes they are merely fanciful. A few of them may be mentioned :—

"Tortoise Back Stone" (*Kiko-seki*).	"Clear Mirror Stone" (*Meikio-seki*).
"Sleeping Tiger Stone" (*Kogwa-seki*).	"Hermit Stone" (*Daruma-seki*).
"Long Boat Stone" (*Chosen-seki*).	"Saddle-shaped Stone" (*Amba-seki*).
"Tiger's Head Stone" (*Koto-seki*).	"Faint Scent Stone" (*Chinko-seki*).
"Magician's Hat Stone" (*Sembo-seki*).	"Priest's Paten Stone" (*Butsuban-seki*).

In some temple grounds many rocks are still named after Buddhas, and Buddhist saints, the system of arrangement followed being simply one of order in theological rank and position (see Fig. 10, page 43). Their object is to assist in the religious contemplation of the priests and acolytes.

STEPPING STONES.

Turf was not used to any extent in ancient Japanese gardens though it has been introduced recently in imitation of foreign methods, and with a view to economise labour in garden-making and tending. In an orthodox garden the plain open portions are spread with sand carefully raked in patterns, or as is still more common, a firm surface of beaten earth, well weeded and swept, is retained. As this is kept slightly damp at all times, and in summer profusely wetted, it presents a cool and fresh surface. In order to preserve such earthen and sanded areas, which the Japanese wooden clogs would cut to pieces, and also as a comfort to the pedestrian when the soil is wet, a pathway is invariably constructed with "Stepping Stones," called *Tsutai-ishi*.

Another name applied to them is *Tobi-ishi*, meaning "Flying Stones," on account of the supposed resemblance in their formation to the order taken by a flight of birds. Such terms as "Sea-gull Style" and "Wild-goose Style" are often employed to describe such arrangements.   These irregular flat stones are, in certain old books, called *Shiki-Shima*, or " Scattered Islands," a name also applied in ancient verse to the islands of the Empire of Japan ; and this fact is quoted by several writers as a proof of the antiquity of the art of gardening in this country.

In the simple rustic gardens attached to Tea Rooms, these " Stepping Stones " constitute one of the principal features, and in all gardens, without exception, they are employed to some extent.

FIG. 11.

It may be observed that nothing could be less artistic than a formal arrangement of such stones at regular intervals.   Everyone, moreover, must have remarked the difficulty of keeping one's balance whilst stepping upon stones placed exactly in a row, a performance resembling that of walking upon a narrow plank.   It is not, therefore, surprising to find that the Japanese gardener follows carefully devised rules for the distribution of " Stepping Stones."   He uses certain special stones and combinations, having definite shapes and approximate dimensions assigned to them, and he connects these with secondary blocks, the whole being arranged with a studied irregularity for both comfort in walking and artistic effect.   This is attained by the employment of ragged slabs of slate, schist, or flint, flat water-worn rocks or boulders, and hewn slabs or discs of granite or some other hard stone. The natural boulders are placed in zigzags of fours and threes, or sometimes in threes and twos, artificially hewn slabs, discs, or strips intervening. Though uniformity of tread is carefully calculated, the different sizes of the stones cause the intervals to vary considerably, and any apparent regularity is avoided. The distance between " Stepping Stones" should not, however, be less than four inches, to allow of the intermediate spaces being kept clean.

The smaller stones are of sufficient size for the foot to rest firmly upon, and should not, as a general rule, be higher than two inches from the soil. In ancient times, it is said that " Stepping Stones" for the Emperor's gardens were made six inches high, those for a Daimio four inches, those for ordinary Samurai nearly three inches, and for common folk an inch and a half in height. The larger stones are intended as a rest for both feet, and two of them should never be used consecutively. Fig. 11 illustrates a small garden, belonging to a merchant at Sakai, in which may be seen several continuous pathways formed of " Stepping Stones." When such walks branch off in two directions a larger and higher stone, called the " Step-dividing Stone" (*Fumiwake-ishi*), will be placed at the point of divergence. This stone is occasionally known by the fancy name of " Snail Stone" (*Garan-seki*), from some supposed resemblance to a gigantic snail or slug. A similar word—*Garan*—written with a different ideograph, means a " Statue Pedestal;" and some writers, in explanation of its application to the " Step-dividing Stone," state that once upon a time a certain priest used the pedestal of a Buddhist statue for the purpose. The above arrangements of " Stepping Stones" are shown in Plate III.

In some places—such as in front of a verandah or a flower bed—it is customary to lay a single rectangular slab of hewn granite, or a number of tooled stones of irregular sizes fitted together in broken bond, and forming a regular strip. The latter arrangement is called " Long-and-short Work" (*Chotan-kaku*), the slabs having wide joints, filled in with a kind of mortar or clay. Sometimes such rectangular strips are composed partly of hewn slabs, and partly of a kind of concrete consisting of large pebbles bedded in mortar.

Other examples occur in which two long strips of hewn granite called " Label Stones" (*Tanzaku-ishi*),—after the oblong strips of card on which Japanese verses are written,—are placed parallel to one another and overlapping about two-fifths of their length. These are frequently seen in front of a flower bed. Similar slips, but of great length in proportion to their width, are called " Girdle Stones" (*Obi-ishi*), after the long, narrow belts used to confine the Japanese robe. Large slabs of wrought granite, of greater height than the above, are employed singly to form a step from the ground to the floor of the verandah, and, in some cases, one of the posts supporting

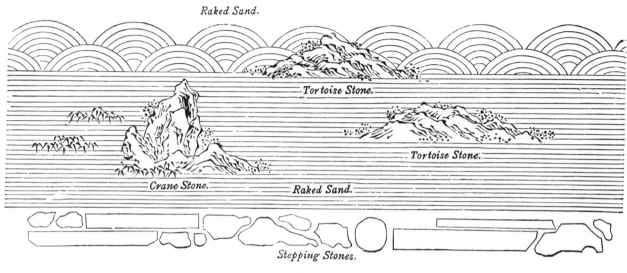

Raked Sand.

Tortoise Stone.

Tortoise Stone.

Crane Stone.

Raked Sand.

Stepping Stones.

FIG. 12.

the gallery floor rests on the edge of such stone or is dowelled into it. Plate IV, illustrates these arrangements of hewn " Stepping Stones," and Fig. 12 shows a combination placed in front of a level area of raked sand.

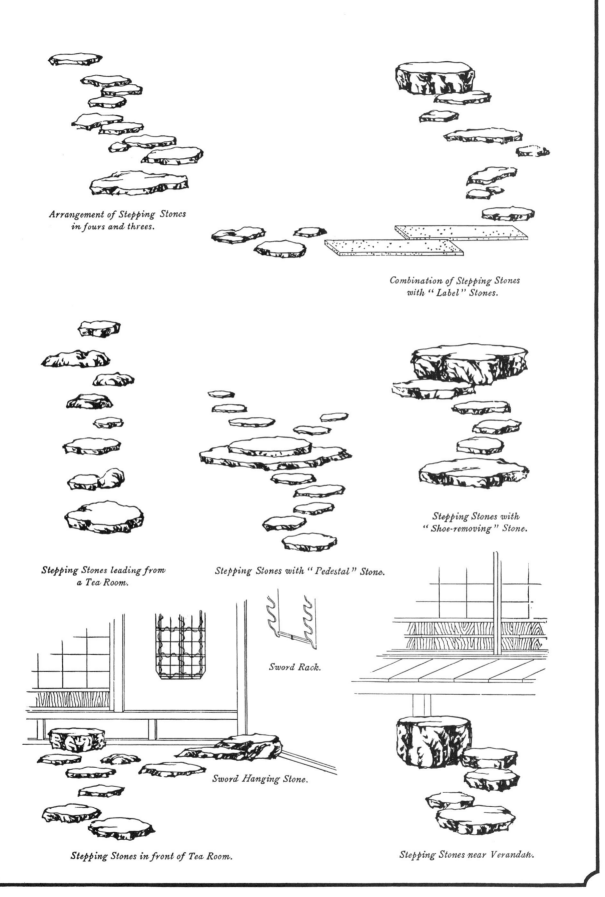

Arrangement of Stepping Stones
in fours and threes.

Combination of Stepping Stones
with " Label " Stones.

Stepping Stones leading from
a Tea Room.

Stepping Stones with " Pedestal " Stone.

Stepping Stones with
" Shoe-removing " Stone.

Sword Rack.

Sword Hanging Stone.

Stepping Stones in front of Tea Room.

Stepping Stones near Verandah.

PLATE JJJ.   STEPPING STONES.

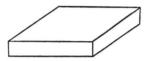

Concrete Stepping Stone.

Verandah Stepping Stone, finished style.

" Worshipping Stone," finished style.

Dowel Hole for Post.

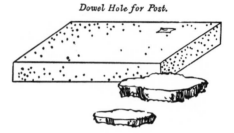

" Worshipping Stone." rough style.

Verandah Stepping Stones, rough style.

" Long and Short" Arrangement, rough style.

" Long and Short" Arrangement, finished style.

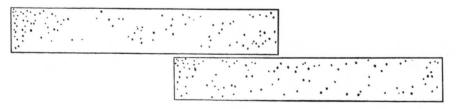

" Label" Stones.

PLATE IV.   STEPPING STONES.

CHAPTER III.

GARDEN LANTERNS.

STANDARD Lanterns form an important feature of all Japanese gardens. It is recorded that the first stone lantern constructed in Japan was erected in the beginning of the seventh century by Prince Iruhiko, son of the Emperor Suiko, at a solitary lake-side spot in the province of Kawachi, as a protection against robbers by whom the locality was infested. It was afterwards removed to the grounds of the temple of Tachibana in Yamato, founded by Shotoku-Taishi. Whether or not this popular story be true, it seems, anyhow, certain that the stone Standard Lantern is of purely Japanese origin. In China, from which country many ideas in gardening were introduced, this particular kind of garden ornament is not to be found. From early times it has been customary in Japan to present Lanterns of stone or bronze to Buddhist temples for the purpose of adorning the courts and paved approaches. The grounds of all the important shrines and mausolea possess large numbers—sometimes amounting to several thousands—which, in many cases, have been brought from great distances as votive offerings from princes and nobles. They vary from six feet to eighteen feet in height, and are arranged in rows and avenues on either side of the paved or gravelled courts. Some authorities state that the use of stone Lanterns as garden ornaments dates from the introduction of the Tea Ceremonies.

Garden Lanterns are used singly in combination with rocks, shrubs, trees, fences, and water-basins. It is an imperative rule that they should harmonise in scale and character with the adjacent buildings and with the magnitude and elaboration of the garden. The usual positions selected are :—at the base of a hill, on an island, on the banks of a lake, near a well, and at the side of a water-basin. The primary intention of introducing such lanterns into landscape gardening is not to illuminate the grounds, but to form architectural ornaments contrasting agreeably with the natural features.   In ordinary grounds they are only occasionally seen lighted at night, and even when thus used the object seems rather to produce a dim and mysterious glow, than to render objects distinctly visible; to obscure the light still more, leafy shrubs and trees are always planted close by.   The idea of placing them on the border of a lake or stream is that their reddish light may be reflected in the water.   The important place which stone Standard Lanterns take in even the simplest designs may be gathered from Fig. 13, representing a small garden belonging to the Zuiun-In, attached to the temple of Mioshinji in Kioto.

FIG 13.

The ordinary material for these ornaments is granite or syenite, of which rocks many varieties exist in Japan.   *Mikage* Stone from the province of Settsu, *Shirakawa* Stone from the province of Yamashiro, *Kido* Stone from the province of Omi, and a kind of rock from Tamba, are much used.

Stone Lanterns are chiefly valued in proportion to their age, and various devices are employed for imparting an antiquated appearance to new specimens. Those rendered weather-worn by long exposure to the elements are mostly brought from old country temples and mountain shrines, and are in special demand.   A fictitious age is given to new Lanterns by attaching, with a gummy solution, patches of green moss, and by fixing to them decayed leaves by means of bird-lime, or by smearing them with the slime of snails; after either of which processes they are kept in the shade and frequently wetted. The result of these methods is to produce on the stone a white lichen and other fungous growths.

Garden Lanterns may be broadly divided into two classes, namely,—the *Standard* class, and the *Legged* class; besides which there are other fancy shapes occasionally employed. The original model for Standard Lanterns dates back from the Ashikaga period, and goes by the name of the "Kasuga Shape," after a Shinto deity to whom one of the ancient temples at Nara is dedicated. The "Kasuga Shape" Lantern has a high cylindrical standard with a small annulet in the centre, erected on a base and plinth of hexagonal plan, and supporting an hexagonal head crowned with a stone roof of double curve, having corner scrolls. The top is surmounted with a ball drawn to a point above. The head of the Lantern, which is technically called the "Fire-box" (*Hibukuro*), is hollowed out, two of its faces having a square opening large enough to admit an oil lamp; and the remaining four sides being carved respectively with representations of a stag, a doe, the sun, and the moon. Enrichments are also applied to the mouldings of the base and fire-box.

The following are examples much resembling the "Kasuga Shape":—

"Lemon Tree Shape" (*Yu-no-ki-gata*),—somewhat ruder and simpler in style than the above, with no annulet to the shaft, and with a cap of flat mushroom-shape instead of the double curved form.

"*Nigatsu-Do* Shape,"—named after another ancient temple, and differing from the "Kasuga Shape" in having the cylindrical standard hollowed out from its central annulet in two flat concavities. The carving is also simpler in character.

"*Shirataku* Shape,"—named after a class of Shinto officials, and distinguishable from the "Kasuga Shape" only in the details of its mouldings and carved enrichments. The subjects represented on the faces of its six-sided fire-box are the sun, the moon, a pine tree, a plum tree, and clouds, supposed in combination to convey some poetical suggestion. It has a circular carved base resting on a rough natural stone.

"*Uzumasa* Shape,"—named after the locality of a famous temple called Koriuji at Saga in the province of Yamashiro, and peculiar for its pyramidal roof of square plan, covering an octagonal head supported upon a cylindrical pillar. It has a broad circular base and no carving. This must not be confounded with the "Uzumasa Owl Shape" which is similar to the "*Nigatsu-Do* Shape" with the exception that it bears the carving of an owl on one of its faces, in historical reference to a romantic spot in Shinano where Fujiwara-no-Nagashige nightly listened to the cry of an owl.

Belonging to the Standard Lantern class, but of somewhat different forms from the above, are the following :—

"Shrine Shape" (*Miya-gata*),—which has an oblong standard with moulded base and neck, supporting a square head covered by a projecting pyramidal roof and resembling the outline of a primitive Japanese temple. The similarity is further assisted by hollowing out and cutting away two of the square sides of the head, so as to leave only a slender stone pillar at one corner, two faces remaining solid and having their surfaces carved. Examples may frequently be seen in which the square fire-box is of wood, the supporting pillar, and even the superincumbent roof, being of stone.

"*Enshiu* Shape,"—named after the famous philosopher Enshiu, who is supposed to have invented it. It is somewhat like the ordinary "Kasuga Shape," except in its peculiar proportions. The cylindrical standard is short, and the head and roof are abnormally elongated, giving the top somewhat the appearance of a high Welsh cap, and to the Japanese suggestive of the long cranium of Fukurokujiu one of the Gods of Fortune. There are two forms of this Lantern slightly different in shape and style of finish.

"*Rikiu* Shape,"—invented by Sen-no-Rikiu, has a slightly hollowed standard carrying a drum-like head crowned with a wide mushroom-shaped roof.

"*Showo* Shape,"—named after another *Chajin*, has a globular fire-box with a flat saucer-shaped cap, and is supported on a high trumpet-like standard, broader above than below.

The "*Soeki* Shape" and "*Sowa* Shape," are rude imitations of the "Kasuga Shape" and "Shrine Shape, and bear the names of their inventors.

The "Lucky Shape" (*Uraku-gata*),—has a globular head with a mushroom-like covering, and a short cylindrical standard. It is very rude and simple in form.

"*Oribe* Shape" is named after the philosopher Furuta Oribe, and used to decorate his tomb. It has a square fire-box in the form of a temple and similar to the "Shrine Shape," supported upon an oblong standard with no base, the lower part of the shaft having its corners hollowed out in two deep chamfers. On one face of the standard a representation of a Buddhist saint is carved.

"Planet Shape," (*Shuko-gata*),—a somewhat simplified form of the above, the wider portion of the chamfered standard forming itself the head of the Lantern, and being hollowed out at one corner in an oblong opening. It is crowned by a flat mushroom-shaped roof and a ball.

"Mile-post Shape" (*Michi-shirabe-gata*),—consists simply of an oblong stone pillar with a cap of very slight projection ending in a flattened pyramid. The shape is copied from the ordinary wooden bridge-newel or gate-post, covered with a metal cap. It has an oblong lamp hole on one side, just below the head, and an inscription is carved on one of the other faces.

Daibutsu Shape,"—named after the temple of Daibutsu, in Kioto. It has a square fire-box with projecting roof of flat slope, and is supported upon a very high oblong stone standard with no base. It resembles more a lamp-post than an ordinary Lantern.

" Dragon Shape" (*Rioto-gata*),—has a globular fire-box with ogee roof and moulded necking, supported upon an attenuated stone pillar of wavy shape and great length, which is supposed to resemble the body of a dragon. It is generally placed beside a high tree.

" Valley Lantern" (*Rankei-gata*),—of peculiar shape, attributed to the invention of the artist Taishin. It has an hexagonal or octagonal head covered with a curved roof of the ordinary " Kasuga" form, carried upon a slender arched stone strut, dowelled at the bottom into a flat boulder from which it springs. This form has a quaint and unstable appearance, and is not often used, but when introduced in gardening it is placed on the border of a lake, so as to project over the water, with the crooked branch of a low pine tree trained over it.

Before leaving the subject of Standard Lanterns, mention may be made of certain lamp-posts which belong more to this class than to any other. They are employed on garden roads or in passage-gardens, chiefly adjacent to the summer-houses and resting-sheds of Tea Rooms, and consist of square or wedge-shaped wooden lanterns covered with roofs of board or thatch and carried on high posts. They are quite rustic in character and are named as follows:—

" Who-goes-there ? Shape." (*Tasoya-gata*),—is square in plan, wider at the top than below, and covered by a gable roof of boards. Its sides are filled in with paper doors and it is supported on brackets attached to a slender square post. It derives this peculiar name from its faint light by which the outline of forms can vaguely be distinguished.

" The Thatched Hut Shape," (*Tomaya-gata*),—the head of which resembles a small thatched cottage, and is carried on brackets attached to a high post.

The class of Garden Lanterns previously referred to under the term of *Legged* Lanterns are also known by the distinguishing name of " Snow-scene" Lanterns (*Yukimi-doro*), on account of the important part they assume during snow time. They are very wide in proportion to their height and are invariably covered by a large umbrella-shaped roof or cap, forming a broad surface to receive snow. The Japanese regard snow scenery as one of the floral displays of the year, and a snow-clad garden is always looked upon with great pleasure. These "Snow-scene" Lanterns are mostly overshadowed by the crooked branch of some evergreen, and form, together with the surrounding foliage, a most picturesque group after a fall of snow.

They have no standard, but their spherical, square, or octagonal heads are supported upon arched legs, crowned with broad mushroom-shaped coverings, resembling the large rush hats worn by the farmers, and surmounted by a bud-shaped ball. The different varieties are distinguished by the number of legs, the principal being :—

"The Three-legged Shape" (*Mitsuashi-gata*),—sometimes called the "Yedo Shape," because most common in the Yedo (Tokio) district,—has an hexagonal body with wide umbrella-like roof supported on three curved legs, like quadrants.

"The Four-legged Shape" (*Yotsuashi-gata*),—common in Osaka and Kioto, very similar to the above, but having four legs instead of three, and covered with a roof of hexagonal plan and double curve.

"The Six-legged Shape" (*Mutsuashi-gata*),—having six curved legs, an hexagonal head, and umbrella-shaped roof.

Sometimes the six or eight-sided heads are rounded above and below so as to approach to a spherical shape, and occasionally the form becomes completely globular. The head, or fire-box, is hollowed out at the side, with openings either square, circular, crescent-shaped, or cusped. A fancy prevails for making such Lanterns of rough unhewn stones, selected to resemble as much as possible the normal shapes, which results in a curious rustic construction. Cases also exist in which wrought stones and natural stones occur in combination. A peculiar kind of stone Lantern, belonging to the "Snow-scene" class, consists of the head and cap alone, without legs, placed upon a low rude stone. This is called the "Crouching Lantern" (*Tsukubai-doro*), and it is generally erected near a very low water-basin, called the "Crouching Water-basin" (*Tsukubai-chozubachi*), and used specially in Tea-Gardens.

Hanging Lanterns of bronze are often suspended by a chain from the verandah eaves of a house or Tea Room, over the garden water-basin, which is placed close by. These are of various design, made in antiquated bronze or iron. The principal Lanterns are illustrated in Plates V., VI., VII., X., and XX.

Bronze Standard Lanterns, such as abound in the courts of temples are seldom introduced into orthodox Japanese gardens. In certain modern gardens they may

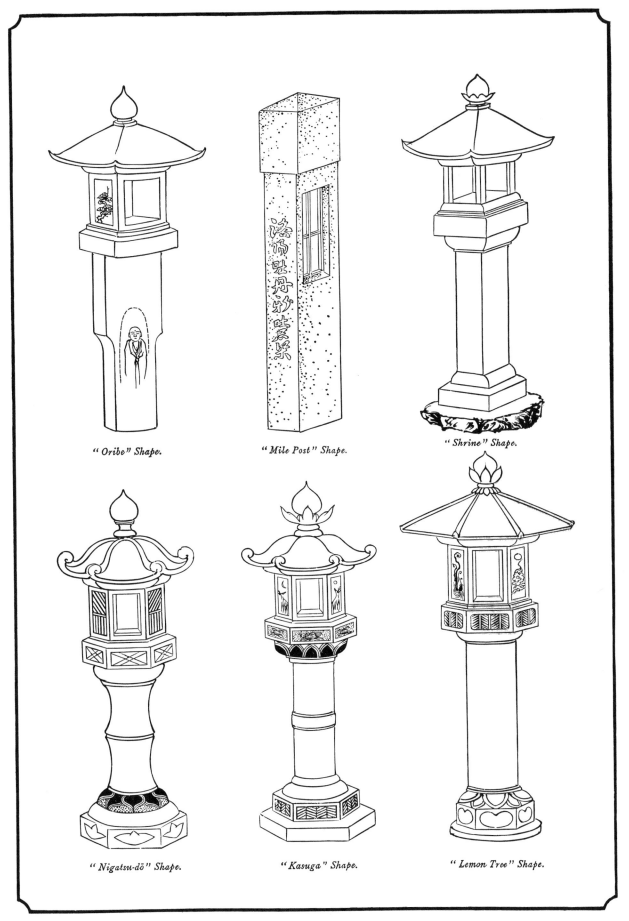

"Oribe" Shape.

"Mile Post" Shape.

"Shrine" Shape.

"Nigatsu-dō" Shape.

"Kasuga" Shape.

"Lemon Tree" Shape.

PLATE V.   GARDEN LANTERNS.

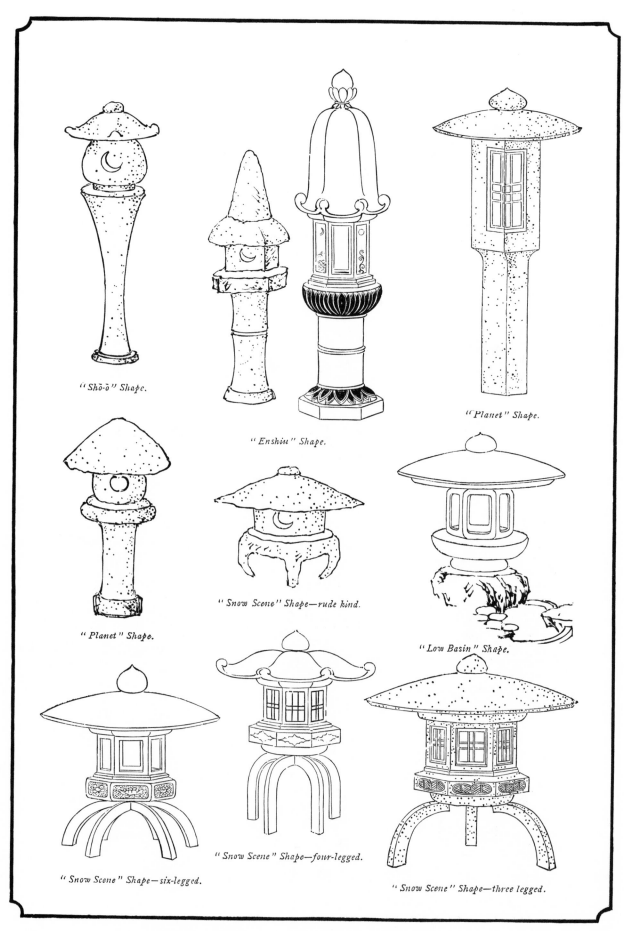

"Shō-ō" Shape.

"Enshiu" Shape.

"Planet" Shape.

"Planet" Shape.

"Snow Scene" Shape—rude kind.

"Low Basin" Shape.

"Snow Scene" Shape—six-legged.

"Snow Scene" Shape—four-legged.

"Snow Scene" Shape—three legged.

PLATE VI.   GARDEN LANTERNS.

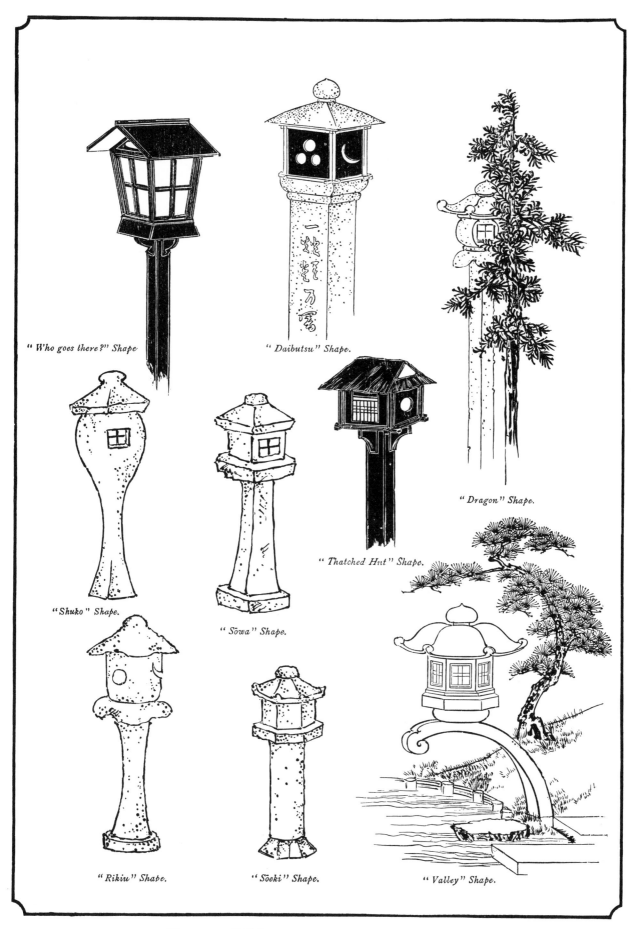

"Who goes there?" Shape

"Daibutsu" Shape.

"Dragon" Shape.

"Shuko" Shape.

"Sōwa" Shape.

"Thatched Hut" Shape.

"Rikiu" Shape.

"Sōeki" Shape.

"Valley" Shape.

PLATE VII.   GARDEN LANTERNS.

be seen, as also bronze images obtained from demolished or despoiled temples. When treated as garden ornaments they have generally been so installed by the foreign purchaser.

Standard Lanterns of porcelain have also lately come into use, but whatever may be their value as successful specimens of keramic art, their decorative appearance ill accords in character with natural scenery, and they are not, therefore, considered desirable ornaments in correct landscape gardening. Natural stones are generally introduced in the vicinity of stone Standard Lanterns, the method of arrangement being similar to that followed in grouping rocks alone,—as already described on page 46,— the Lantern itself occupying the place of the " Statue Stone " in such combinations. One of the adjacent stones, called the " Lamp-lighting Stone " (*Tenkwa-seki*), is employed for the purpose of reaching the fire-box of the Lantern, and is made higher than the adjacent " Stepping Stones," being often of a double-stepped form.

CHAPTER IV.

GARDEN PAGODAS.

A favourite ornament in Japanese gardens of the better class is the stone Tower, or Pagoda. It is a structure in two, three, five, or more separately roofed stages, somewhat similar in shape to the large Chinese pagodas, though of ruder proportions. In certain examples, each storey has vertical sides which

Garden of Jojiu-In, Kiyomizu.

FIG. 14.

are cut into cusped openings, but in others the upper stages consist merely of a series of curved roofs placed immediately one over the other. Garden Pagodas are either supported upon curved stone legs, like the "Snow-scene Lanterns," or are carried solid to the ground. Their roofs are cut into plain concave slopes with projecting tilted eaves,—occasionally ornamented with rolls representing roof-tiles,— and are surmounted by long stone finials, consisting of several successive rings and a crowing ball or jewel. The most usual forms are copied from ancient monuments to be seen in the mortuary grounds of many old temples and mausolea, and as in the case of standard lanterns, these ornaments appear to have had a religious origin. Applied to gardening, however, they are purely decorative, and present a very pic- turesque appearance amid the foliage of the gardens, imparting to the composition the suggestion of actual landscape upon a diminutive scale. Fig. 14 illustrates the garden of Jojiu-In, attached to the Temple of Kiyomizu, in which a Pagoda is shown as a central feature ; Fig. 15 represents another ancient garden designed by

Garden belonging to Tei-ami, at Maruyama.

FIG. 15.

Sho-ami, which contains two of these ornaments. The ordinary name given by the Japanese to these garden structures is "Korean Tower" (*Koraito*), and they are described according to their number of stories, some being of considerable height. They are extensively employed in the gardens of China, whose arts, as is well known, first reached Japan through the medium of Korea.

The example of an ornament of this kind, given in Plate XXIX., occupies a central point in the garden; Plate VIII. illustrates geometrically several of the ordinary shapes. There are, however, an infinite variety of designs, almost every old garden displaying some novel and interesting shapes. In fact, more variety and license seem to have been allowed in the forms of Pagodas than in that of any other garden ornament.

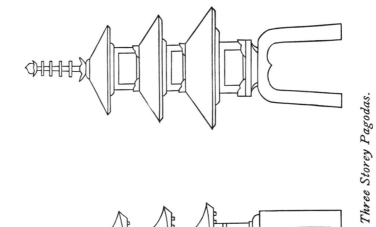

Three Storey Pagodas.

Five Storey Pagodas.

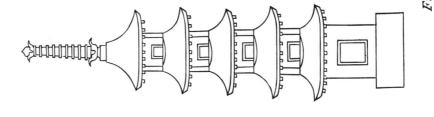

PLATE XIII. GARDEN PAGODAS.

CHAPTER V.

GARDEN WATER BASINS.

THE Water Basin is found in all Japanese gardens, situated generally in close proximity to a building, but forming a part of the garden composition. Its purpose is to provide water for rinsing the hands, and it is therefore placed so as to be easily reached with a ladle from the gallery or verandah leading to the more private parts of the residence. As a screen between it and the wall of the neighbouring lavatory, a low ornamental fence of bamboo or rush-work is placed on one side, also a stone lantern half hidden by trees and shrubs; all of which are scrupulously kept free from dirt, webs, or insects. Fig. 16 illustrates one of the many designs of screens serving such a purpose. The size of a Water Basin should, strictly speaking, be proportionate to the character of the building, and its distance from the verandah should also accord with the general dimensions adopted. As the ordinary distance of a Basin from the outer gallery of a small residence is about eighteen inches, and its height from the ground about three or four feet, it follows that, in front of a building of large proportions, the Basin becomes at least four or five feet removed, and its height seven or eight feet from the soil. It is consequently out of reach for practical purposes, and in connection with religious and palatial buildings of large size and importance, in which due proportions are carefully followed, the large Water Basin becomes merely an ornament, another smaller Basin and draining floor, called *Nure-En*, attached to the verandah, being provided for service. Such large ornamental Basins, removed to a distance from the building and beyond the shelter of its projecting eaves, are provided with some kind of decorative lid or cover to keep out the rain.

In small town buildings the lavatory may be found disconnected from the dwelling and placed in the garden or yard, in which case the Water Basin stands near it, removed from the house, and approached by stepping stones leading from the verandah.

Certain kinds of Basins of very low form, which cannot be used in an erect position, and employed mostly in Tea-Gardens, or Passage Gardens, are called " Crouching Water Basins" (*Tsukubai-chozubachi*). Their original purpose was for collecting spring water, and they had no connection with the out-buildings. In the gardens

FIG. 16.

of modern Tea Rooms they are placed in front of the lavatory, detached, and filled with perfectly clean water; when introduced into larger grounds they occupy quite a secondary position.

The principal kinds of Water Basins are as follows:—

The "Ornamental Water Basin" (*Kazari-chozubachi*) consists generally of a large natural rock of some interesting shape, flat on the top, and hollowed out as a basin. It is adorned with a little wooden construction, like a miniature shed or temple, to protect the clear water from rain, falling leaves, and sunshine.

The "Date-shaped Basin" (*Natsume-gata*) is of simple oval form, made of roughly wrought granite, with a shallow hollow above for holding the water.

The "Bridge-post Basin" (*Hashigui-gata*),—in imitation of the cylindrical posts used for the newels of wooden and some stone bridges, is hollowed out on the top to form a basin, and has an oblong slit in the side, representing the mortise into which the horizontal balustrade of a bridge is tenoned. It appears probable that the design was copied from an old bridge-post originally used by some noteworthy personage for the purpose of a Garden Basin.

The "Oven-shaped Basin" (*Doko-gata*) is of an elongatéd cubical form, with a curious curved opening in the side, representing the fire-hole of a Japanese stove. It has a circular hollow on the top to hold the water.

The "Round Star Basin" (*En-Shoshuku-gata*) is simply a short granite cylinder hollowed out to hold water at the top, and inscribed with an astronomical ideograph. This kind of Basin is placed immediately on the ground, without any stand.

The "Square Star Basin" (*Ho-Shoshuku-gata*),—an elongated cube, in granite, similarly hollowed at the top, also inscribed with an astronomical ideograph.

The "Stone Bottle Basin" (*Sekibin-gata*),—of an irregular oval form, somewhat resembling an ordinary stoneware filter, with ears on the sides, and a shallow hole at the top.

The "Stone Jar Basin" (*Sekisui-gata*) is of plain oval vase-shape, its surface sometimes carved with an inscription.

The "Bubble Shape Basin" (*Wakutama-gata*),—a simple globular stone Basin roughly carved on the side with the representation of a saint or hermit, and carried on the head of a wooden pile.

The "Iron Basin" (*Tetsubachi-gata*),—almost similar to the former, but having a somewhat more flattened shape, to imitate the metal bowl used by mendicant priests.

The "Four Deities Basin" (*Yoho-Butsu-gata*),—a basin of rude oval or melon-like shape, carved with representation of four Buddhist deities. This kind of Basin should have a base stone.

The "*Naniwaji*-shape Basin" (*Naniwaji-gata*),—having two octagonal faces, placed vertically, one inscribed with the name of Naniwaji, a temple near Osaka. It is of narrow width, having the uppermost facet of the octagon hollowed out for holding water.

The "Priest's Scarf Basin" (*Kesa-gata*),—of a flattened oval form, a little broader below than above, decorated with geometrical carving representing the pattern of a priest's scarf. This kind should have a base.

The "*Genkai*-shaped Basin,"—formed of a slender arched bar of granite, in imitation of a Japanese curved stone bridge, and hollowed out at the crown as a bowl. Its name is derived from the Genkai Straits on the West Coast of Japan.

The "*Shiba Onko* Basin," also called the "Decayed Pine Basin," is in the shaped of a broken jar, somewhat resembling a decayed and hollowed stump of wood. Shiba Onko was a man of learning who showed his precocity in boyhood by breaking a large jar of water to deliver his playmate who had fallen into it. This kind belongs to the low form of Water Basins before referred to.

The "*Fuji*-shaped Basin,"—another low vessel, made in the shape of Fujisan, and hollowed out at the top, the crater forming the water-holder.

The "Chinese Junk Basin,"—also of the same class, roughly resembling a Chinese boat or junk.

The "Ray-fish-shaped Basin" (*Anko-gata*),—a low Basin of irregular shape, supposed to resemble in outline a fish of the ray species.

The "Running-water Basin" (*Kakehimizu-gata*) is a bowl or pot of stone or earthenware with a broad rim. It is placed on a stone or wooden pillar, filled with running water conveyed to it by means of bamboo aqueducts, and consequently kept in an overflowing condition. Ornamental stones and a sunk drain are arranged around the base of the supporting post.

In addition to the above, Bronze Basins,—some vase-shaped (see Fig. 16), some bowl-shaped, and some in the form of an urn with a small tap and bronze lid,— are often used. These are generally placed upon a high rock or stone.

The "Hand-pail Basin" (*Teoke-gata*) is a small tub of white wood, provided with a lid, with a little brass tap in the side for serving the water. Such Basins are used in connection with the simpler class of buildings, and are hung from the roof eaves; they can hardly, therefore, be properly classed as garden ornaments.

Attached to all open Basins is a small wooden ladle, called *Hishaku*, for baling the water and pouring it over the hands. The most important Basins are illustrated in Plates IX., X., and XX.

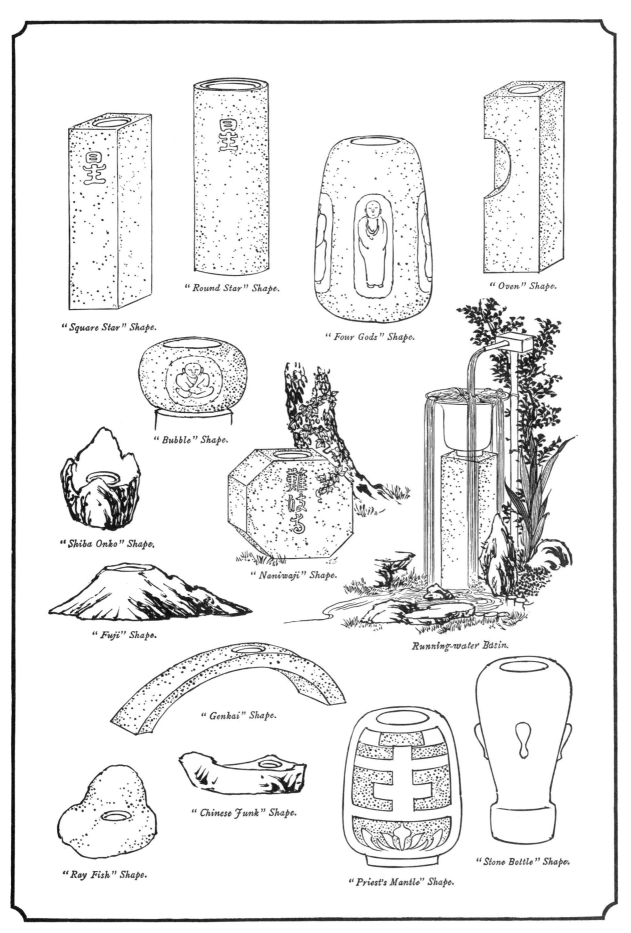

"Square Star" Shape.

"Round Star" Shape.

"Four Gods" Shape.

"Oven" Shape.

"Bubble" Shape.

"Shiba Onko" Shape.

"Naniwaji" Shape.

"Fuji" Shape.

Running-water Basin.

"Genkai" Shape.

"Chinese Junk" Shape.

"Ray Fish" Shape.

"Priest's Mantle" Shape.

"Stone Bottle" Shape.

PLATE IX.   GARDEN WATER BASINS.

Fig. 1.

Fig. 2.

Fig. 3.

Fig. 4.

PLATE X.   GARDEN WATER BASINS.

CHAPTER VI.

GARDEN ENCLOSURES.

JAPANESE gardens are bounded by walls, fences, or hedges. Walls serve more as a general enclosure to property, and belong rather to the province of the architect, than to that of the landscape gardener; but in cases where gardens are carried to the outer boundary, and not preceded by gravelled courts and paved approaches, the style of the outer wall and its gateways are more or less influenced by the character of the garden. The walls surrounding the grounds of the old palaces consist of a thick battering construction of clay and tiles, neatly plastered, and enclosed in a stout timber framework, having elaborate wooden bracketting as a cornice, and being crowned with a roof of ornamental tiles. Intercepted at intervals by handsome roofed gateways, they present a strikingly grand appearance, as may be seen around the Imperial Palace and the Temple called Higashi Honganji, at Kioto.

FIG. 17.

Commoner mud-and-tile plastered walls, having no wooden framing, and carrying a tile roof of smaller projection, are often employed to enclose grounds of less importance. Examples may be seen in those surrounding the property of H.I.H. Prince Arisugawa, and in parts of the Imperial Palace, in Tokio. A similiar form of enclosed wall, in simpler construction, is shown in Fig. 17, which serves also to illustrate a common practise of planting trees in the corners of such boundaries.

Brick and stone enclosing walls are of quite modern introduction. The

Japanese have never been accustomed to employ solid walls in gardens as a means of cultivating wall-fruit or climbing plants, wall-fruit being unknown in the country as such, and the creepers being grown upon light trellises and open fences.

GARDEN FENCES.

Garden enclosures are sometimes constructed with a framework of posts and horizontals, filled in with wattling, and afterwards plastered. The faces of the timbers in these constructions remain visible, and support a projecting roof of boards or tiles. Round the small gardens of buildings in crowded towns, where it is absolutely necessary to obtain privacy and seclusion, these wood and plaster Fences are of a considerable height, sometimes attaining fifteen or twenty feet; the upper portions are supplied with square, circular, or multi-foil openings, railed or latticed, by which means the interior light and ventilation of the narrow courts is increased, and a very ornamental appearance produced externally. This kind of Fence may be frequently seen in Osaka and Kioto, but is not so common in Tokio.

Another kind of enclosure is made with a similar framework filled in with boarding, instead of plastering, thus coming under the head of Wooden Fences. The simplest sort of Wooden Fence consists of square posts and a ground sill with two narrow horizontal strips between the posts, against which the intermediate boarding is nailed. Broad planks are fixed vertically, first on one and then on the other side of the horizontals, and slightly overlapping, in such a way that a space for the passage of air is left between the boards. The whole is covered with a capping, cut into two slopes on the top to carry off the rain. The posts are sometimes continued above the capping, their extremities being crowned with little roofs and ridges of board. The planking of such structures, in some examples, is not carried to the bottom, a space of a foot or more being left open below. Simple Fences of the above kind are not intended to be thoroughly private and secure enclosures, but are merely regarded as light boundaries, only partially screening from publicity. In the construction of some boarded Fences the planks instead of being nailed overlapping on alternate sides of the cross pieces, are kept flush with one another, and the open joints covered by thin strips of wood or bamboo. In addition to the interval left at the bottom, a similar open space is often introduced between the top of the boarding and the capping of the fence, and this space is filled in with narrow bars or lattice-work, or sometimes with slender intersecting diagonals. Through the interstices thus left may be seen the blossom-clad branches of trees, the planting of which in the corners of such enclosures is a favourite device.

Leaving out of consideration the gorgeously decorated woodwork of certain temple buildings, the Japanese prefer always to exhibit the natural grain of timber in their wooden constructions. The boarding of Fences is occasionally ornamented by a method of removing the softer parts of the wood to some depth by means of sand, which leaves the harder portion of the grain standing in relief. This produces a very effective marking, similar to that observed in timber which has been long exposed to the weather. Sometimes the worm-eaten and weather-worn planks of old boats are introduced into such constructions, to produce rustic effects.

Another method applied both to the boards and posts of Garden Fences is that of charring the wood in patches,—a process which gives to it a piebald aspect. Different ways of roughly tooling and chipping timber posts, so as to show the markings of the adze or chisel, are also employed, for the purpose of giving them a picturesque effect. Various kinds of Wooden Fences are shown in Plates XI., XII., and XIII.

Apart from the idea of privacy and protection, Garden Fences are considered an important ornament of the grounds, and with this view they are frequently introduced to divide and give interest to different portions of the same garden (see Fig. 18).

FIG. 18.

They were first extensively employed in the *Kamakura Period*. Later, when the Tea Ceremonies came into vogue during the supremacy of the Ashikaga Shoguns, there are said to have been twenty-five different kinds of Fences invented. Other books refer to as many as thirty-five varieties, but in some of these the points of difference seem to have been very trifling.

BAMBOO FENCES.

Close Fences of bamboo are very commonly employed in Japanese gardens. These are called *Kenninji*, after a noted temple of that name, and are constructed of closely packed strips of freshly cut bamboo, placed vertically and double, so as to show their green outer surface on both sides. The degree of roughness or delicacy of workmanship in these structures is carefully observed, and they are known as belonging respectively to the *rough*, *finished*, or *intermediary* styles. For making the common *Kenninji*, tubes of bamboo are split into four pieces, and the strips are, therefore, very convex in shape; but for the more elaborate class of constructions narrower and flatter laths are employed. These vertical strips are connected by

FIG. 19.

means of two or three horizontal bars, formed of half sections of a stouter kind of bamboo, to which they are bound by dyed cords, care being taken in arranging the filling-in, that the knots of the bamboo-work alternate.   The   top   is   sometimes

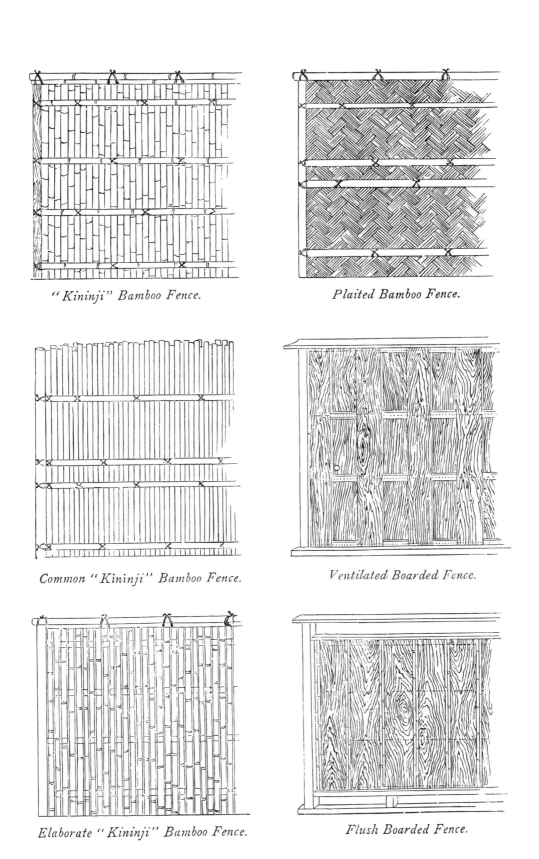

"Kininji" Bamboo Fence.

Plaited Bamboo Fence.

Common "Kininji" Bamboo Fence.

Ventilated Boarded Fence.

Elaborate "Kininji" Bamboo Fence.

Flush Boarded Fence.

PLATE XI. GARDEN FENCES.

finished with a large bamboo pipe or a round pole as a capping, ornamentally tied with coloured cords at intervals. One way of arranging the vertical strips, which form the body of Bamboo Fences, is to thread them alternately in and out of horizontal strips so as to produce a kind of coarse plaiting; and other examples are constructed with thin strips diagonally interwoven, forming a kind of rattan work, and strengthened with horizontal rails and borders of thick bamboo, tied to the body of the fence. There is a special kind of Bamboo Fence, called the "*Daitokuji* Fence," after a famous temple of that name; it differs from the ordinary *Kenninji* in having its vertical lathing bound with wire.

Some Bamboo Fences are made of thin unsplit stems packed closely together, and held between horizontal strips of larger size. Slender twigs of a birch-like wood—(*Lindera sericea*)—are sometimes similarly employed in combination with posts and longitudinal bands of stout bamboo. In such structures the top is left ragged to produce a rustic appearance, and they receive the poetical name of " Nightingale Fence " on account of their rural character.

The kinds of cord used to bind together the parts of Bamboo Fences, as well as the manner of looping and tying, are of no small importance. Sometimes the stems of vines or wistaria creepers are used, but oftener hemp cords, or the fibres of the *Pteris aquilina*, dyed of a brown or black colour.

Another sort of Bamboo Fence, which will be seen illustrated, is filled with upright bamboo strips in its lower division, terminating at the top in an open framework adorned with delicate diagonal bracing; the intermediate portion consists of close reed-filling or rush-work pierced with hexagonal barred openings. The whole is strengthened with a bottom sill, a top cap-piece of wood, and occasional verticals of stout bamboo. All of the above enclosures, though frequently provided with ornamentally barred or latticed openings, are classed as Closed Fences. Illustrations of Bamboo Fences are shown in Plates XI., XVI., and XVII.

OPEN FENCES.

The next to be mentioned are Open Fences of bamboo, called *Yotsume-gaki*, generally decorated with climbing plants,—the convolvulus, wild rose, passion-flower, and in some cases the wistaria, being applied to this purpose. They consist of occasional wooden posts—with or without a ground sill—between which are placed verticals and horizontals of thin bamboo, having open intervals; the whole is tied together with cords, and presents a series of open checkers. The uprights, which consists of single or double stems, are arranged of different lengths, sometimes regularly recurring, and sometimes without any apparent system. A flat middle bar of wood is occasionally introduced longitudinally to strengthen the construction, the stems being arranged alternately on each side of it, and the whole secured with dyed cord. Open Fences are seldom more than two or three feet in height, with their style of fabrication distinguished by the three degrees of elaboration. A rare example of a very simple and rustic kind is made with thin leaf-clad branches of bamboo fixed in the ground at intervals of five or six inches, bent in different directions, and tied together at the crossings; this produces a kind of curved lattice-work, the leaves partly filling up the intervals. Occasional wooden posts are necessary to strengthen and bind together such constructions. Illustrations of Open Fences are shown in Plates XII., and XVIII., and Fig. 19 gives an example taken from a small Tea-Garden.

GARDEN HEDGES.

The use of Hedges as garden enclosures is very common in suburban and rural localities. It is not unusual to see thick Hedges, as high as fifteen or sixteen feet, made of closely planted Kaname (*Photinia glabra*), Sugi (*Cryptomeria japonica*) Maki (*Podocarpus macrophylla*), Tsuge (*Buxus japonica*), or Kashi (*Quercus lævigata*). As some of these trees do not send out branches close to the ground they are often surrounded by an outer bamboo fence about six feet high. Such natural enclosures are carefully trimmed and clipped, generally to a square form, and they are sometimes pierced with arched openings. These archways may be seen fitted with a square timber frame-work, having recessed wooden gates of very ornamental appearance. The Camellia tree is occasionally used for Hedges in country districts.

The short, clipped Hedge is a favourite enclosure for portions of Tea-Gardens, some thickly growing bush—such as box—being used, closely planted and cut square to the height of about six feet. The garden of the temple Kaifuku-In, in Kioto, illustrated in Fig. 20, has such a hedged enclosure. Wooden gates and gate-posts are employed in conjunction with this form of boundary; and it is by no means uncommon to see a bamboo or boarded fence on one side of a gateway with a natural hedge as a continuation on the other,—a method exemplified in Fig. 20. Short Hedges

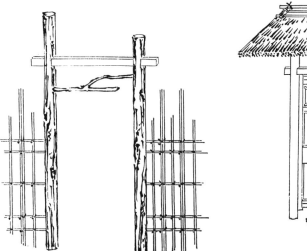

Rustic Garden Gateway.

Thatched Roof Gateway.

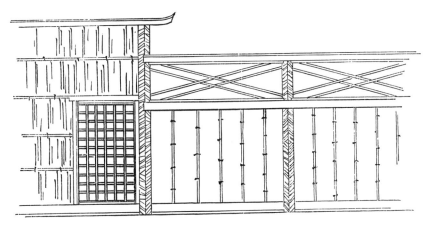

City Garden Fence and Gate.

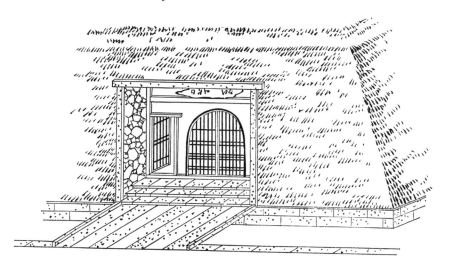

Hedge-framed Gateway.

PLATE XII.   GARDEN GATEWAYS.

often serve as screens in the interior of a garden, or the outer Hedge is continued inwards in two right angles, just within a gateway, so as to screen the view immediately in front, on entering. The use of the Kuromoji (*Ilex integra*) for such constructions is considered a great luxury; this wood has a sweet cedar-like scent, on which account, as well as owing to the hardness of its slender twigs, it is much used for toothpicks. The skeleton of light Hedges is often formed of open bamboo-work on which is grown

Garden in Kaifuku-In, Kioto.

FIG. 20.

the Kikoku (*Citrus fusca*), a kind of thorny shrub bearing small citrons. Such borderings are rarely more than three or four feet high, and are elevated on grass-covered embankments, called *Dote*,—an arrangement which may be observed round the grounds of some of the palaces and the residences of the nobles. Different sorts of Hedges are illustrated in Plates XII., and XXXI.

GARDEN GATEWAYS.

The enclosures of gardens are provided with various kinds of entrances. It is considered imperative that even the smallest garden should have two Gateways,—one forming the principal entrance, and the other a back entrance, called

Soji-guchi, or "Sweeping Opening," because of its use when clearing away the litter and rubbish from the garden. The back entrance is generally a wooden or bamboo gate of the simplest kind, but its position is of great importance. The form of Entrance Gateway varies with the kind of enclosure in which it is placed. The outer

boundaries of large gardens will be provided with handsome gate-buildings including a porter's lodge, double-barred doors, and a gate for pedestrians which often contains a small wicket. Elaborate architectural constructions of this sort are, however, somewhat ouside the subject of gardening. The ordinary garden entrance-way, suitable for boarded or bamboo fences, consists of two vertical posts having a cross-tie framed between them at a point some little distance below the top. Occasionally an extra cross-piece or lintel of

FIG. 21.

crooked wood is added below this, to impart an antiquated character to the construction. The style of the garden—rough or elaborate—determines whether the timbers of such Gateways should be squared, planed, and provided with metal cappings, or simply left round, and rough; in some cases the wood will be charred or worm-eaten. The fancy for quaintness and artistic dilapidation is carried so far that in

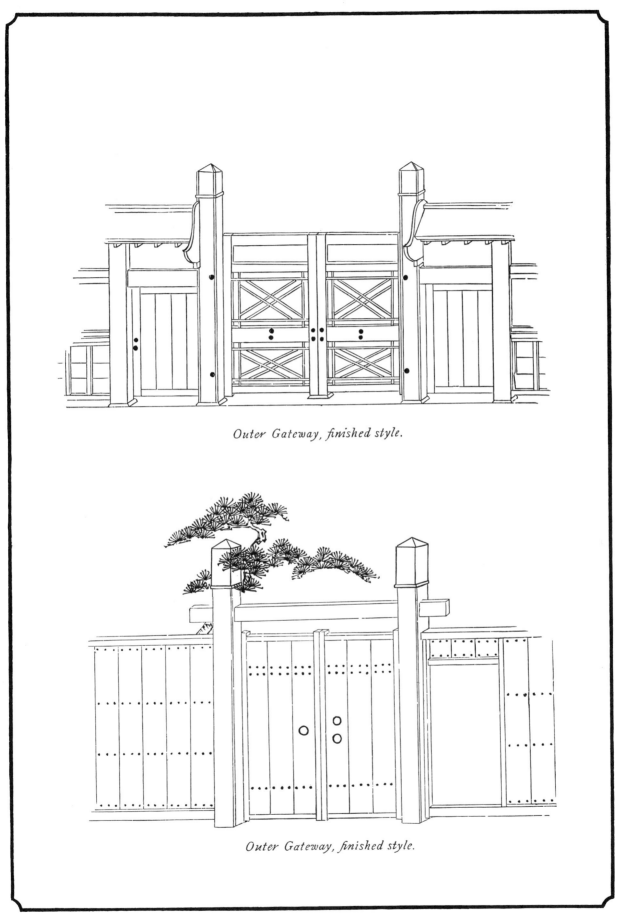

Outer Gateway, finished style.

Outer Gateway, finished style.

PLATE XIII. GARDEN GATEWAYS.

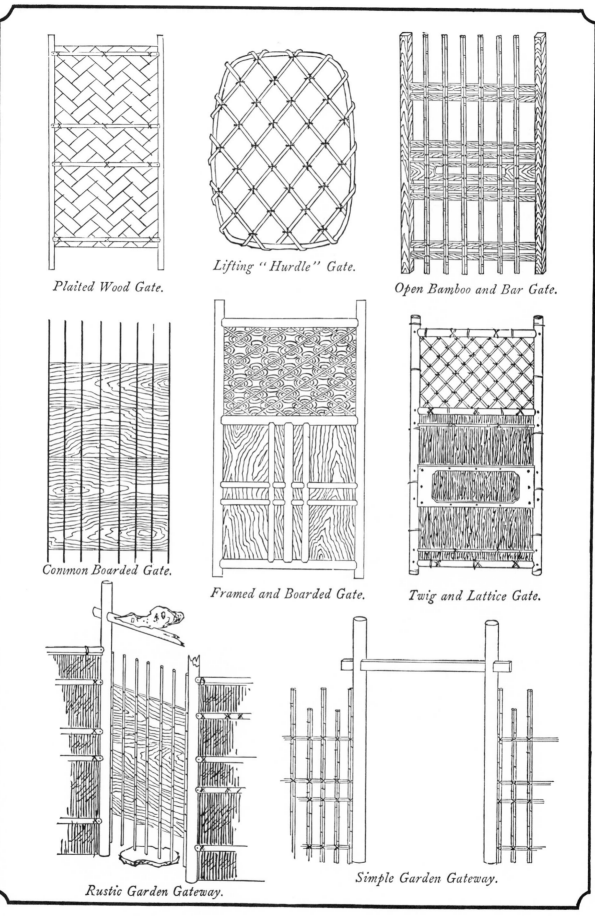

Plaited Wood Gate.

Lifting "Hurdle" Gate.

Open Bamboo and Bar Gate.

Common Boarded Gate.

Framed and Boarded Gate.

Twig and Lattice Gate.

Rustic Garden Gateway.

Simple Garden Gateway.

PLATE XIV. GARDEN GATES.

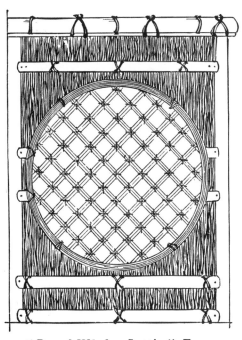

"Round Window Lattice" Fence.

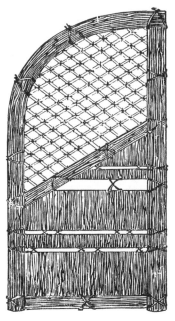

Low Korean Screen Fence.

"Clothes-horse" Fence.

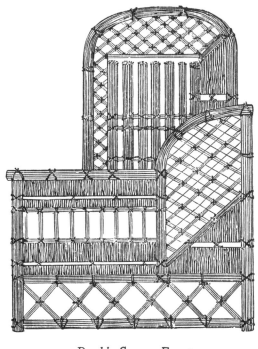

Double Screen Fence.

PLATE XV. GARDEN SCREEN FENCES.

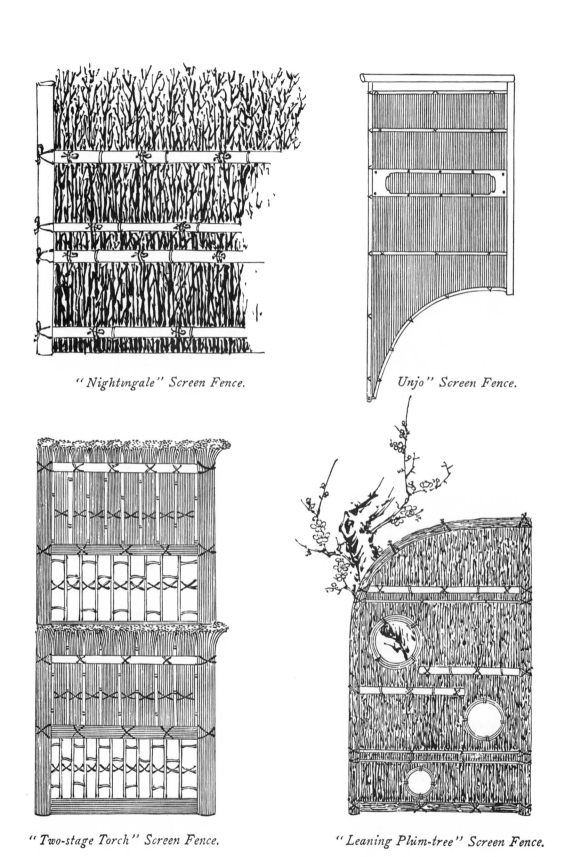

"Nightingale" Screen Fence.

Unjo" Screen Fence.

"Two-stage Torch" Screen Fence.

"Leaning Plum-tree" Screen Fence.

PLATE XVI. GARDEN SCREEN FENCES.

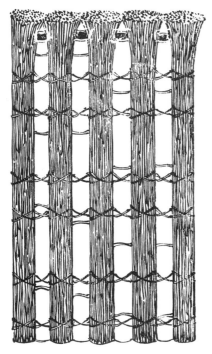

Reed Bundle Screen Fence.

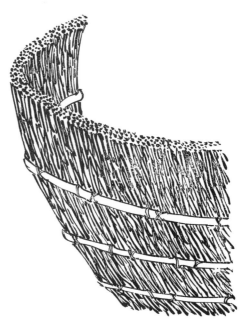

"Hurdle" Fence.

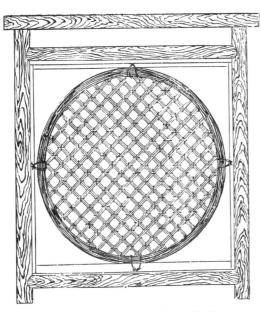

"Round Window Clothes-horse" Fence.

"Bent-branch" Fence.

PLATE XVII.   GARDEN FENCES.

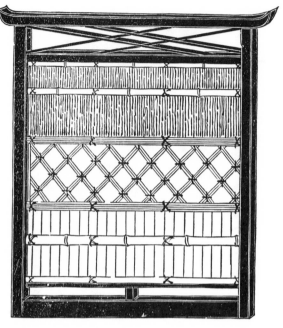

"Komachi" or "Hiding" Screen Fence.

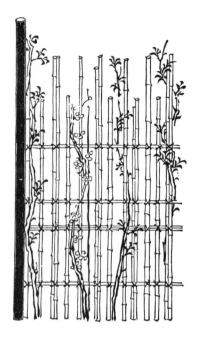

Open Fence.

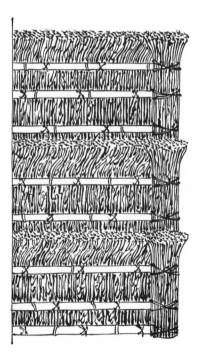

"Triple Stage" Screen Fence.

"Looking-through" Screen Fence.

PLATE XVJJJ. GARDEN SCREEN FENCES.

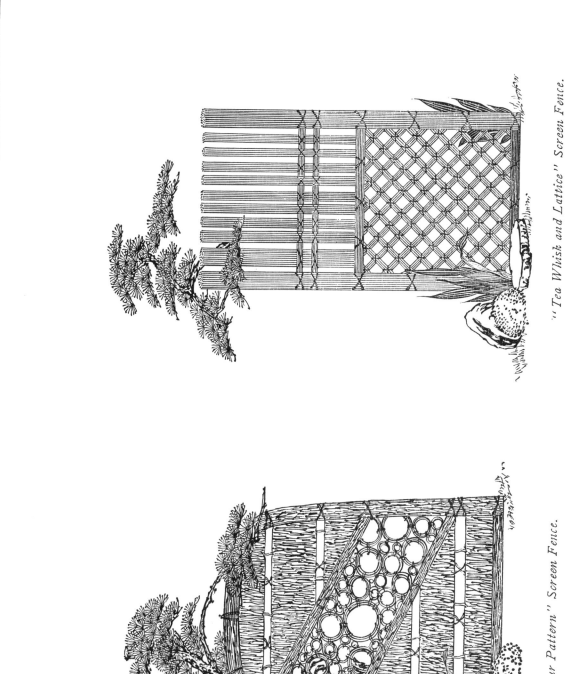

"Tea Whisk and Lattice" Screen Fence.

"Armour Pattern" Screen Fence.

PLATE XIX.   GARDEN SCREEN FENCES.

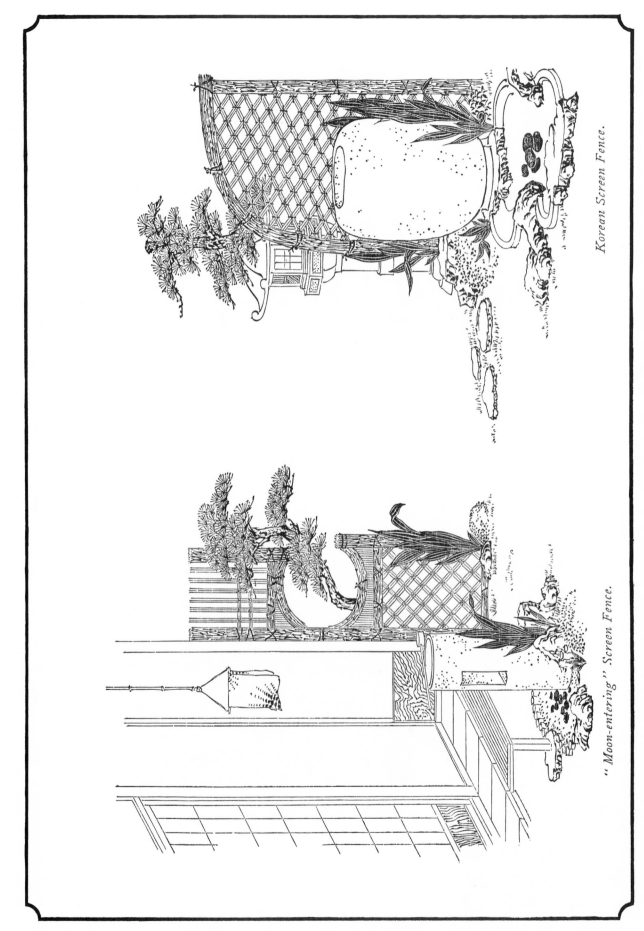

Korean Screen Fence.

"Moon-entering" Screen Fence.

Plate XX. Garden Screen Fences.

some instances the horizontal tie is broken off short at one end in a ragged manner, suggestive of decay. Antique looking tablets of wood containing an inscription are also introduced between the two lintels. The words inscribed may be briefly descriptive of the style of garden,—such as "*Tamagawa Tei*," meaning "Gem River Garden;" or they may merely convey a pretty sentiment in keeping with its character. The doors of such Gateways are constructed of light frames filled in with boarding, and furnished with cusped panels, pierced carving, or lattice-work. Some gates are formed of rail-work, with portions made to slide open, like the outer doorways to ordinary city dwellings.

Roofed Gateways, somewhat similar to the English lich-gate, are very common, the side-posts having cross-pieces and bracketing at the top, which carry a light thatched, boarded, or shingled roof of considerable projection. Some are curiously ornamented with heavy raised ridges constructed of bamboo poles, and tied with thick wisps of dark red rope. The posts of such Gateways are steadied by the addition of wooden buttresses on the inner side. Occasionally the roof is merely a sloping open trellis entwined with creeping plants. Ornamentally framed panels of wood containing inscriptions are placed over the architraves of these entrances. One part of an extensive garden will often be divided from another by a light fence with miniature thatch-roofed Gateways.

It is a common practice to plant a pine or some picturesquely bent tree beside a Gateway, in such a manner that one of its branches may overhang the portal. Fig. 21 illustrates an arrangement of this sort, together with an arched entrance-way of a peculiar kind, occasionally found in gardens.

For the internal fences of Tea Gardens very light Gates of odd designs are often used. One of these,—the *Saimioji-shiwori-do*, or "Lifting Gate of *Saimioji*,"—is of a rounded oblong shape, measuring about two and a half feet in width, and constructed of light basket-work of crossed bamboo rods. This Gate is peculiar inasmuch as it is made to swing from above, and is propped up when open by a bamboo rod. The construction is supposed to be in imitation of the doorways used in the most primitive Japanese dwellings.

Gates of a kind of rattan work, called *Ajiro*, with bamboo frames, measuring two feet wide and three and a half feet high, are also common. This class of Gate develops into a light ornamental appendage which affords scarcely any real protection against violence. Weather-worn and vermiculated wood is much fancied for the boarding of Gates used in Tea Gardens, and occasionally the planks of old boats, with the partially decayed dowel and nail holes intact, are applied to this purpose. Various Gateways and Gates are illustrated in Plates XII. XIII. and XIV.

SCREEN FENCES.

Screen Fences,—called by the Japanese " Sleeve Fences " (*Sode-gaki*),—are short screens helping to conceal some object in the garden, but mainly ornamental in purpose. They are chiefly arranged near the verandah of a house, or at the side of a water basin,—generally on one side attached to a wall or verandah post—and are about three or four feet wide, and from five to seven feet high. In form they are sometimes rectangular, sometimes curved at the top on one or both corners, and occasionally of irregular shape. The designs are numerous, and are distinguished by many odd names as follows:—

" Tube Screen Fence " (*Teppo-sode-gaki*),—a fence made with stout bamboo tubes like organ pipes, alternately long and short. Sometimes other materials, such as slender poles of scorched wood, and round bundles of reeds or twigs, are combined with the bamboo tubes. The whole is bound with horizontal strips of bamboo tied with stained cord.

" Sliding-door Fence " (*Fusuma-gaki*). This resembles in shape the summer rush-work door-slide of a Japanese chamber. It is constructed of slender reeds or rushes strengthened with thin wooden frames and cross-bars.

" Peeping Fence " (*Nozoki-gaki*),—a fence about six feet high, built of reeds or *lespedeza* branches, with a long barred opening in the middle.

" Clothes-horse Fence " (*Kicho-gaki*),—so called from its resemblance at the top to the ornamental clothes-horse used in a Japanese dressing or sleeping apartment. It is arched below, leaving an open quadrant, and it has a large circular orifice in the centre, ornamentally barred with bamboo strips. It is made of water reeds bound with wistaria stems, its height being five feet, and width nearly two feet.

" Tea-whisk and Lattice Screen Fence " (*Chasen-bishi sode-gaki*). This kind of fence is so called from the whisk-like form of the standard heads, which are composed of round bundles of reeds or twigs tied with cord or wistaria stems. The lower half is composed of lattice-work.

" Double-Screen Fence " (*Yaye-sode-gaki*). This example is designed with double borders to look as if one fence overlapped another. It is of irregular stepped shape, curved at the top, and with the filling-in of complicated design.

"Korean Screen Fence" (*Korai-sode-gaki*). A fence five feet high, and three and a half feet wide, curved at the top in a quadrant, constructed with reeds arranged in diamond-shaped lattice-work and bordered with a thick roll of the same material. It is illustrated, in combination with a water basin and lantern, in Plate XX.

"Low Korean Screen Fence" (*Koshi-korai-sode-gaki*),—similar to the former but of less height.

"Moon-entering Screen Fence" (*Haso-getsu sode-gaki*). This kind is about seven feet high and three feet wide, having in the centre a circular hole from which it receives its name. The vertical border on one side is broken off at the edge of the orifice so that the circle is not complete, and this gives it the form of a three-quarter moon. Above the hole, the bundles of reeds are arranged vertically, like bars, and below in a diagonal lattice-work, tied with hemp cords.

"Armour Pattern Screen Fence" (*Yoroi-gata sode-gaki*),—receives its name from a diagonal band in the centre, filled with numerous rings made of wistaria tendrils, tied together somewhat after the manner of chain-mail. The construction is arched at the top, and consists chiefly of vertical twigs or reeds bordered with a heavy roll, and barred with cross-pieces of stout bamboo.

"Nightingale Screen Fence" (*Uguisu-sode-gaki*),—so called on account of its rustic character. It is a rough fence constructed of irregular twigs of *Ilex integra* arranged vertically, left untrimmed at the top, and held by horizontal cross-pieces of bamboo tied to a bamboo tube border. This is a favourite design for Tea Gardens, in which it is used both as a short screen and as a continuous fence.

FIG. 22.

"Bent-branch Fence" (*Eda-ori-gaki*),—constructed of leaf-clad branches of bamboo bent in diagonal curves crossing in a kind of coarse lattice-work, the interstices being partly filled by the leaves. The branches are tied with cords at their crossings.

"Hurdle Fence" (*Mase-gaki*),—a kind of rough fence constructed of twigs of ilex or rushes arranged vertically in a bowed form, and fastened to horizontal bamboo strips.

"*Komachi* Fence" (*Komachi-gaki*), also called *Shinobi-gaki* (Hiding Fence),—a construction seven feet high, and about four feet wide, resembling in design the pierced walls in front of certain city buildings. The middle portion is of reeds with hexagonal barred windows, the bottom of split bamboo, and the top has a wooden cap-piece and open trellis. Komachi,—generally known as Ono-no-Komachi,—was a heroine of great beauty, the idea conveyed by the name as applied to a Screen Fence being that of a suitable retreat for lovers.

"Triple-stage Fence" (*Sandan-kasane-gaki*),—a fence constructed of twigs of ilex mixed with slender branches of bamboo, arranged overlapping in three stages, with thick rolls at the edge and intermediate bands of bamboo.

"Looking-through Fence" (*Mitoshi-gaki*). This is a construction seven feet high and six feet wide, very similar to the "Komachi Fence," but having a band of open trellis-work in the centre, instead of window-like openings. The border is framed in wood, lacquered black, with projecting corners, and the rest is in bamboo and reeds. The design resembles the divisions used in the galleries of palaces.

"Leaning Plum-tree Fence" (*Koboriume-no-sode-gaki*),—has a semi-curved top and three circular holes arranged irregularly in its surface, through which the stem of a leaning plum tree may be seen. It is built of slender bamboo or *lespedeza* twigs, strengthened with a roll border and with horizontal bamboo strips; its height is five feet and its width three feet.

"Two-stage Torch Fence" (*Taimatsu-no-niju-gaki*),—a high fence constructed chiefly of bundles of twigs like torches, combined with bamboo work, and made to look as if built in two stages. It is seven feet high and three feet wide, and is only used in large gardens.

"*Shinto* Arch Fence" (*Torii-gaki*),—so called from its resemblance to the trabeated gate-like erections in front of Shinto temples.

"Light-revealing Fence" (*Kwato-gaki*),—has a round opening at the top revealing the light of a stone lantern placed behind it.

"Round Window-lattice Fence" (*Enso-bishi-no-sode-gaki*),—a low square fence of twigs and bamboo-work, containing a large circular hole filled with lattice-work.

"*Unjo* Screen Fence" (*Unjo-sode-gaki*),—named after the title of a Court official. It is hollow below, being made to arch over the verandah floor, and is constructed of reeds with a narrow border and a pierced band of cryptomeria wood. It is five and a half feet high, and three feet wide.

"*Hokumen* Fence" (*Hokumen-gaki*),—named after another rank of Court official.

It is seven feet high, made of wooden frames and broad planks of deeply grained wood, the joints of the boarding being covered with bamboo strips. Some of the chief Screen Fences are illustrated in Plates XV., XVI., XVII., XVIII., XIX., and XX. Figure 22, on page 83, represents an example of somewhat unusual design, made in imitation of a framed screen such as is used in entrance halls, and called *Tsuitate.*

Drawings exist of hundreds of such fences as the above, slightly differing in design and material. As exact forms for these fences are by no means so rigidly established as that of many other garden features, the gardener has much more license in dealing with them; appropriateness to surroundings, in scale and degree of elaboration, is always kept in mind, and the dimensions given are therefore not absolute but only proportionate. Whether the Garden Fences be heavy or frail in design and execution depends greatly on the style or character of the garden.

Among the Screen Fences specially referred to, the " Tube Screen Fence " is deemed the grandest in style, and is suited for large gardens in front of, or in proximity to, buildings of fine proportion. As with other lightly constructed fences, the cords and knots employed in the binding of Screen Fences, receive much attention. The material is generally made from the fibres of the sago palm dyed to a deep brown or black colour; in many cases the stems of creepers are preferred.

In the gardens of the nobility high moveable Screen Fences, forming a temporary square enclosure, were used for the purpose of screening games of football,—a favourite pastime of the upper classes in former times. They are called " *Mari-gaki,*" or " *Mari-oki,*" meaning " Ball Fence." The " Ball Fence " is framed with wooden bars carried to a considerable height, like a cage, and finished at the top with ornamental open lattice-work. They are often handsomely lacquered or ornamented in colour.

CHAPTER VII.

GARDEN WELLS.

THE Well is an indispensable ornament of many gardens; very often it is purely ornamental, another being provided for use in the court or kitchen yard. The Well frequently assists to express the *mood* of the garden, and some designers have used it to imply a sentiment, not unlike the familiar scriptural analogy of Eternal Life. The presence or suggestion of water, in some shape or other, is an absolute necessity in Japanese gardens. As an ornament the Well consists of the well-hole border or frame, the pulley with its supporting post and cross-bar, a little roof to protect the pulley and cord from rain, the rope, and the buckets. Its necessary accessories are the drain, stepping stones, and other ornamental rocks; also a stone lantern, and certain suitable trees and shrubs to form a group with it. Sometimes instead of the pulley, rope, and double bucket arrangement, a single bucket is suspended from a thin bamboo rod, hinged to a long pole fixed in the socket of a short post of wood or stone, and acting as a lever. The other extremity of the lever is weighted with a heavy stone, so that with the addition of slight pressure it will raise the filled bucket from the well; when at rest the bucket is suspended in the air. Other kinds of Wells are those which have no suspended bucket, but are served by one attached to a long bamboo rod and used independently. Another example is that in which the pulley is suspended to an overleaning tree instead of a well-frame.

The well-border or frame is sometimes a continuation of the boarded lining of the well, projecting like an inverted tub or barrel from the ground, and bound with hoops of twisted bamboo strips. Such a Well will generally have a sloped, boarded drain, and a single long flat stone near it. This is the most commonplace kind of construction, rarely employed as an ornament in gardens, but kept for use in the kitchen court. Another more picturesque kind of well-frame is made of a square border of rough logs in several courses, crossing like an Oxford frame at the angles, and tied with coarse black or brown cords. Thick half decayed and irregular boards, used alone, or in combination with round logs or squared timbers, forming square or octagonal borders to Wells, are not uncommon. For the more important gardens a well-border of stone is generally preferred. One kind consists of a solid square structure of worked granite or some other hard stone, rounded off at the top and containing a circular well-hole neatly hewn; it should have a finely tooled oblong step-stone in keeping with the border. But a more favoured arrangement is that of irregular slabs of unhewn stone, roughly jointed together and forming a shell of rude shape round the opening. Occasionally upright slabs of stone of better finish are used after the manner of wood-work, being halved at the angles like a box. The size of such well-borders is three feet square and eighteen inches high. Well-frames are often covered with a mat or flexible lid constructed of close bamboo strips, to keep out insects and rain.

The buckets used are both round and square in plan, and generally wider above than below. Their attachment to the well-rope or bamboo rod is effected by means of a flat wooden bar fixed across the mouth. For Garden Wells the buckets, pulley, and rope are purposely made as antique looking as possible. Porcelain rope pulleys are occasionally introduced. The overhanging pulley-frame or gallows is made of squared timbers or of irregularly rounded logs, to be in accord with the rough or elaborate character of the well-frame. The designs for the roof over the pulley are also numerous and quaint, some-times affording examples of most exquisite joinery work, and at other times purposely rough and decayed looking. Occasionally the roof is made large enough to cover the whole Well, and is supported by two posts and a lintel instead of a projecting

FIG. 23.

bracket. The use of a complete well-shed, covering the whole of the Well together with the draining floor around, is common in kitchen yards, and in a more elaborate form may be seen in temple grounds; but it is not usually an adjunct of Wells when considered merely as garden ornaments.

The drain for ornamental Wells consists of an irregular bed of pebbles surrounding the well-frame, with a hidden outlet. The ornamental rocks are distributed outside this stony bed. The trees, shrubs, lanterns, and rocks appropriate to Wells will be noted under their respective heads. Various Garden Wells are illustrated in Plates XXI., XXVIII., XXIX., XXX., and XXXI.; and Fig. 23 shows the situation of a simple Well in relation to the verandah of a house.

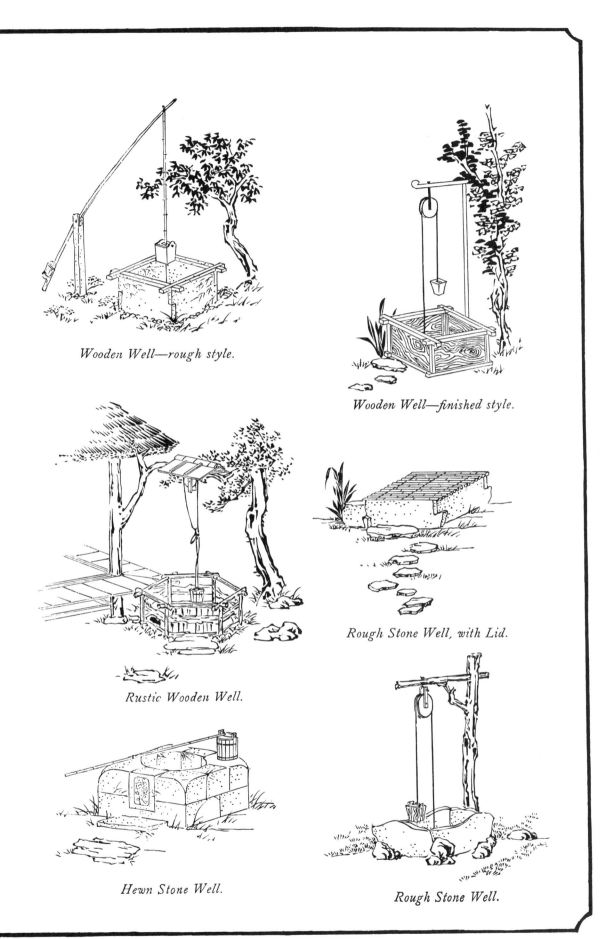

Wooden Well—rough style.

Wooden Well—finished style.

Rustic Wooden Well.

Rough Stone Well, with Lid.

Hewn Stone Well.

Rough Stone Well.

PLATE XXI.   GARDEN WELLS.

CHAPTER VIII.

GARDEN BRIDGES.

THERE are many kinds of Bridges for spanning streams, or for reaching islands in garden lakes. Some are of stone, some of wood, and others of wattle-work covered with earth. The Stone Bridges are often formed of a single rough slab of some kind of schist, or more generally, of a fine piece of wrought granite slightly arched. Where very large spans occur, two parallel blocks may be used, overlapping in the centre of the stream, and supported upon a trestle-like construction. An example of a monolithic Stone Bridge may be seen in Fig. 24, illustrating a small garden at Kamakura, called the Sho-fu-tei. Constructions of this kind are only used in level situations. Elaborate Stone Bridges formed of several spans of stone, supported upon intermediate granite piles, are used in important gardens, provided with moulded or carved parapets and posts. The manner of fitting partakes of the character of carpentry, even the large stone piles and newels being scarfed together like timber, and tenons and mortises being frequently employed. Arched Stone Bridges are found in some gardens, notably in the Koraku-En at Koishi-kawa (see page 31). This particular form is of Chinese origin, and is supposed to suggest the full moon, the semi-circular arch combined with its reflection in the stream below making a complete circle. The quick curve of its roadway, which corresponds almost with the extrados of the arch, necessitates the floor of the bridge being stepped.

Wooden Bridges are of various designs, from those made of single planks to elaborate constructions resembling the engineering bridges of the country. An old form of Wooden Bridge, used chiefly to cross the swampy iris-beds, consists of wide planks arranged one by one in a zigzag manner, supported by short wooden piles or stakes driven into the mud. This is called the " Yatsuhashi Bridge," to which allusion has already been made on page 11. The intention of its winding shape is to allow one to loiter above the beds of water-plants. The Japanese conception of a Garden Bridge is not, by any means, that of a quick and direct passage across a watery space ; the love of picturesqueness,—as well as a fondness for lingering above an expanse of water, to enjoy the cool breezes and watch the gold fish disporting in the stream,—has led to a preference for crooked and tortuous constructions. Even in the simplest stone-slab Bridges, one span will often be carried to an intermediate rock planted in the stream, and the next be made to branch off from this point in an entirely different direction. Some highly finished and roof-covered Wooden Bridges are built so as to take several right-angle turns in crossing a lake, each bend forming a nook or recess for loitering in. It is a favourite device to train trellises of wistaria creepers over such constructions, which, in the early summer, form a rich flowering

Sho-fu-tei, Kamakura.

FIG. 24.

canopy. Such an arrangement may be seen in the garden of the Hama Rikiu, in Tokio. Other Wooden Bridges are constructed with planks laid cross-wise, and supported upon arched beams with an intermediate trestle-like support fixed in the bed of the stream. In long structures of this sort, when owing to the nature of the river bottom no intermediate support is feasible, the curved bearers are strengthened by an arrangement of wooden bracketing, built out from the two opposite banks. The name of "Bracket Bridges" (*Rankan-bashi*) is given to those made in this style.

Certain constructions, called "Earth Bridges" (*Dobashi*), consist of bundles of faggots or small logs laid across a timber frame-work, and covered with about six inches of earth and gravel; both edges are planted with a strip of turf bound with bamboo and cord, to prevent the loose earth from falling away. Bridges of this kind are provided with no hand-rail. Another kind is built of triangular heaps of logs supported underneath by leaning timbers presenting the outline of a pointed arch below, the top surface being covered with earth. Such structures are named "Genkai Bridges," after the Genkai Straits, and are used when the soil of the banks is so hard that it will not allow of piling being driven in.

Garden of Joko-In, Temple of Miidera.
FIG. 25.

A rustic sort of Bridge is sometimes made with a single balk of half-decayed timber, or a row of parallel logs, and even the worm-eaten side of an old boat will at times be employed. A combination of bridge and stepping stones occasionally serves to cross a stream or lake, when a favourite form for the bridge is that of a short rising curve arranged with its outer end higher than that towards the shore, appearing as if an ordinary arching Wooden Bridge had been cut through at some distance beyond the centre of the curve. This kind goes by the curious name of the "Peeping Bridge" (*Nozoki-bashi*). The above described Bridges are illustrated in Plates XXII., XXIII., XXVI., and XXVII.; and Figure 25,—representing the garden of the Joko-In, attached to the temple of Miidera,—exhibits two different examples of such structures.

Wooden Trestle Bridge.

"Peeping" Bridge.

Curved Bracket Bridge.

Earth Bridge.

"Yatsu-hashi" Bridge.

"Genkai" Bridge.

Wooden Bracket Bridge.

PLATE XXII.   WOODEN GARDEN BRIDGES.

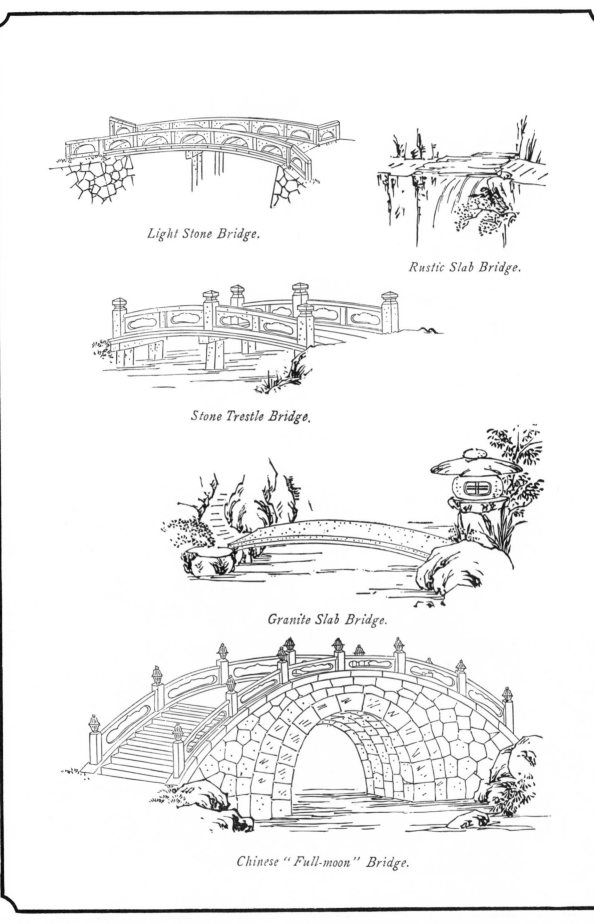

Light Stone Bridge.

Rustic Slab Bridge.

Stone Trestle Bridge.

Granite Slab Bridge.

Chinese "Full-moon" Bridge.

PLATE XXIII.   STONE GARDEN BRIDGES.

CHAPTER IX.

GARDEN ARBOURS.

THE larger Japanese gardens are invariably provided with one or more Summer-houses or Arbours, placed on prominent elevated spots, in order that they may afford either a charming view of the garden itself, or of a beautiful outside prospect. These structures vary from the simplest open shed, sheltering a few moveable seats, to elaborate miniature houses with raised and matted floors, doors, and windows. The latter kind merge into the class of buildings specially intended for performing the Tea Ceremonial,—structures to be noticed later under the head of Tea Gardens.

The simplest garden shelter consists of a central post carrying a broad roof, square or circular on plan, and—in the latter case especially—suggestive in its shape of a large umbrella. Seen from underneath, this roof shows a neat arrangement of rafters, boarding, and bracketing; externally it is covered with shingling or straw thatch. The central post is of rough wood fixed in the soil. Moveable seats are furnished in the shape of porcelain tubs or blocks of wood, placed on

Fig. 26.

the sward. Another example is that of a four-post shed having carved lintels, bracketed cornice, and curved tile roof adorned with heavy hip and ridge ornaments, the whole being made in imitation of the structures found in temple grounds. A tiled or stone-paved floor is generally provided, and the pillars are supported upon small stone bases.

Other open structures present a more rustic character, with thatched roofs and delicately framed ceilings, and some of these have two sides partly filled in with a low railing or paneling, which forms the back to fixed interior benches.

FIG. 27.

Hexagonal and octagonal Arbours may be observed, with cusping between the heads of the pillars, and balustrade-work below, displaying a Chinese character in their ornamentation. The arrangement of the fixed seats inside is generally irregular, a symmetrical distribution being in most cases avoided.

A number of Garden Arbours are illustrated in Plate XXIV. Figures 26, 27, and others scattered through the text, show the arrangement of these structures in landscape gardens.

Summer House.

Hexagonal Arbour.

Resting Shed.

Umbrella-shaped Arbour.

Summer House.

Matted Arbour

PLATE XXIV. GARDEN ARBOURS.

CHAPTER X.

ORNAMENTAL WATER.

IN one or other of its many forms of lake, river, stream, torrent, or cascade, Water is an almost indispensable feature of Japanese gardens. Even in localities where no natural supply can be obtained, the idea of Water Scenery is expressed in the design by the arrangement of surrounding hills, stones, and plants. A sunken stretch of bare beaten earth or well-raked sand, with isolated boulders scattered here and there, will often indicate a lake or sea with its islands or jutting rocks. In other cases, a meandering bed, spread with pebbles and crossed by a small bridge or stepping stones, will serve to convey the impression of a stream, which is further sustained by distributing water plants, rushes, and rounded river boulders on its banks. There are certain kinds of level gardens—including the ordinary Tea Garden—into which Water Scenery is rarely introduced, but in such cases an antique well or water-basin, or the suggestion of a natural spring will be added to make up the deficiency. It is essential that a garden should, above all things, look cool and refreshing in the summer-time, and such a character is best maintained by the presence—or at least the idea—of Water. Shallow and clear running Water is held to have a much cooler and refreshing effect than deep, stagnant, and weed-covered expanses. Water plays a most important part in the *Sansui*, or " Hill Gardens," which form the principal models for all Japanese landscape gardens. Imaginative writers compare the hills of such grounds to the Emperor, the rocks to his Officials, and the surrounding water to his Courtiers. As the Emperor must be advised and protected by strong Officials to guard him from the intrigues of insinuating Courtiers, so, they say, must the artificial hills of gardens be strengthened by firm stones against the encroachment of the water. Fig. 28 illustrates a famous *Sansui* garden from an ancient temple at Kioto, in which an artistic balance between rocks, hills, and water is cleverly maintained, and a profound and serene effect created.

The direction taken by the current of lakes and streams in gardens is considered of much moment. The inflow should if possible be from the east, the main direction of the current southerly, and the outlet towards the west ; a circuitous route

Fig. 28.

from north to east, then round by south and west, is not uncommon, but a course from west to east is deprecated as sinister and unpropitious.

GARDEN LAKES.

According to the character of landscape indicated, the Lakes of gardens may represent mountain lochs, lagoons, and occasionally the open sea. The favourite classical model is the extensive lagoon of Che Chiang in China,—called Seiko by the Japanese,—remarkable for its wealth of lotuses. It is this expanse of water that is invariably represented in the lotus ponds of temple and monastery grounds. Another imaginary model, is the China Sea, in which were supposed to exist the three Elysian Islands of Chinese mythology. When—as in this and similar examples—the open ocean is suggested in a Garden Lake, the illusion is assisted by means of a beach of pebbles or sand, with sea-rocks scattered in the foreground. Island bridges and water plants, both of which characterise ordinary lake scenery, are purposely avoided, as the idea of a sea view must be consistently maintained. Native writers classify Lakes according to their shapes, as round, square, half-moon shape, crescent-shape, flowing-water shape, *water* (ideograph) shape, *heart* (ideograph) shape, and dragon shape. The principal forms will be understood from Figure 29, in which ideographs are appended to the shapes named after them, and the inlets and outlets of the water are indicated by the letters *I* and *O*. The round, square, and half-moon shapes are rarely found, except in the tiny ponds for gold fish which adorn some small gardens. The geometrically designed canals and fountain-basins of European gardens have no counterpart in Japan, but the capricious irregularity of natural water scenery is studiously imitated, and if the source of supply be of necessity artificial, it is carefully concealed, and the semblance of a natural inlet is created.

Whichever of the above normal shapes a Garden Lake approaches, its complete outline must never be clearly and distinctly visible. Portions of the boundaries are purposely obliterated by shrubs, trees, or stones, with a view to indicate an undefined extent, and add to its mysterious grandeur. Especially is this the case in following classical models. These sheets of water must,

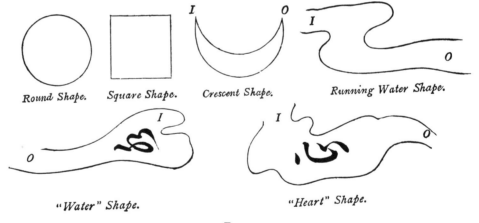

Round Shape.   Square Shape.   Crescent Shape.   Running Water Shape.

"Water" Shape.   "Heart" Shape.

FIG. 29.

above all, offer to the observer a logical reason for their presence in the scene. The source of supply, whether it be a stream or waterfall, must be prominently shown, and the outlet of the current should also be represented. Water deprived of either of these essential features is called *dead water*, and regarded with the professional contempt bestowed upon all shams and falsities in art. Sometimes the inflow of a Lake may be indicated by a stream curving from behind a garden hillock which serves to hide the artificial character of the source; or, occasionally, a deep pool of clear water, with rocks and moss, may suggest the proximity of a spring or underground supply.

A feature frequently introduced into garden Lakes is the *Iriye*, or Inlet, in imitation of the creek or cove of a natural scene.

The islands and peninsulas of Lakes will be considered under a separate heading.

GARDEN CASCADES.

The source of a lake is frequently represented by means of a waterfall, real or expressed. This may be simply a low mountain torrent, or a precipitous cascade. The latter kind are often suggestive of sea scenery, as in Fig. 2.

The term *Taki-guchi*, or "Cascade-mouth," is a common one in gardening, and even in waterless grounds certain cliff-like rocks, backed by hills and overhung with vegetable growth, are arranged in a prominent spot to indicate this feature. Gardeners distinguish Cascades by different names applicable to the character assumed by the falling water, as follows:—

"Thread-falling,"—a term used when the water pours over the rough surface of a rock in such a way as to fall in thread-like lines.

"Right-and-left-falling,"—applied to a Cascade dividing on two sides.

"Side-falling,"—to indicate water falling on one side only.

"Folding-falling,"—a Cascade bounding from rocks in several steps or falls.

"Front-falling,"—a Cascade pouring evenly over a rock or cliff in full front view of the spectator.

"Stepped-falling,"—a Cascade which is broken into steps like a torrent.

"Leaping-falling,"—a Cascade shooting out with great force from its source.

"Wide-falling,"—descriptive of a Cascade of great width in proportion to its height.

"Heaven-falling,"—a Cascade of great elevation in which the water tumbles in layers.

"Linen-falling,"—to indicate a weak and wavy fall, suggestive of a sheet of linen in the wind.

It is laid down as a rule that waterfalls of great width should not be employed for the principal Cascade of a garden, but a low and wide fall may be introduced as subsidiary to the main one, which is high and narrow in proportion. The two together form a pair, the principal fall being considered *male*, and the secondary one *female*.

Even for the lower fall a width greater than two feet is not recommended, for the reason that too great a size detracts from the scale of the artificial lake adjoining. Fine natural Cascades abound all over Japan, but, on the principle of following classical models, it is customary, in a elaborate garden, to represent a famous waterfall in the South of China known to the Japanese as Rozan. Close to this Chinese lagoon is a high mountain called Riumon, the subject of frequent poetical allusions; for this reason custom prescribes the introduction of a high mound or hillock opposite to a Garden Cascade. In temple grounds the priests delight to associate such water scenery with a noted landscape in the Himalayas, renowned in Buddhist lore for its cataract, lake, and four rivers issuing therefrom. Fig. 30 represents an ideal scene of this character reproduced in the garden of the Temple called Kotokuji, at Kioto.

Garden of Kotokuji, Kioto.
FIG. 30.

In accordance with the fancy for suggesting in limited areas natural scenery of extensive proportions, rules exist for veiling portions of a waterfall so as to assist in creating the illusion of a cataract of indefinite height. A tree should be placed so that its branches hide the outlet of the Cascade, which is also surrounded by thick foliage to give it a solitary and profound appearance. Elevated ground, suddenly interrupted, and presenting a vertical face of some hard material proof against speedy disintegration, being the essential of all natural waterfalls, it is necessary, in artificial landscapes, to comply with the same conditions. The earthen mounds behind the Garden Cascade have to be cut off to an almost vertical face, which is strengthened and adorned by means of high rocks forming the cliff over which the water pours. The principal rock amongst these, broad at the base, tapering above, and presenting a flat face in front, constitutes at the same time the most important stone of the whole garden, and receives the name of *Shugo-seki*, translateable as "Guardian Stone," or "Immoveable Stone." Generally paired with it is another rock, of lower and more rounded shape; in addition to which are various smaller stones, with names implying different functions in connection with the waterfall. These are all fully described under the head of Garden Stones.

GARDEN RIVERS.

When fresh running water can be easily obtained, it is usual to introduce streams into a garden, arranged to wind through the grounds in an irregular and interesting manner. A Garden River may have its source indicated by a low water-fall or it may appear to originate in a pool with a mossy spring. A rivulet is often constructed in conjunction with a lake of which it forms the natural outlet. In the famous Koraku-En garden at Okayama, a small stream is carried from the lake in a ser-pentine course, part of it supplying water to a marsh planted with irises and water-lilies, and a portion serving to carry the current through a building intended for certain summer pastimes.

When garden streams are introduced, unconnected with lake scenery, they are often intended to represent one or more of the six *Tamagawa*, or "Gem-rivers" of Japan. The Tamagawa near Tokio consists of rapid shallows occupying the centre of a wide pebbly bed, and the banks at its sudden bends are strengthened with piling and breakwaters formed of heaps of bamboo baskets containing stones. The artificial introduction of such features, bordering garden streams, and the planting of kerria and other river-side plants and grasses on the banks, assist in reproducing the effect of the natural scenery. Gardens with a river and no lake are often designed to represent some wild-moor scenery; the river should in such cases be given a broad channel.

In what is technically termed by the Japanese "Dry-river Scenery," the deep winding bed of a river or torrent is represented by means of an excavated channel, covered with pebbles or sand, and strewn with occasional rocks and stepping stones. Such dry river-beds are moreover crossed by rusticated bridges of planks or logs, in the same way as if actual water existed. Many examples may be seen in which the flowing current is actually represented as distinct from the gravelled bed, black stones, broken like macadam, being used for the water, and ordinary white pebbles and boulders for the exposed portions of the beds.

GARDEN ISLANDS.

Four important Garden Islands are introduced into water scenery. The first of these is called the "Elysian Isle" (*Horai-jima*), the conception of which has been already explained. Intended to represent a sea island, it is placed near the centre of a garden lake, and on no account should a bridge connect it with the neighbouring land. Its beach should be spread with sea sand, pebbles, and shells, and the cultivation on its surface of all fresh-water vegetation must be avoided. A fancy has arisen for making the "Elysian Isle" in a form suggestive of the tortoise, and adorning it with rocks and stones representing the head, legs, and tail of this animal (see page 51).

The second goes by the name of the "Wind-swept Isle" (*Fukiage-jima*), and also simulates an ocean island. It should therefore never be used in a running stream, but may be introduced into a garden lake, when such is intended to express the idea of the open sea. No moss, river plants, or growths of any kind peculiar to fresh-water islands are permitted on the "Wind-swept Isle;" like the "Elysian Isle," its shores should be spread with sand, shells, and sea rocks.

The other two islands are called respectively the "Masters's Isle" (*Shujin-to*), and the "Guest's Isle" (*Kiakujin-to*); and they are rarely used separately. The "Master's Isle" is specially appropriated to the owner of the garden, and is placed in the foreground of the landscape, easily accessible from the front banks of the lake by a bridge, or, as is sometimes the case, by a picturesque combination of bridge and stepping stones. It often happens that this so-called island is connected with the shore by a narrow neck of land and becomes, strictly speaking, a peninsula or promontory (*Dejima*), and not an island in the proper sense of the word. A little resting-shed or summer-house is often built upon the "Master's Isle," over-looking the water of the surrounding lake. In Fig. 31 may be seen a repre-sentation of an island of this kind, carrying a rustic arbour, as designed in the ancient garden of the Jizo-In at Mibu. The different stones adorning the "Mas-ter's Isle" have names implying functions of ease and recreation, as already explained on page 51.

The "Guest's Isle" receives its name in honour of visitors to the garden. It is located more in the background of the scene, approached by bridges and stepping stones from the banks, and adorned with ornamental rocks specially devoted to the purposes of hospitality (see page 51).

Garden of the Jizo-In, Mibu.
FIG. 31.

The above four Islands are considered strictly according to rule for gardens, but others are often arbitrarily introduced. In the garden of Kinkakuji, for example, the Islands of the lake are said to represent in form and distribution the Empire of Japan; and in the lake of the Mangwanji at Nikko they are outlined to pourtray the felicitous emblems of the crane and tortoise. Many terms descriptive of Islands of different form and character are employed, among which the following may be mentioned : —

The "Mountain Isle" (*Yama-jima*), as its name implies, is shaped like a mountain rising from the water. Two peaks,—one higher than the other,—adorn its summit, and its sides are planted with numerous evergreens. Encircling it is a stretch of flat beach, on which sand and occasional rocks are spread; mosses and autumn grasses are cultivated between the stones.

The "Forest Isle" (*Mori-jima*) is of low elevation, covered with a plantation of straight trees, placed sufficiently apart to allow of a view from between their trunks. Sand should be spread and short grasses planted between the trees.

The "Rock Island" (*Iso-jima*) is rugged and precipitious in form, like a huge sea-rock, having vertical crags above, and detached fragments at the water's edge. It should be adorned with one or more crooked pine trees, suggesting in their contorted shapes long exposure to the wind and tempest. This kind of Island is often employed to represent the scenery of Matsushima (see page 37).

FIG. 32.

The "Bare Beach Isle" (*Suhama-gata-jima*) is so called because it is flat, like a sand-bank, and has its surface furrowed with undulating patterns in imitation of the wrinkled marking which the waves leave on a soft sandy beach at ebb-tide. It is spread with fine sea sand, and planted with young pine trees such as thrive on the sandy coast.

The " Tide-ebb Isle " (*Hikata-jima*) is somewhat similar to the " Bare Beach Isle," but is half immersed below the water, with only a few rocks visible, and no trees or plants.

The " Pine-bark Isle" (*Matsu-kawa-jima*),—so called from the resemblance which the rough coriaceous markings of its surface bear to the bark of the Japanese pine tree. The use of trees and stones on this kind of Island is said to be optional.

The " Cloud-shaped Island" (*Kumo-gata-jima*) receives its name on account of the imaginary resemblance it bears in scenery to the form of a streaky cloud. This Island therefore occupies a distant position in the view; it should be covered with white sand, without either rocks or trees.

The " Mist-shaped Isle" (*Kasumi-gata-jima*) resembles in the outline of its shores the serpentine curves or streaks used to represent mist in Japanese conventional designs. It is employed in the remoter parts of lake scenery, strewn with white sand, and bare of vegetation.

Fig. 32, illustrating an ancient landscape garden from one of the old Kioto temples, shows two Islands of different kinds, connected by a monolithic bridge. One of these is a " Mountain Isle," adorned with a handsome leaning pine tree stretching over the water, and several maple trees; the other is composed almost entirely of rocks of different character, having one or two small shrubs planted between them.

An extended beach, covered with sand, pebbles, or shells, whether attached to an island, or forming a portion of the shores of the lake itself, is, in some form or other, invariably introduced into artificial water scenery. A group of rocks, a " Snow-view Lantern," and often a few shrubs and plants, add interest to these pebbly reaches.

DUCK PONDS.

A indispensable attraction of most modern parks and spacious gardens in Japan is the decoy duck-pond, used for the sport of netting wild fowl,—a recreation of the nobility and gentry, and one often enjoyed in the very centre of the most populous cities. As a decorative feature of the grounds it is unimportant, presenting from the garden side the appearance of an extensive mound crowned with thickly planted trees, and surrounded by wide sanded or turfed walks and spinnies for purposes of isolation ; but a notice of Japanese landscape gardening might be thought incomplete without some brief mention of the arrangement followed. An oval or circular pond is constructed, surrounded with high irregular slopes, thickly planted with wild bushes and leafy trees contrived to look as natural as possible. This pond is provided with numerous bent inlets, having steep sides and raised turf-covered banks, additionally screened at their extremities by mounds on the garden side. These grassy mounds support little sheds or arbours with peep-holes and shoots for grain, carefully hidden from the pond by bushes. The wild fowl, which are attracted to these ponds by means of tame decoys during the winter months, are allured by baiting into the inlets, and the sportsmen who approach stealthily from the sides net them with hand nets as they fly upwards to escape.

DRAINAGE.

Though it is an important axiom that a garden lake should have the outflow of its water clearly defined, the drainage of the grounds is on no account permitted to mix with the current of the lake. The low and level parts of the garden should be provided with several concealed outlets for rain water, which are carried underground to a drain beyond the site, or which may occasionally be connected with the extremity of the stream forming the lake-outlet, provided that it be at a point far removed from the ornamental areas. In certain small gardens, which represent mountain dells and are completely enclosed by artificial hills and banks, an elaborate system of hidden drainage becomes most essential, and little bamboo pipes may be discovered in places, forming the inlets to such a system. The levelling of large gardens is also carefully attended to, and the general surface drainage is carried away from the buildings in a gentle and almost imperceptible slope.

CHAPTER XI.

GARDEN VEGETATION.

THE distribution of suitable trees, shrubs, and plants in a garden comes up for consideration after the contours of land and water and the principal rocks and stones have been arranged. Primary as is the importance attached to the disposal of garden rocks, they form but the skeleton of the design, and can only satisfactorily fulfil their purpose when embellished with suitable vegetation. In some cases, trees or shrubs are planted so as to branch over and partially conceal these lithic ornaments; in other instances they serve as a background to bring into relief their picturesque shapes. Japanese gardeners studiously avoid regularity in the disposal of vegetation.

In connection with the temples of the country, magnificent avenues and groves are to be seen arranged with the same formality adopted in certain European gardens; and some of the rows of pines and cryptomerias which line the country roads are hardly surpassed in grandeur by anything similar in the West. But in landscape gardening,—and all gardening in Japan comes under this head,—

"Saigio" Willow Tree.
FIG. 33.

such formal arrangements are seldom if ever resorted to. When trees are grouped together in numbers, they are generally of different species specially selected to contrast with one another; unless, as is sometimes the case, it is the designer's intention to represent a natural forest or woodland. Contrasts of form and line receive primary attention, though contrasts of colour in foliage are also considered, especially in the distribution of shrubs and bushes. Such combinations as that of the twisted and rugged pine tree with the spreading cherry tree or drooping willow, are purposely devised. A rule has been established that, when several trees are planted together in gardens, they should never be placed in rows, but distributed in open and irregular files, so that the majority of the group

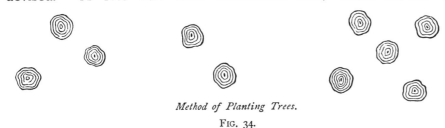

Method of Planting Trees.
FIG. 34.

may be seen from different points of view. Fig. 34 exemplifies how trees may be arranged in groups of two, three, or five. If quite a number are clumped together, they will be disposed in a varied series of double, triple, and quintuple combinations, with wider spaces dividing them. The space left between individual trees varies according to the size and scale of the grounds, from about three to six feet; in a very diminutive garden as little as eighteen inches will suffice. This rule does not, however, apply to trees intentionally planted in pairs, as twins or consorts, which are often arranged quite close together.

The noted landscape gardener Sen-no-Rikiu was accustomed to employ higher trees in the foreground than in the background of his compositions, but his successor, Furuta Oribe, followed an exactly contrary method. It is constantly laid down as a most important axiom, that trees and plants,

"Saigio" Pine Tree, Sagami.
FIG. 35.

however desirable as ornaments, must not be used in positions at variance with their natural habits of growth; a plant which, when undomesticated, grows upon the hill or mountain side, must not be placed in a garden plain or valley, nor should vegetation produced in low damp situations be transferred to elevated spots. Not only is the violation of this rule detrimental to the freshness and vitality of growths, but it is condemned as leading to incongruity and falseness in design. Deciduous trees are not much favoured for the foreground of a garden, because of their bare and cheerless aspect in the winter-time. An exception is, however, made with plum and cherry trees, which, on account of their early blossoming, as well as the high rank they hold in public estimation, are often planted in the foreground, close to the chambers of the dwelling.

The clipping and shearing of evergreens is much practised in Japan, though seldom executed in a manner violently inconsistent with the nature of the vegetation dressed. Reference has previously been made to the conspicuous ability possessed by the Japanese,—also displayed in the Western arts during the middle ages,—of seizing upon the fundamental and characteristic qualities of natural forms, and creating a sort of shorthand or contracted representation for decorative purposes.

" Kwannon's Seat " Pine Tree, Sagami.
FIG. 36.

A favourite object for such treatment is the native pine tree, in which, with all its irregularity and ruggedness of growth, can be discerned the tendency to group its fisculated leaves into arched masses of foliated shape. This prevailing form supplies the conventional outline so often applied to the decoration of household objects. The gardener, in a similar way, when trimming garden trees, aims at a somewhat abbreviated expression of characteristic outlines, and seldom produces shapes violently at variance with nature. The ornamental pine tree passes through a sort of surgical treatment for the purpose of producing a shape of acknowledged beauty, as displayed in some of the finest natural trees of its species. Its branches are bent, broken, and bandaged with splints and cords, until they assume unassisted the fancy shapes desired. Figures 1, 6, 35, and 36, scattered through the text, as representative of famous wild pine trees of Japanese scenery, will suffice to show the faithful resemblance which the garden pine bears to its natural prototype. Similar examples are given in Figures 33, 37, and 40, of wild willows and plum trees exhibiting the ideal forms attributed to their species, which the gardener seeks to imitate with his handicraft. Besides the training of the branches of the pine tree, its foliage is subjected to different methods of trimming. The style called *Tamatsukuri,* or " Ball Treatment," consists in clipping the short twigs and fasciculated leaves into the shape of a number of discs or flattened spheres. Another favourite manner is known by the name of the *Fuse-tsukuri*, or " Fraying Treatment," by which the different stems are extended along numerous horizontal strips of bamboo, so that the pine needles arrange themselves in radiating lines and ridges. There is still another treatment called the *Korin* style, after a noted painter of that name, and supposed to be in imitation of his peculiar man-nerism in delineating the pine tree. This method shows the branches trained in a pendent arched form, suggestive of the curves of a cascade.

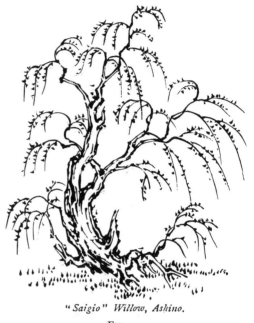

" *Saigio*" *Willow, Ashino.*

FIG. 37.

In dressing low garden shrubs, they are generally clipped into hemispherical forms, present-ing rounded masses of varying shades of green upon the hill-sides, and between rocks and monu-ments, and classed under the native term of *Marumono*, or " Round Material." Different kinds of junipers, box bushes, azalea bushes, and dwarf *Thuyæ obtusæ*, are the most common shrubs treated in this manner. Such spherical masses are fre-quently arranged in clumps on sloping ground, towering one above the other, so as to give the appearance of green hills. This art was carried to perfection in some of the ancient temple gardens, of which Fig. 3 is an example, taken from the grounds of the Banto-In, a monastery in Kioto.

Cases occur in which similar bushes are cut into cubical shapes, in sug-gestion of large wrought blocks of granite, or even into multi-arched outlines, rep-resenting cascades and torrents. Such fantastic and artificial treatments are, how-ever, somewhat uncommon. In certain gardens, trees or shrubs are trained and trimmed into forms intended to imitate a ship or junk in full sail ; even a lantern or a shrine may be represented in such greenery, but these exceptional examples possess always the merit of pourtraying objects not out of place in natural scenery. The hewn stone monument, the junk, the shrine, and lantern, though the product of human handicraft, are nevertheless objects associated with rural landscape.

The Japanese gardener masses his trees at particular points in his design and seldom follows a method of equal distribution. In so doing, he bears in mind the particular value and function of each group,—one to express distance; one to give a shady, solitary impression; one to receive and intercept the glare of the setting sun; one to serve as a partial veil or screen; and one to give reflection and shadow in the water. The chief localities chosen for such trees or groups of trees are:—valleys, river banks, island shores, slopes of hills, cliffs behind cascades, and flat open expanses. Secondary vegetation is placed between rocks and stones, near garden wells and springs, and close to fences, lanterns, or basins. It is a common saying that four-fifths of the trees and shrubs of a garden should consist of evergreens; and indeed, in most Japanese gardens, it will be found that, with the exception of a few flowering trees and certain species of the oak, ash, and maple, valued on account of their blossom-like tints in spring and autumn, comparatively few deciduous trees are used.

The following list of Japanese domesticated trees, shrubs, and plants may be found to some extent wanting in completeness. The numerous fanciful names given by the gardeners of the country to different varieties of certain *genera* have in many cases not yet received exact botanical classification; and though the vernacular terms alone can convey little or no meaning to the uninitiated, to omit all mention of them would be misleading and fail to give a correct idea of their rich diversity. These unclassified names refer, in some instances, not so much to distinct varieties of species, as to peculiarities due to special methods of nursing; but in other examples they relate to striking differences in colour or form of leaf or flower. In either case they imply an important addition to the landscape artist's stock of material for designing with. Free English translations have therefore been appended to those terms for which no botanical equivalents are yet at hand.

EVERGREENS.

Among the coniferous evergreen trees and shrubs of Japan found in gardens are many varieties of the Pine, such as:—*Pinus desiflora* (Aka-matsu), *Pinus thunbergii* (Kuro-matsu), *Pinus parviflora* (Go-yo-matsu), and *Pinus koraiensis* (Chosen-matsu, or Chosen-go-yo-matsu). Under the vernacular term of Matsu are included *Larix leptolepis* (Kara-matsu)—called also Rakuyosho, and not strictly speaking an evergreen,—*Abies mairiesii* (Todo-matsu), *Picea microsperma* (Yezo-matsu), and certain unclassified varieties known to gardeners by names, either entirely fanciful, or descriptive of their peculiarities of growth or colour of foliage, as: Midori-matsu, or Yellow Pine; Asagi-matsu, or Blue Pine; Shidare-matsu, or Weeping Pine; Mandai-matsu, or Everlasting Pine;

Senzai-matsu, or Pine of a Thousand Years; Tan-yo-matsu, or Short-leaved Pine; Kanoko-matsu, or Spotted Pine; Izari-matsu, or Creeping Pine; Kinsen-matsu, or Ring-leaved Pine; Kin-matsu, or Golden Pine; Janome-go-yo-matsu or Disc-leaved Pine; Shiraga-matsu, or Grey-hair Pine; and Torafu-matsu, or Tiger Pine.

FIG. 38.

There are several kinds of Firs or Spruces, as follows:—*Abies firma* (Momi), *Abies brachyphylla* (Awobo-momi), and *Abies mariesii*,—mentioned above under the name of Todo-matsu. Various garden varieties of *Cryptomeria japonica* are known by fancy names, as :—Kusari-sugi, or Chain-like Cryptomeria; Howo-sugi, or Phœnix Cryptomeria; Ogon-sugi, or Golden Cryptomeria; Kifu-sugi, or Yellow-leaved Cryptomeria; Shirofu-sugi, or White-leaved Cryptomeria; Enko*-sugi, or Monkey Cryptomeria; Yore-sugi, or Twisted-leaved Cryptomeria; Kara-sugi, or Chinese Cryptomeria; Fuiri-sugi, or Spotted-leaved Cryptomeria; Sendai-sugi, or *Sendai* Cryptomeria; and Tamatori-sugi, or Dragon Cryptomeria. The *Thuya orientalis*, var. *pendula*, is also classed with these, and called Ito-sugi, or Thread-like Cryptomeria.

Other kinds of the *Thuya* are common, as: *Thuya obtusa* (Hinoki, Kamakura-hiba, or Chabo-hiba), *Thuya dolabrata* (Asunaro), *Thuya gigantea* (Goro-hiba), *Thuya occidentalis* (Niwoi-hiba), *Thuya orientalis* (Konote-gashiwa), *Thuya pendula* (Hiyoku-hiba), *Thuya pisifera* (Sawara or Shinobu-hiba), and *Thuya squarrosa* (Himuro). Also varieties of the *Podocarpus*, such as :—*Podocarpus nageia* (Nagi), and *Podocarpus macrophylla* (Maki), and, under the Japanese generic names of Maki and Nagi, are several fancy kinds known as :—Hana-maki, or Flowering Podocarpus; Enko*-maki, or Monkey Podocarpus; Rankan-maki, or Arhat's Podocarpus; Nagaha-maki, or Long-leaved Podocarpus; Tateba-shiroba-maki, or Erect-white-leaved Podocarpus; Kifu-Namban-maki, or Yellow-spotted Chinese Podocarpus; Kuyo-maki, or Nine-leaved Podocarpus; Sunago-maki, or Tiny-leaved Podocarpus;

---

* Enko,—a term referring to a long-armed monkey but frequently applied to trees with long clambering branches.

Fukurin-maki, or White-edged-leaved Podocarpus; Shirofu-maruba-nagi, or White-spotted-leaved Podocarpus; Asagi-jima-nagi, or Blue-striped-leaved Podocarpus; Shirofu-hosoba-nagi, or White-narrow-leaved Podocarpus; Konjima-nagi, or Dark-blue-streaked Podocarpus; Sajiba-nagi, or Spoon-leaved Podocarpus; Aocha-nagi, or Olive-green Podocarpus; Kin-gin-nagi, or Gold-and-silver Podocarpus; Maruba-nagi, or Round-leaved Podocarpus; Ogon-nagi, or Golden Podocarpus; Aode-nagi, or Blue-leaved Podocarpus; and Hosoba-nagi, or Narrow-leaved Podocarpus. Classified with these under the name of Koya-maki is the *Sciadopytis verticillata.*

Next may be mentioned several kinds of the Juniper, such as :—*Juniperus rigida* (Nezu or Muro-no-ki), *Juniperus littoralis* (Hai-nezu), *Juniperus taxifolia* (Shima-muro), *Juniperus chinensis* (Ibuki); and under the class of Ibuki are included Shirofu-ibuki, or White-spotted-leaved Juniper; Ogon-ibuki, or Golden Juniper; and Barafu-ibuki, or Centre-spotted-leaved Juniper.

Other coniferous evergreens are :—*Tsuga sieboldii* (Tsuga), *Torreya-nucifera* (Kaya), *Cephabolaxus drupacea* (Inu-gaya), *Libocedrus decurrens* (Oni-hiba), *Cupressus corneyana* (Suiriu-hiba or Kanaami-hiba), *Taxus cuspidata* (Ichii), *Taxus tardiva* (Kiaraboku), and *Picea alcockiana* (Toki).

Among non-coniferous evergreens are many varieties of Box and Holly, as ;—*Buxus japonica* (Asama-tsuge), *Buxus japonica*, var. *macrophylla* (Kusa-tsuge), *Ilex crenata* (Inu-tsuge), *Ilex crenata albo-marginata* (Shiro-fukurin-tsuge), *Ilex integra* (Mochino-ki), *Ilex rotunda* (Kurogane-mochi), *Ilex latifolia* (Tarayo), *Ilex crenata fulvo marginata* (Cha-fukurin-tsuge), *Ilex sieboldii* (Ume-modoki), *Ilex serrata* (Hiragi-gashi), *Ilex pendunculosa* (Soyogo), and *Ilex crenata macrophylla* (Oba-tsuge). The gardeners also include under the terms Tsuge and Mochi the following fancy varieties :—Yanone-tsuge, or Arrow-headed-leaved Box; Keshiha-tsuge, or Grass-leaved Box; Kikko-boshi-tsuge, or Tortoise-shell-marked Box; Makiba-mochi, or Curled-leaved Box; Edo-mochi, or Edo Box; Toyama-mochi, or *Toyama* Holly; and Ao-mochi, or Blue Holly. Classed with these as Fukuro-mochi is the *Ligustrum japonicum fol. crispis.* There are also certain evergreen Oaks, such as :—*Quercus acuta* (Aka-gashi), *Quercus cuspidata* (Shii-no-ki), *Quercus dentata* (Kashiwa), *Quercus glabra* (Mate-gashi), *Quercus seosilifolia* (Yanagi-gashi), *Quercus solicina*, (Hosoba-gashi), and (Hira-gashi) *Quercus glavca.* Other evergreens extensively used in gardens are :—*Cleyera japonica* (Sakaki), *Photinia glabra* (Kaname-mochi), *Ternstrœmia japonica* (Mokkoku, Hana-mokkoku, and Tobera-mokkoku), *Nandina domestica* (Nanten), *Camellia japonica*

(Tsubaki), *Camellia sasanqua* (Sazankwa), *Camellia theifera* (Cha), *Camellia theifera*, var. *macrophylla* (To-cha), *Cytrus aurantium* (Yudzu), *Citrus bigaradia* (Dai-dai), *Citrus decumana* (Zabon), *Citrus fusca* (Kikoku), *Citrus japonica* (Kinkan), *Citrus nobilis* (Mikan), *Cupressus corneyana* (Suiriu-hiba), *Daphniphyllum macropodum* (Yuzuri-ha and Hime-yuzuri-ha), *Cercidiphyllum japonicum* (Katsura), *Cinnamonium camphora* (Kusu-no-ki), *Cinnamonium loureirii* (Nikkei, Kinkei, and Tora-nikkei), *Andromeda japonica* (Asebo), *Aucuba japonica* (Aoki),—of which four or five kinds are known,—also *Viscum album* (Yadori-gi), *Photinia japonica* (Biwa), *Olea fragrans* (Mokusei), *Olea aquifolium* (Hiragi), and several fancy varieties of the Olea, called :—Ogon-hiragi, or Yellow-leaved Olea ; Chirimen-hiragi, or Silk-crape Olea ; Kin-mokusei, or Golden Olea ; Gin-mokusei, or Silver Olea ; Shiki-mokusei, or Olea of the Four Seasons ; also *Dendropanax japonicum* (Kakure-mino), *Silene Keiskei* (Biranji), *Cornus officinalis* (Sanshiyu), and others.

DECIDUOUS TREES AND BUSHES.

The principal deciduous trees consist of Sycamores, Maples, Chestnuts, Elms, Beeches, Hornbeams, Birches, Ashes, Limes, Willows, Poplars, Mulberry trees, etc., as follows:—*Acer argutum* (Miyama-momiji), *Acer buergerianum* (Hana-kaede), *Acer carpinefolium* (Yama-shiba or Chidori-no-ki), *Acer cissifolium* (Mitsude-kaede), *Acer diabolicum* (Oni-momiji), *Acer distylum* (Hitotsuba-kaede), *Acer parvifolium* (Tetsu-kaede), *Acer pictum* (Tsuta-momiji), *Acer palmatum* (Yama-momiji), *Acer japonicum* (Meigetsu-kaede), *Acer rufinerve* (Urihada-kaede), *Acer purpurascens* (Kachi-kaede), *Castanea vulgaris*, var. *japonica* (Kuri), *Celtis cinensis* (Yenoki), *Ulmus montana* (Atsuni), *Ulmus parvifolia* (Akinire), *Ulmus campestris* (Yagiri or Kobu-nire), *Zelkowa keaki* (Keyaki), *Fagus sieboldi* (Shiro-buna), *Fagus sylvatica* (Buna-no-ki), *Betula alba* (Kaba-no-ki), *Betula corylifolia* (Mehari-no-ki), *Betula lenta* (Kawara-buna), *Betula ulmifolia* (Yoguso-mine-bari), *Fraxinus longicuspis* (Aodako), *Fraxinus mandschurica* (Shoji), *Fraxinus pubinervis* (Toneriko), *Tilia cordata* (Shina-no-ki), *Tilia miqueliana* (Bodaiju), *Salix babylonica* (Shidare-yanagi), *Salix brachystachys* (Neko-yanagi), *Salix japonica* (Shiba-yanagi), *Salix nipponica* (Tachi-yanagi), *Salix padifolia* (Yama-yanagi), *Salix purpurea* (Kawa-yanagi), *Salix rubra* (Saru-yanagi), *Salix sieboldiana* (Iwa-yanagi), *Salix subopposita* (Kuro-yanagi), *Populus tremula* (Hako-yanagi), *Populus suaveolens* (Poplar), *Spiræ thunbergii* (Yuki-yanagi), *Morus alba* (Kuwa), *Lagerstrœmia indica* (Hiakujikko or Saru-suberi), *Alnus firma* (Minebari), *Alnus maritima* (Han-no-ki), *Alnus incana* (Yama-ban-no-ki), *Sambucus racemosa*, var. *sieboldiana* (Niwatoko), *Paullownia imperialis* (Kiri), *Sterculia plantanifolia* (Aogiri), and several garden varieties of the Kiri species known as:—Shiro-giri, Iigiri, Akame-giri, Oka-giri, Fuyu-giri, Goto-giri, Abura-giri, To-giri, Shina-giri, and Shima-giri. Also *Æsculus turbinata* (Tochi-no-ki), *Diospyros kaki* (Kaki), of which there are five or six varieties, *Ginkgo biloba* (Icho), *Catalpa kæmpferi* (Adzusa), *Sophora japonica* (Yenju), *Albizzia julibrissin* (Nemu-no-ki), *Actinidia polygama* (Matatabi), *Ficus carica* (Ichijiku), *Corylus heterophylla* (Hashibami), *Aphananthe aspera* (Muku-no-ki), *Hovenia dulcis* (Kempo-nashi), *Lindera sericea* (Kuromoji), *Lindera triloba* (Shiromoji), *Rhus vernicifera* (Urushi-no-ki), *Rhus succedanea* (Haze-no-ki), *Vaccinium ciliatum* (Natsu-haze), *Euonymus europæus* (Mayumi), *Euonymus alatus* (Nishikigi), *Edgeworthia papyrifera* (Mitsumata), *Quercus crispula* (O-nara), *Quercus glandulifera* (Ko-nara), *Cedrela chinensis* (Chanchin), *Tamarix chinensis* (Gioriu), *Cornus macrophylla* (Mizuki), *Clethra barbinervis* (Riobu), *Melia japonica* (Ko-sendan), *Melia tosendan* (To-

Maple trees of Tsuten, Kioto.
FIG. 39.

sendan), *Crataegus sanguinea* (O-sanzashi), *Crataegus cuneata* (Sanzashi), *Rhamnus crenata* (Iso-no-ki), *Meliosma myriantha* (Awa-buki), *Ehretia serrata* (Chisha-no-ki), *Broussonetia kasinoki* (Kaji-no-ki), *Pterostyrax corymbosum* (Asagara), *Ligustrum ibota* (Ibota-no-ki),

Ligustrum medium (Oba-itabo-no-ki), *Sapindus mukurosi* (Mukuroji), *Viburnum dilatatum* (Gamadzumi), *Gleichenia glauca* (Urajiro), *Sophora japonica* (Enju), *Cladrastis amurensis* (Inu-enju), *Juglans regia* (Oni-gurumi), *Juglans cordiformis* (Hime-gurumi), *Pterocarya rhoifolia* (Sawa-gurumi), and *Platycarya strobilacea* (No-gurumi).

Certain of the above are classed separately by the Japanese as *Koyo-mono*, or Trees of Reddening Leaf, and as such, may be recapitulated :—*Acer palmatum* (Yama-momiji), *Acer japonicum* (Meigetsu-kaede and Hauchiwa-kaede), *Acer rufinerve* (Uri-hada-kaede), *Acer buergerianum* (Hana-kaede), *Acer purpurascens* (Kachi-kaede), *Acer cissifolium* (Mitsude-kaede) ; and belonging to the same species are certain garden varieties known as :—Chishiwo-momiji, or Blood Maple; Tora-kaede, or Tiger Maple ; O-sakazuki-momiji, or Wine-cup Maple ; Benishida-momiji, or Pink Maple ; Kara-kaede, or Chinese Maple ; Jiman-zome-momiji, or Maple of Rich Dye ; Genji-momiji, or Red Maple ; Nomura-momiji or Copper-coloured Maple ; Hitotsuba-momiji, or Single-leaved Maple. The Blood Maple, Pink Maple, Copper-coloured Maple, and others, are classed as "Spring Maples," their colour being brightest when their leaves are young. Maples which show green leaves in the spring-time, produce the richest tints in Autumn. (Figure 39 illustrates one of the spots in Kioto noted for its wild Maple trees.) Also belonging to the same class of *Koyo-mono* are :—*Rhus vernicifera* (Uru-shi-no-ki), *Rhus sylvestris* (Haze-urushi), *Rhus succedanea* (Haze-no-ki), *Vaccinium ciliatum* (Natsu-haze), *Euonymus europæus* (Mayumi), *Euonymus alatus* (Nishikigi), *Edgeworthia papyrifera* (Mitsumata), *Quercus crispula* (Onara), *Quercus glandulifera* (Ko-nara), *Fraxinus pubinervis* (Toneriko), *Ginkgo biloba* (Icho), *Diospyros kaki* (Kaki), and *Enkianthus japonicus* (Dodan-tsutsuji).

FLOWERING TREES AND SHRUBS.

Among the flowering trees and shrubs are many kinds of Plum and Cherry, also Peach, Quince, Pear, Pomegranate, and other fruit trees, Magnolias, Camellias, Azaleas, Rhododendrons, Wistarias, Tree-peonies, Daphnes, and Hydrangeas. The following are the principal kinds of Cherry-trees :—*Prunus cerasus* (Mizakura), *Prunus pseudo-cerasus* (Yama-zakura), *Prunus buergeriana* (Inu-zakura), *Prunus incisa* (Mame-zakura), *Prunus spinulosa* (Shiro-zakura), *Prunus subhirtella* (Higan-zakura). Also numerous varieties—distinguished by the native gardeners, but classed by botanists merely as garden varieties—are :—Shidare-zakura, or Weeping Cherry ; Yaye-zakura, or Double Cherry ; Ito-zakura, or Thread-like Cherry ; Niwa-zakura, or Garden Cherry ;

Jizenkoji-zakura, or *Jizen-koji*[*] Cherry; Taizanji-zakura, or *Taizanji*[*] Cherry; Yokihi-zakura,[†] or Lovely White Cherry; Miyama-zakura, or Distant Mountain Cherry, Asagi-zukura, or Pale Blue Cherry; and Kuruma-gayeshi-zakura.[‡]

The Japanese Plum-tree is even more prolific in varieties, but under the native term for Plum (Ume) are included one or two kinds of the *Jasminum* and other species.   They may be enumerated as follows:—*Prunus mume* (Ume), *Prunus japonica* (Niwa-ume), *Prunus mume, fl. coceinea* (Kobai), *Prunus tomentosa* (Yusura-ume), *Prunus mume,* var. *pleiocarpas* (Mizaron-ume), *Jasminum sieboldianum* (Obai), *Jasminum floridum* (Riu-kiu-obai), *Potentilla fructicosa* (Kin-robai), *Raphiolepis japonica* (Sharin-ume).   Other distinguishing names for garden varieties are:— Shichi-gwatsu-ume, or July Plum; Tobi-ume, or Flying Plum (see Fig. 40); Shidare-ume, or Drooping Plum; No-ume, or Wild Plum; Hai-ume, or Crawling Plum; Tomeko-ume, or Small Blossom Plum; Gin-ume, or Silver Plum; Ogawa-ume, or River Plum; Chigo-

The Flying Plum.
FIG. 40.

ume, or Tiny Blossom Plum; Kikkwa-bai, or Chrysanthemum Blossom Plum; Yama-ume, or Mountain Plum; Asagi-ume, or Pale Blue Plum; Mochi-ume, or Cluster Blossom Plum; Fuyu-ume, or Winter Plum; Saigio-ume, or *Saigo* Plum; Bungo-ume, or *Bungo*§ Plum; Miyagi-ume, or *Miyagi*§ Plum; Suzunari-ume, or Rich Cluster Plum; Yaye-riokugaku-bai, or Double-emerald-blossom Plum; Hanazaron-ume, or Ephemeral-blossom Plum; Suo-kobai, or Deep Red Plum; Kan-kobai, of Winter Red Plum; Rioku-gaku-bai or Emerald-blossom Plum; Shidare-midori-ume, or Drooping-emeraled Plum; Mikaiko-ume, or Light Red Plum; Oshuku-bai, or Nightingale-dwelling Plum; Yokihi-ume, or Lovely White Plum; Toji-bai, or Chinese Plum; Naniwa-ume, or *Naniwa*§ Plum; Eizan-kabai, or *Eizan*§ Red Plum; Hassaku-bai, or Eighth Month Plum; Miuki-ume, or Fruit-growing Plum; Ogon-ume, or Golden Plum; Chirimen-kobai,

---

[*] Taizanji and Jizenkoji are names of noted temple groves.

[†] Yokihi, the name of a beautiful Chinese Princess, is often applied to blossoms of special whiteness and loveliness.

[‡] Kuruma-gaeshi—means "to send back the carriage" and refers to the gorgeously trapped bullock waggons in which the ladies of the Court were driven to view the flowers.   The idea conveyed in its present context is that the beauty of the blossoms, requires a long day for the full enjoyment of them, and that carriages should be sent back.

§ Bungo and Miyagi are names of provinces, and Naniwa and Eizan names of places in Japan.

or Crape-like Red Plum; Fudan-ume, or Common Plum; Goshiki-ume, or Prismatic-coloured Plum; Futairo-ume, or Double-coloured Plum; Kuro-ume, or Dark-coloured Plum; Haya-haku-bai, or Early White Plum; and Yaye-kobai, or Double Red Plum. Other blossoming fruit trees are:—*Prunus armenica* (Anzu), *Prunus communis* (Amendo), *Prunus macrophylla* (Biran), *Prunus spinulosa* (Rinboku), *Prunus triflora* (Sumomo), *Jasminum grandiflorum* (Sokei), *Pyrus japonica* (Boke, Haruboke, Shiroboke, and Koboke), *Pyrus japonica*, var. *pygmæa* (Kusa-boke), *Pyrus malus* (Ringo), *Pyrus cydonia* (Marumero), *Pyrus ussuriensis* (Nashi), *Pyrus spectabilis* (Kaido, Yama-kaido, and Shidare-kaido), *Cyrus chinensis* (Kwarin), *Punica granatum* (Zakuro), *Photinia japonica* (Biwa), *Meliosma pungens* (Yama-biwa), *Diospyrus kaki* (Kaki), and *Zizyphus vulgaris* (Natsume).

The Camellia, which has been mentioned among evergreens, is one of the most important flowering trees. The classified kinds are:—*Camellia japonica* (Tsubaki), *Camellia japonica*, *luteo-variegata* (Kifu-tsubaki), *Camellia japonica*, *flore pleno* (Otome-tsubaki), *Camellia japonica*, *fol. aculeato serratis* (Hiragi-tsubaki), *Stuartia pseudo-camellia* (Natsu-tsubaki or Shara-tsubaki). Fancy names applied to garden varieties of the above are:—Yaye-amegashita-tsubaki, or Celestial Double Camellia; Kara-tsubaki, or Chinese Camellia; Gegan-tsubaki, or Double Pale Red Camellia, Shiratama-monoguruitsubaki, or White Curled Blossom Camellia; Bingo-shibori-tsubaki, or *Bingo** Variegated Camellia; Miorenji-tsubaki, or *Miorenji** Camellia; Kumagaye-tsubaki, or *Kumagaye** Camellia; Suisho-tsubaki or Crystal Blossom Camellia; Sarasa-fukurin-tsubaki, or Coloured-edged Blossom Camellia; and Iwashibori-tsubaki, or Variegated Rock Camellia.

Next may be mentioned different varieties of the Magnolia:—*Magnolia conspicua* (Haku-mokuren), *Magnolia grandiflora* (Taizen-boku), *Magnolia hypoleuca* (Hono-ki), *Magnolia kobus* (Kobushi), *Magnolia obovata* (Shimoku-renge), *Magnolia obovata*, var. *purpurea* (Sarasa-renge), *Magnolia parviflora* (Oyama-renge), *Magnolia pumila* (Shiratamamokuren), and *Magnolia stellata* (Hime-kobushi).

The following are different kinds of the Azalea and Rhododendron:—*Rhododendron albrechti* (Murasaki-yashio-tsutsuji), *Rhododendron brachycarpum* (Shiro-shakunage), *Rhododendron dilatatum* (Mitsuba-tsutsuji), *Rhododendron indicum*, var. *macranthum* (Satsuki), *Rhododendron kamschaticum* (Yezo-tsutsuji), *Rhohodendron keiskei* (Me-shakunage), *Rhododendron ledifolium* (Mochi-tsutsuji), *Rhododendron ledifolium*, var. *narcissiflorum* (Ye-

---

* Bingo, Miorenji, and Kumagaye are names of places.

dogawa-tsutsuji), *Rhododendron ledifolium*, var. *leucanthum* (Riukiu-tsutsuji), *Rhododendron metternichii* (Shaku-nage), *Rhododendron quinquefolium* (Goro-tsutsuji), *Rhododendron schlippenbachii* (Kuro-fune-tsutsuji), *Rhododendron semibarbatum* (Baikwan-tsutsuji), *Rhododendron serpillifolum* (Unzen-tsutsuji), *Rhododendron sinense* (Kirenge-tsutsuji), and *Rhododendron chrysanthum* (Kibana-shakunage). The Japanese put in the same class with the above:—*Andromeda campanulata* (Furin-tsutsuji), *Andromeda japonica* (Abura-tsutsuji), *Andromeda cernua*, var. *rubens* (Beni-dodan), *Enkianthus japonicus* (Dodan-tsutsuji), *Menziezia cilii-calix* (Tsurigane-tsutsuji), and *Menziezia purpurea* (Yashio-tsutsuji).

Under the head of flowering bushes may be also included many varieties of the Olea, mentioned among evergreens. The *Wistaria chinensis* (Murasaki-fuji), and *Wistaria brachybotrys* (Shira-fuji), play an important part in gardens, and, classed with them as a Yellow Wistaria, is the *Stachyurus præcox* (Ki-fuji). Other flowering shrubs are:—*Daphne zenkwa* (Fuji-modoki), *Daphne jesoensis* (Naniwazu), *Daphne kiusiana* (Kosho-no-ki), *Daphne odora* (Jinchoke), *Hydrangea hirta* (Yama-ajisai), *Hydrangea hortensis*, var. *japonica* (Beni-gaku), *Hydrangea hortensis*, var. *ajisai* (Ajisai), *Hydrangea thnnbergii* (Amacha), *Lespedeza bicolor* (Hagi), *Lespedeza bicolor*, var. *sieboldi* (Natsu-hagi), *Lespedeza buergeri* (Ki-hagi), *Lespedeza cyrtobotrya* (Maruba-hagi), *Lespedeza tomentosa* (Shira-hagi), *Lespedeza virgata* (Makiye-hagi), *Kerria japonica* (Yamabuki), *Pæonia moutan* (Ki-botan and Yamato-botan), *Cytisus scoporius* (Enishida), *Acacia farnesiana* (Kiugo-kwan), *Spriæa cantoniensis* (Kodemari), *Spiræa japonica* (Shimotsuke), and *Deutzia sieboldiana* (Utsugi).

FLOWERING PLANTS.

The principal flowering plants are Chrysanthemums, Asters, Carnations, Lilies, Gentians, Irises, Jonquils, Lotuses, Peonies, Anemonies, Orchids, etc. as follows:—*Chrysanthemum coronarium* (Shun-giku), *Chrysanthemum frutescens* (Moku-shun-giku), *Aster dimorphophyllus* (Tateyama-giku), *Aster fastigiatus* (Hime-shion), *Aster glehni* (Komame-giku), *Aster hispidus*, var. *isochætus* (Yamaji-nogiku), *Aster microcephalus* (Mizu-giku), *Aster scaber* (Shiro-yama-giku), *Aster tataricus* (Shion), *Aster trinervius*, var. *congesta* (Kon-giku), *Aster trinervius*, var. *ovata* (Yamashiro-giku), *Aster tripolium* (Ura-giku), *Aster spathulifolius* (Daruma-giku), *Boltonia indica* (Chosen-giku), *Boltonia insisa* (Noshun-giku), *Erigeron thunbergii* (Azuma-giku), *Pyrethrum marginatum* (Iwa-giku), *Pyrethrum indicum* (Abura-giku), *Pyrethrum senticuspe* (Korin-giku), *Pyrethrum decaisneanum* (Shiogiku or Shiokaze-giku), *Pyrethrum sinense* (Yama-giku or Riuno-giku), *Mallopus japonicus* (Kuma-giku), *Leucanthemum nipponicum* (Hama-giku), *Leucanthemum vulgare* (Furansu-giku), *Anemone japonica* (Kitsune-giku), *Tripleurospermum amdiguum* (Shika-giku), *Seneccio nikoensis* (Sawa-giku), and *Arnica angustifolia* (Usagi-giku).

Dianthus chinensis (Kara-nadeshiko), *Dianthus japonicus* (Fuji-nadeshiko, *Dianthus superbus* (Nadeshiko), and *Gypsophia saxifraga* (Hari-nadeshiko).

Lilium auratum (Eizan-yuri and Horaiji-yuri), *Lilium callosum* (Nohime-yuri), *Lilium candidum* (Yoriba-yuri), *Lilium concolor* (Hime-yuri), *Lilium cordifolium* (Uba-yuri), *Lilium japonicum* (Sasa-yuri and Tamoto-yuri), *Lilium longiflorum* (Teppo-yuri, Hakata-yuri, Nioi-yuri, and Tametomo-yuri), *Lilium speciosum* (Shiratama-yuri and Kanoko-yuri), *Lilium thunbergianum* (Haru-zukashi-yuri and Natsu-zukashi-yuri), *Lilium tigridum* (Oni-yuri), *Lilium maximowiczii* (Ko-oni-yuri), *Lilium medeoloides* (Kuruma-yuri), *Lilium medeoloides*, var. *obovatum* (Takeshima-yuri), *Lilium thunbergianum*, var. *venustium* (Hirado-yuri), *Fritillaria japonica* (Tengai-yuri), *Fritillaria thunbergii* (Ami-gasa-yuri), *Fritillaria camtschatensis* (Kuro-yuri), *Polygonatum canaliculatum* (Naruko-yuri), and *Disporum smilacinum* (Chigo-yuri).

Iris japonica (Shaga), *Iris lævigata* (Kakitsubata), *Iris lævigata*, var. *kæmpferi* (Hana-shobu), *Iris sibirica*, var. *orientalis* (Ayame), *Iris tectorum* (Ippatsu), *Narcissus jonquilla* (Kin-dzuisen), *Narcissus tazetta*, var. *chinensis* (Suisen), *Amaryllis belladonna* (Natsu-dzuisen), *Amaryllis candida* (Tama-sudare), and *Lycorus aurea* (Jagatara-dzuisen).

Gentiana scabra (Rindo), *Gentiana thunbergii* (Haru-rindo), *Gentiana triflora* (Oyama-rindo), *Pæonia albiflora* (Shakuyaku), *Melastoma macrocar* (No-botan), *Dahlia variabilis* (Tenjiku-botan), *Clematis tubulosa* (Kusa-botan), *Rosa indica* (Koshin-bara), *Rosa rugosa* (Hama-nasu), *Rosa lævigata* (Hatoya-bara), *Platycodon grandiflorum* (Ki-kio), *Lobelia sessilifolia* (Sawa-gikio), *Eupatorium chinense* (Fujibakama), *Aconitum fis-cheri* (Torikabuto), *Aconitum lycoctonum* (Reijinso), *Aconitum uncinatum*, var. *japonicum* (Hana-kazura), *Wahlenbergia marginata* (Hina-gikio), *Campanula medium* (Furinso), *Campanula lasiocarpa* (Iwa-gikio), *Campanula punctata* (Hotarubukuro), *Alcea rosea* (Tachi-aoi, and Hana-aoi), *Malva pulchella* (Fuyu-aoi), *Monochoria vaginalis* (Mizu-aoi), *Monochoria plantaginea* (Sasanagi), *Glaucidum palmatum* (Shirane-aoi), *Malva sylvestris* (Zeni-aoi), *Patrinia scabiosæfolia* (Ominaeshi), *Patrinia villosa* (Otokoeshi), *Sedum kamtschaticum* (Korinso), *Sedum erythrostictum* (Benkeiso), *Impatiens balsamina* (Hosenkwa), *Hermerocallis flava* (Wasure-gusa), *Hermerocallis dumortieri* (Hime-kwanzo), *Hermerocallis minor* (Beni-kwanzo), *Hermerocallis fulva* (Yabu-kwanzo), *Hibiscus mutabilis* (Fuyo), *Hibiscus syriacus* (Mokuge), *Gardenia florida* (Kuchinashi), *Gardenia radicans* (Ko-kuchinashi), *Polygonum cuspidatum* (Itadori), *Polygonum tinctorum* (Ai), *Primula cortu-soides* (Sakuraso), *Viola patrinii,* var. *chinensis* (Sumire), *Cnicus brevicaule* (Hama-azami), *Cnicus japonicus* (No-azami), *Cnicus nipponicus* (Ho-azami), *Cnicus ovalifolius* (Hime-azami), *Cnicus spicatus* (Yama-azami), *Cnicus purparatus* (Fuji-azami), *Begonia evansiana* (Shiukaido), *Gomphrena globosa* (Sennichi-so), *Adonis amurensis* (Fukujiso), *Manettia cordifolia* (Kwaenso), *Caltha palustris,* var. *siberica* (Yenkoso), *Helianthus annuus* (Himawari), *Papaver somniferum* (Keshi), *Papaver rhoeas* (Hina-geshi), *Cotyledon spinosa* (Tsume-renge), *Lysimachia leucantha* (Sawa-tora-no-o), *Lysimachia clethroides* (Tora-no-o), *Poterium officinale* (Waremoko), *Scabiosa japonica* (Matsu-mushi-so), *Celosia argentea* (Keito), *Lychnis grandiflora* (Ganpi), *Lychnis forma floribus congestis* (Kuruma-gampi), and *Calendula officinalis* (Kinsenkwa).

CREEPING PLANTS.

The principal creeping plants grown on trellises and fences are :—*Vitis inconstans* (Tsuta), *Vitis vinifera* (Budo), *Vitis pentaphylla* (Bimbo-kazura), *Vitis labrusca* (Yama-budo), *Vitis Iceoides* (Udo-kazura), *Clematis japonica* (Tsurigane-kazura), *Clematis paniculata* (Senninso), *Clematis patens* (Kazaguruma), *Clematis florida* (Tessen), *Clematis apiifolia* (Botan-dzuru), *Trachelospermum jasminoides* (Teika-kazura), *Tecoma grandiflora* (Nozen-kazura), *Convolvulus japonicus* (Hirugao), *Convolvulus soldanella* (Hama-hirugao), *Ipomœa pes-capræ* (Uchiwa-kazura), *Ipomœa hederacea* (Asagao), *Ipomœa bona-box* (Hari-asagao), *Ipomœa purpurea* (Maruba-asagao), *Kadsura japonica* (Binan-kazura), *Vicia amœna* (Tsuru-fujibakama), and *Vicia cracea,* var. *japonica* (Kusa-fuji). The wistaria —a gigantic creeper—has been mentioned among trees.

LARGE LEAVED PLANTS.

The Japanese class, apart from ordinary flowering plants, under the name of *Ha-no-mono,* those which are remarkable for their large handsome leaves, and the blossoms of which, if existing at all, are comparatively insignificant. The principal specimens are as follow :—*Nuphar japonicum* (Kohone), *Rhodea japonica* (Omoto), *Tradescantia discolor* (Murasaki-omoto), *Veronica murorum* (Kuwagata-omoto), *Funkia ovata* (Giboshi), and *Canna indica* (Dandoku). Also numerous species of Orchids :—

Arethusa japonica (Sawa-ran), *Bletia hyacinthina* (Shi-ran), *Cephalanthera falcata* (Kin-ran), *Lecarnorchis japonica* (Muyo-ran), *Cymbidium ensifolium* (Oran), *Cymbidium virens* (Shun-ran), *Marsdenia tomentosa* (Fuyo-ran), *Chloranthus inconspicuus* (Cha-ran), *Cremastra wallichiana* (Saihai-ran), *Luisia teres* (Bo-ran), *Gymnadenia rupestris* (Seki-ran), *Phajus maculatus* (Kinkei-ran and Token-ran), *Phajus grandiflorus* (Kaku-ran), *Calanthe textori* (Kinsei-ran), *Oeceocladus falcata* (Fu-ran), *Canarium commune* (Kan-ran), *Lycapodium cryptomerinum* (Sugi-ran), *Lycopodium sieboldi* (Himo-ran), *Lycopodium phlegmaria* (Nankaku-ran), *Liparis plicata* (Chikei-ran), *Liparis bambusæfoia* (Sasaba-ran), *Liparis cornicaulis* (Yukoku-ran), *Goodyera schlechtendaliana* (Kamome-ran), *Goodyera repens* (Shusu-ran), *Sarcanthus scolopendrifolius* (Mukade-ran), *Saccolabium japonicum* (Kashinoki-ran), *Dendrobium reptans* (Osa-ran or Bakkoku-ran), *Bulbophyllum inconspicum* (Mugi-ran), *Anodendron laeve* (Nishiki-ran), *Psilotium triquetrum* (Matsuba-ran, or Chiku-ran), *Ophiopogon jaburan* (Noshi-ran), *Metanarthecium luteo-viride* (Nogi-ran), *Epilobium angustifolium* (Yanagi-ran), *Clintonia udensis* (Tsubame-ran), *Hoya carnosa* (Sakura-ran). Other large leaved plants are :—*Musa basjoo* (Basho), *Musa cococinea* (Hime-basho), and *Dawallia bullata* (Shinobu). The following are other plants of the fern species :—*Pteris aquilina* (Warabi), *Pteris quadriaurita* (Hachijo-shida), *Pteris semipinnata* (Amakusa-shida), *Polypodium linearifolium* (Birodo-shida), *Polypodium maximowiczii* (Fuji-shida), *Polypodium phegopteris* (Usu-warabi), *Polypodium tricuspe* (Iwa-omodaka), *Polypodium buergerianum* (Tanone-shida), *Adiantum pedatum* (Kujaku-shida of Howo-shida), *Aspidium falcatum* (Oni-shida), and many varieties of Aspidium and Asplenium. Palmaceous trees are :—*Chamærops excelsa* (Shuro), *Cycas revoluta* (Sotetsu), *Trachycarpus excelsus* (To-juro), *Onoclea germanica* (Kusa-sotetsu or Yamasotetsu), and *Onoclea orientalis* (O-kusa-sotetsu).

BAMBOOS, RUSHES, AND GRASSES.

There are numerous kinds of bamboos, bamboo grasses, and other long grasses, cultivated in gardens, namely :—*Bambusa nana* (Kan-chiku), *Bambusa aurea* (Howo-chiku), *Bambusa chino* (Kanzan-chiku), *Bambusa senanensis* (Suzu-take). *Bambusa senanensis*, var. *albo marginata* (Kuma-zasa), *Bambusa sterilis* (Hotei-chiku), *Bambusa variegata* (Chigo-dake, Chigo-zasa, and Ogon-chiku), *Phyllostachys kumazasa* (Gomai-zasa), *Phyllostachys bambusoides* (Ya-dake), *Phyllostachys nigra* (Kurorchiku, Ha-chiku, or Ma-dake), *Arundinaria japonica* (Me-daka or Ne-zasa), *Alisma plantago* (Omo-daka), *Phragmitis communis* (Yoshi or Ashi), *Eularia japonica* (Susuki), and *Eularia cotulifera* (Abura-susuki). Among turfs are :—*Zoysia pungens* (Chosen-shiba, Korai-shiba and No-shiba), and *Selaginella involvens* (Iwa-shiba). And among mosses :—*Selaginella kraussiana* (Eizan-goke), and other kinds known as Yama-goke, Ja-goke, Zeni-goke, Matsuba-goke, and Hinata-goke.

Old books on Japanese gardening contain injunctions as to the selection of trees and plants, which, though often conflicting, and seldom closely followed in practise are interesting as showing the ideal standards by which the early designers were guided, and reveal much of the true spirit of the art. One ancient authority remarks that the first trees to be chosen for a garden are Pines and Cherries. Of the former, he gives preference to the *Pinus parviflora*, and among the latter, trees of single blossom are most favoured. Cherry trees of double blossom—in early times confined to the Nara district —were looked upon as an abnormal production; the beautiful groves at Yoshino, the wild trees at Arashiyama (see Fig. 41), and even the *Sakon-no-sakura*, or Imperial Cherry tree, planted in front of the Kioto Palace, were of single flower. Among Plum trees the same authority prefers those of single and pinkish blossom, which bloom early in the

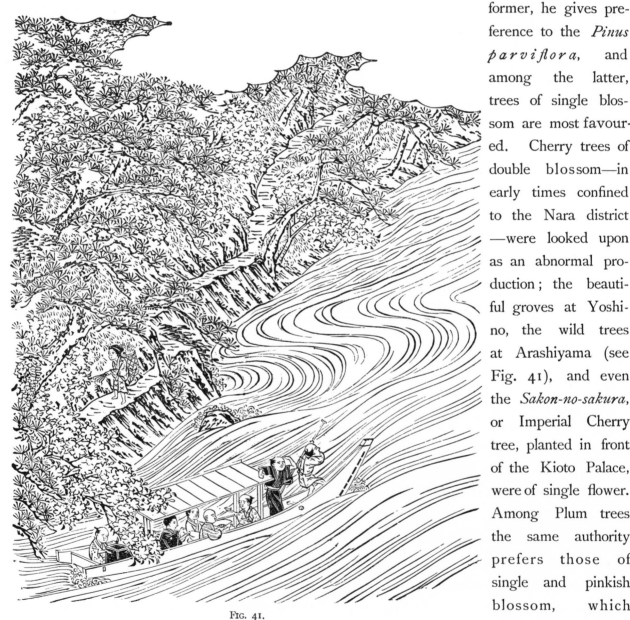

Fig. 41.

season, but sanctions the limited use of certain double-blossomed kinds on account of their delicious fragrance. He deprecates, however, the employment of the most luxuriant species in gardens, because they flower late in the season, and contemporaneously with the Cherry-blossom, by the side of which they always appear at a disadvantage. Willows, young Maples, and the *Podocarpus macrophylla* are also much favoured among trees. Referring to plants and grasses, the Kerria, Wistaria, Platycodon, Dianthus, Patrinia, Euphatrium, Poterium, Gentian, Chrysanthemum, Eularia, and Anthistiria are mentioned as invaluable in their respective seasons, and suitable for planting in front of ornamental fences. Very rare flowers, however beautiful, are not considered desirable material for gardens, the scarce and unfamiliar being favoured only by vulgar and ignorant persons.

Another writer discourses on the fancy for planting Plum and Cherry trees in front of a guest's chamber, a custom said to have originated as a token of hospitality. A verse in an ancient collection of poems, called *Tsurezure-gusa*, runs :— " On a lovely day in spring-time, it is hard to pass by a garden resplendent with blossoming trees ; we are unconsciously constrained to enter, though uninvited ! " A similar sentiment, attributed to a Chinese poet, forbids the owner of fine flowering trees to close his gates to the passer-by.

The above observations regarding the choice of trees and plants appear chiefly to refer to the areas immediately around a residence. In the background of a large landscape garden, flowering trees and shrubs are sparingly scattered between the evergreens, by which means they are set off to better advantage when in bloom, and cause no perceptible bareness between seasons. The judicious use, in this manner, of the Camellia, Plum, Cherry, Peach, Magnolia, Wistaria, Azalea, Hydrangea, Daphne, Kerria, and Lespedeza, add to the vivid and ever-constant verdure of the Japanese garden a successively varying increment of gay colouring.

Flowering plants are not much employed in the body of the landscape, exceptions being :—the Flag or Iris, planted on the edge of a stream, or in marshy beds ; the Lotus, grown in some garden lakes ; and certain choice flowering plants and grasses belonging to the late autumn. Even the use of the " Seven Autumn Plants " (*Nana-kusa*) is restricted to particular parts of an artificial landscape, or to special types of smaller gardens. Chrysanthemums and Peonies—the two most beautiful floral productions of the country, and those on which considerable horticultural skill is lavished—find no place in a landscape garden proper ; their display is restricted to flower-beds arranged in level areas, which are generally placed near the ladies' apartments. In the grounds of the palaces the open space facing the ladies' chambers, (notably those called Komachi-no-ma, and Tsubone-beya), are adorned in this fashion. Such arrangements partake rather of the character of flower shows, specimens of the same plant being grouped together, with rarely any attempt to produce colour patterns, as in the Western parterre.

What has been stated above as to the limited use of deciduous flowering trees and shrubs must not be understood as ignoring the introduction of groves or

Outer Passage.

Tea Room.

Gateway and
Resting Shed.

FIG. 42.

orchards of such trees. The favourite pastime of "Flower-viewing" and picnicking beneath the blossoms has led to the massing of Plum trees and Cherry trees in public grounds; and a wealthy land-owner will often devote a portion of his park or garden to a similar purpose. Such groves of blossoming trees are placed apart from the general landscape composition. With a similar object, high garden banks are sometimes exclusively devoted to the display of Azalea blossoms.

There are also exceptional cases in which landscape gardens are purposely designed to satisfy special fancies, or to serve as an attraction in one particular season. An example of this is shown in Fig. 42, representing a Tea Garden designed by a priest called Saito Dosan, and intended to suggest the pictorial style of a Chinese painter famous for his paintings of hills of wild Cherry trees.

Five evergreens are mentioned as the most important and essential in a *Sansui* garden, namely :—the *Ternstrœmia japonica* (Mokkoku), the *Olea fragrans* (Mokusei), the *Podocarpus macrophylla* (Maki), the *Pinus parviflora* (Matsu), and the *Quercus dentata* (Kashiwa); and it is stated that, whatever other vegetation be added, the above should never be dispensed with in even the smallest garden, unless it be a Tea Garden. It does not follow, however, that these five kinds of trees all occupy positions of prime importance; numerous other species are introduced to give variety and to fulfil special functions in the landscape. Certain shrubs and trees may be enumerated according to the particular localities and surroundings to which they are considered appropriate.

Trees and plants specially selected for adorning the sides of hills are :— the Maple, Oak, Daphne, *Gardenia, Eugenia, Pueraria thunbergiana,* Wistaria, Azalea, Juniper, Box-tree, *Ginkgo biloba, Jasminum sieboldianum, Hibiscus mutabilis, Thuya obtusa,* Iris, Rhodea, and Plum tree. Some of these,—namely the Iris, Rhodea, and Plum,— are confined to the proximity of water, placed only on hilly islands, or on the edges of hills bordering lakes. Large trees should never be placed near the brow of a garden hill; they are best planted near its base, and a little to the rear, so that their branches partly overhang it.

The following are generally confined to the valleys or level parts of Hill Gardens :—Chrysanthemums, Asters, Peonies, *Petasites japonicus, Bletia hyacinthina, Funkia ovata,* and *Manettia cordifolia.*

For well-sides, Pines, Plum trees, Willows, or Bamboos are considered suitable, but not in too great numbers. The roots of the Willow are apt to push out the stones of a rubble-lined well, if planted too near. Plants infested by noisome insects and all poisonous growths must on no account be placed near wells or water-basins.

Particularly suited for the vicinity of water-basins are the *Andromeda japonica, Aucuba japonica, Nandina domestica, Astragalus reflexistipulus, Phellodendron amurense,* and the *Cleyera japonica.* Any of these may be planted so that a branch extends over the basin, but at sufficient height not to interfere with its use.

The following may be employed at the base of rocks and boulders :—*Rhodea japonica, Aspidium tripteron, Rhododendron indicum,* var. *macranthum, Polypodium lingua, Arundinaria japonica,* and *Senecio kœmpferi.* It is not usual to place plants in front of single stones, but between groups of two or more.

For arranging near a garden boundary, Pines, Oaks, the *Abies firma,* and the *Euonymus japonicus* are preferred.

Immediately in front of a house, Willow-trees may be planted on the east, Plum-trees to the west, the *Paulownia imperialis* to the south, and the *Sophora japonica* on the north. Plum-trees may be placed quite close to the verandah on account of their fragrant and early blossoms. In front of temples, Bamboos are often planted, and should be to the east of the buildings.

Shady, spreading trees, among which may be mentiond Pines, Cryptomerias, Chestnuts, and Persimmon trees, are selected for positions near an arbour or garden shrine.

Still stricter rules exist for the employment of particular trees in Tea Gardens. A sequestered and sombre effect being principally aimed at, evergreens and trees of thick foliage are preferred; but a few deciduous trees, such as Oaks, may be placed in the background, and an old Plum tree planted near the enclosing fence. The following are the trees and plants most used for Tea Gardens :—the Pine, Maple, Oak, *Aucuba japonica, Andromeda japonica, Gardenia florida, Euonymus alatus, Euonymus europœus, Aralia, spinosa, Elœagnus glabra, Deutzia sieboldiana, Euxus japonicus, Citrus aurantium, Eularia japonica, Lespedeza bicolor, Equisetum hyemale, Vitis inconstans, Pteris aquilina, Pelasites japonicus,* and certain Ferns. Bushes clipped into rounded shapes, called *Maru-mono* (see page 109), are not generally admitted into orthodox Tea Gardens, being considered too artificial, and detracting from the natural wildness aimed at in such gardens.

Other directions are given for the treatment of vegetation employed in different parts of ornamental grounds. Trees planted near a garden river or lake should lean over the water so as to shade it, and be reflected in it; beside a garden bridge some tree of quaint shape will often be placed and treated in this manner. Foliage surrounding a cascade should be arranged to hide a portion of the water fall. A stone lantern requires a tree or shrub near it, with one of its branches crossing in front of the fire-box, and partially intercepting the light. Shrubs or plants grown beside screen-fences are oddly called *Sode-ga-ka,* or " Scent of the Fence," not with reference to their perfume, but simply implying attractiveness. Growths thus used should be of picturesque shape, and trees with open branches and sparse foliage, such as the *Nandina domestica* and *Lespedeza bicolor,* are mostly chosen.

Careful consideration is bestowed upon the proportions of the trees selected for gardens; such proportions being controlled primarily by the scale of the whole composition, and secondarily by the relative position in the landscape. Very high trees are but sparingly employed, even for extensive grounds, and special attention is given to their aspect in relation to the building. Though the setting sun may with advantage be screened by a clump of large trees, particular care must be taken not to hide the rising moon from view. Another objection made to the unlimited use of large timber in a garden is that it excludes light and air and is therefore unhealthy.

Pollards,—called by the Japanese *Bo-mono*,—are not much favoured, though one or two may be introduced in the foreground of a garden, near the dwelling. In Tea Gardens, however, the use of pollard trees is very common. A prejudice exists against the *Shichiku*,—a kind of purple-leaved bamboo, supposed in legend to have derived its unusual colour from the tears of an inconsolable heroine of Chinese legend; also against all fragile reeds and rushes easily injured by the wind, and vegetation possessing real or imaginary poisonous properties. Terms are applied to the principal trees or tree-clumps indicating their relative functions and importance in the composition. These will be explained when treating in detail of the arrangements for different styles of gardening.

CHAPTER XII.

GARDEN COMPOSITION.

BEFORE referring in detail to the models followed in the arrangement of different kinds of gardens, it is interesting to note instructions laid down by various writers as to garden composition in general. From a European standpoint, many of these maxims may appear to present no great novelty or originality, but they will serve to show the basis upon which the theory and practice of the art is founded. Principles of design, not unlike those pursued in the West, often lead to curiously dissimilar results in the hands of the Eastern artist.

Teachers of the craft insist that, as a preliminary education for garden designing, every opportunity should be taken of visiting natural scenery for the purpose of taking notes and sketches. Such out-door sketching should not be made from a single point of view, with the object of producing a mere picture, but should be fragmentary and analytic. The best method is to copy the scenery in detail from different stations, delineating and studying separately the principal contours and features of both the foreground and the distance. It must be remembered that in a landscape garden, the various objects will be regarded from several positions, and the designer must, therefore, render himself familiar with the altered aspects which irregular contours and masses present under such varying circumstances. Notes and sketches from actual scenery are not intended to be closely followed in preparing designs, but supply suggestions and inspire originality in composition. The detailed execution is subject to constant variations, influenced chiefly by the accidental facilities of the site or surroundings; and, to a lesser extent, by the size, shape, and character of the stones, trees, lanterns, and other materials available.

The designer is repeatedly warned against attempting to follow too closely in his work the details of a real landscape, a habit leading invariably to false and unsatisfactory results; and in this respect the work of the landscape gardener is compared with that of the painter. For, according to the principles of Japanese pictorial art, though a painter will faithfully copy a natural object, mentally retaining a clear conception of its form and character, his finished work will show changes and modifications imposed upon it by the conventional rules of his art. It is the same in the art of gardening. A rural pathway through cultivated fields, for example, should be carefully studied from nature, but in its application the details must be modified and refined to suit the stately elegance of a garden.

Before proceeding with the garden construction, a complete survey and thorough examination of the site and of its surroundings are required. Its size, peculiarities of shape, levels, and drainage must be all considered. If the area be a bare and level one, the designer has considerable license, provided that he keeps in mind the aspect, neighbouring prospects, and the character of garden best calculated to suit his client. Guided by these limitations, he will consult his sketches, and perhaps make frequent visits to existing gardens, to assist him in originating a design. This he will subject to thorough reconsideration in every detail. If, however, the locality selected possesses certain natural facilities, such as fine clumps of trees, natural hills, a stream, or a cascade, the artist's controlling motive will be to work these features cleverly into his design. In the same way, a neighbouring view may be skilfully taken advantage of, the garden being so arranged that it appears, when regarded from the foreground, as a part of the general composition.

Aspect must be considered as well as prospect. An open view to the south or south-east is a great natural advantage, as is also an elevated wooded bank or a grove of high trees to the north or west. In Japan, a southern aspect is always sought for the principal rooms of dwellings. The summer breezes mostly blow from this direction, and the altitude of the sun when in this quarter prevents its glare penetrating the eave-shaded chambers. Next in favour is the eastern aspect, because it receives the pleasant and comparatively harmless morning sunshine. The north is, of course, the coldest and most cheerless quarter, but the west is even more disliked, on account of the fierce glare of the low afternoon sunshine which enters every opening. Moreover, the bitterest and bleakest winds of winter blow from the north and west. In the neighbourhood of Tokio, however, the world-famed mountain Fujisan is to be seen towards the west, for which reason it is customary to seek a partially open prospect in this direction, some important room in the dwelling having a small round window to afford a view of this peerless peak. Rules governing the aspect of apartments must necessarily control, to a great extent, the whole garden composition. The principal living and receptions rooms of a residence form the central point of view from which the artificial landscape is regarded. Within the compass of the grounds may be several distinct views, each seen to greatest advantage from certain secondary stations, but the united composition as a whole, must be best commanded, from the dwelling itself.

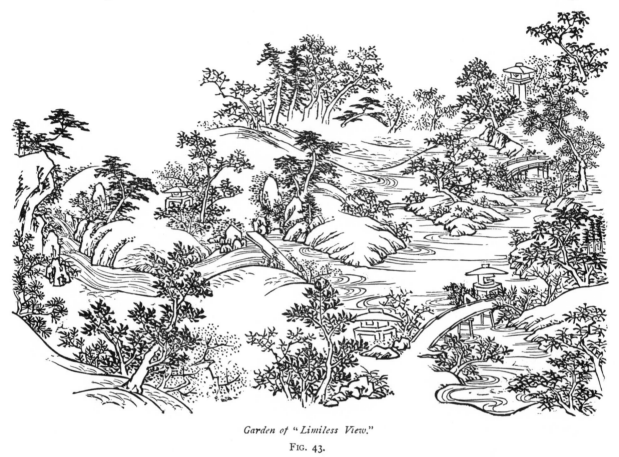

Garden of "Limitless View."
FIG. 43.

From here, also, should be obtained the finest prospect of some central object in the distance which dominates the landscape.

If a garden be constructed in a place where fine trees already stand, others of the same species should be planted beyond them, so that they may appear to blend into the composition. The same method should be followed with regard to any existing rocks or boulders of a picturesque appearance; they should be retained, and reinforced by additional stones harmonising with them in character, and arranged so as to unite them to the general landscape. In taking advantage of an outside view to impart the idea of expanse, it is recommended to plant within the grounds trees of the same kind as those seen in the distance, their heights being gradually raised or lowered so as to lead the eye by degrees to the scale of the background.

Somewhat conflicting instructions are laid down as to the portion of a land-scape garden which should first be worked upon, some writers holding that the fore-ground takes precedence, and others contending that the background should receive primary attention. All agree, however, that the mid-distance is of less import-ance, and may be finished last. The best method is probably that recommended

Garden of Tarioji no Zushi, Kotokuji.

FIG. 44.

by one authority of roughing out almost simultaneously, and elaborating alternately, step by step, both the foreground and the distance; for though it is generally considered that the background ranks first in importance, its true value is best secured by accommodating it to the scale and character of the nearer portions of the garden.

As mentioned previously, Sen-no-Rikiu is said to have taught a system of composition by which larger trees were planted in the front parts of the grounds, and lower ones in the background, thus assisting the effect of perspective distance,— an advantage particularly desirable in small gardens. On the same principle he maintained that more distant hillocks should be made lower than the nearer ones, and the level of artificial water higher in the background than in the foreground. This method is known by the name of the "Distance-lowering Style" (*Saki-sagari*), as distinct from the "Distance-raising Style" (*Saki-agari*), attributed to another artist—Furuta Oribe. The latter treatment consisted in placing the taller trees and more elevated hills behind, and gradually lowering the heights of objects towards the front of the garden.

In designing Hill Gardens, the hillocks should first be arranged, and then the water channels; the principal rocks and stones are next distributed, and lastly the trees and shrubs are planted. When constructing garden hills, in lake gardens, it must be remembered that their bases will be partly immersed after the water has been let into the adjacent lake or river bed, and an allowance in altitude must be made on this account. A good average proportion for such eminences is that of a height equal to one half of their breadth at the base. But this is not absolute, distant hills being designed higher, and nearer hills lower, in proportion to their widths. Sharp broken edges to hills are carefully avoided. If the site already possesses fine clumps of trees, the arrangement of stones may be subjected to such conditions; but with this exception the vegetation is always disposed last, and in a subsidiary manner to the principal lithic features.

A landscape garden may be of any size from fifty or sixty square yards to several acres. The Japanese maintain that it is much easier to design a large garden than a small one. Great care is recommended in fixing the scale of a composition. If a small garden be slavishly copied from a larger model, it will appear weak and unsatisfactory in design; and, on the same principle, if a large garden be composed on the lines of a smaller model, it will be totally lacking in grandeur. To take an example, the arrangement of two or three massive rocks in front of a clump of handsome trees would look more imposing in a large garden than a number of smaller stones; but within the compass of a miniature garden, multiplicity of detail is often necessary in order to add to its apparent scale, and to impart sufficient interest to its limited area. Stone lanterns and monuments introduced must be strictly kept in appropriate scale; large objects suited to extensive grounds would entirely destroy the *values* in a small enclosure. The size of the garden, together with its mood or character, determine whether it will be treated in the *finished*, *rough*, or *intermediary* style. A landscape garden may be of large scale, and yet treated in the *finished* style; or it may be small in size, and in the *rough* style.

The impression of coolness considered so desirable in a garden, is not produced by planting trees too densely and crowding the area with many objects, but by a few masses of foliage judiciously arranged. There must be a total absence of litter and untidiness. Large open spaces partly overgrown with moss and kept cleanly swept should occupy the background, stretches of white sand or gravel being spread in the foreground. Even in the gardens attached to Tea Rooms, where rustic dilapidation is particularly affected, the most scrupulous cleanliness is exacted, an important distinction being always observed between natural decay and litter.

HILL GARDENS.

The Hill Garden (*Tsukiyama-niwa*) style of design is taken as the model for the most complete gardens, such as those suited to large areas in front of important buildings. An ideal Japanese landscape must contain mountain and water scenery in combination, and the term *Sansui*—used to denote such natural views—is also applied to the best class of artificial landscapes. The favourite classical model for these compositions is derived from the scenery of the Lake Seiko in China, having high surrounding hills and cliffs, with a cascade leaping from the rocks in several falls (see Fig. 2, page 14). There are five different styles, any of which may be attributed to Hill Gardens :—

Firstly,—the " Rocky Ocean Style," in which the stones selected should be sea rocks, the banks of the lake for the most part high and rugged, with steep cliffs for the cascade, and portions of the shore spread with white sand and planted with crooked pine trees, looking as if bent by the sea wind.

Secondly,—the " Wide River Style," in which river boulders are employed and the waterfall kept low ; the source may sometimes be a real or suggested stream issuing from behind a hill. The lake should resemble in form the spreading bed of a broad river, its sides being strewn with pebbles or sand. A broad sand-bank, on which water plants are grown, occupies the centre of the lake.

Thirdly,—the " Mountain Torrent Style," in which a wild mountain torrent and a small lake or pool are indicated. A number of river boulders aud stepping stones are arranged in the stream, which is specially designed to suggest both swiftness and shallowness.

Fourthly,—the " Lake Wave Scene," representing the wide inlet of a river expending into a lake, with no islands and very few stones, but having numerous water plants and grasses on the banks. Connected with the principal sheet of water in this design is a narrow tributary stream. A garden of this sort has no actual waterfall, but a source of water supply merely indicated and mysteriously hidden by hills or trees.

Fifthly,—the "Reed-marsh Scene," in which style all hills are low and rounded like dunes, and only flat stones employed. On one side of the water extends a heath or moor covered with reeds, rushes, and bamboos, and having river plants and grasses near the banks. Close to the water-side may be planted plum and willow trees.

Other special designs are mentioned, such as : — the "Style of Nine Hills and Eight Rivers," which should have four cascades in different parts of the lake; and the "Style of the Three Islands," in reference to the three Elysian Islands, called Horai, Hojo, and Eishu.

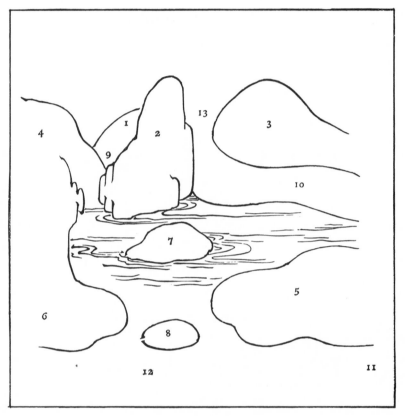

FIG. 45.

Fig. 45 shows the radical distribution of land and water intended as a general key to garden designs of the landscape type. The numbers in the figure refer to the following features :— 1, "Distant Mountain ; " 2, "Guardian Stone ; " 3, "Near Mountain ; " 4, "Side Mountain ; " 5, "Guest's Island;" 6, "Master's Island ;" 7, "Central Island ;" 8, "Worshipping Stone;" 9, "Cascade Mouth ;" 10, "Sand-blown Beach ;" 11, "Lake Outlet ;" 12, "Wide Beach ;" 13, "Mountain Road." The influence of this model, which has been handed down from ancient times, may be traced to some extent in all garden designs.

A Hill Garden may be in any of the three styles of elaboration, *finished,* *intermediary,* or *rough.* Plate XXV illustrates the model for an ordinary Hill Garden of the *finished* style, The positions of the principal hills, stones, tree clumps,

PLATE XXV. HILL GARDEN—FINISHED STYLE.

Tree 1. Principal Tree.
Tree 2. View perfecting Tree.
Tree 3. Tree of Solitude.
Tree 4. Cascade-screening Tree.
Tree 5. Tree of the Setting Sun.
Tree 6. Distancing Pine.
Tree 7. Stretching Pine.

A. Garden Well.
B. Snow-view Lantern.
C. Garden Gate.
D. Boarded Bridge.
E. Plank Bridge.
F. Stone Bridge.
G. Water Basin.
H. Lantern.
I. Garden Shrine.

Hill 1. Near Mountain.
Hill 2. Companion Mountain.
Hill 3. Mountain Spur.
Hill 4. Near Hill.
Hill 5. Distant Peak.

Stone 1. Guardian Stone.
Stone 2. Cliff Stone.
Stone 3. Worshipping Stone.
Stone 4. Perfect View Stone.
Stone 5. Waiting Stone.
Stone 6. Moon Shadow Stone.
Stone 7. Cave, or Kwannon Stone.
Stone 8. Seat of Honor Basin.
Stone 9. Pedestal Stone.
Stone 10. Idling Stone.

cascade, bridges, and islands are all relatively established by rule and for the purpose of reference are figured on the Plate. Hill 1 forms the central feature of the nearer distance; it represents a mountain of considerable size, and should have broad sweeping sides. It may have a pathway near its base, and a little pavilion on its slope, but in the present illustration a pathway only is indicated. The position of this garden hill must be determined after settling the general distribution of the landscape, for it is important that the lake inlet or cascade should be arranged just in front of it. Hill 2 is employed as a companion to No. 1, to which it should be adjacent; it is somewhat lower and of secondary importance. A cascade and rocks often mark the division between the two. Hill 3 is placed on the opposite side of No. 1, near the base of its broad slope, and somewhat more in the foreground; it is intended to represent a lower hill or spur divided from the principal mountain by a depression. This depression is supposed to be occupied by a hamlet, road, or stream, and it should be planted with a few trees or shrubs of thick foliage, giving the idea of a sheltered and inhabited dale. Hill 4 is a small eminence generally introduced in the near foreground and on the same side of the composition as Hill 2; it should be low, rounded, and covered with detail in the form of stones and shrubs, and must have none of the characteristics of a large or distant mountain. Hill 5 is placed in the remotest part of the garden, visible over the sides of Hills 1 and 2; as it is meant to represent a distant peak in mountain scenery, it should be steep in form and partially hidden below, with little or no detail upon it.

The present model shows ten important rocks or stones. No. 1 is generally called the " Guardian Stone," but sometimes it corresponds to the " Stone of *Fudo*," or the " Cascade-supporting Stone," which have been separately described. under the head of Cascade Stones. It is a high *standing* stone, occupying the most central position of the background, and is supposed to be the dedication stone of the garden. In the present illustration it forms—as one of its names implies—the flank of the cliff over which the cascade pours. Sometimes it is roughly carved with a representation of Fudo, the patron god of waterfalls; or it carries on its crown a small statuette of that deity. Stone 2 is used as a mate to No. 1, being placed on the opposite side of the fall; it is of lower altitude, with a flattish top, and arches over slightly so as to screen a portion of the torrent. Various names are given to it, such as :—" Cliff Stone," " Wave-dividing Stone," and " Water-receiving Stone." No. 3, which is broad and flat, is called the " Worshipping Stone," and is placed more in the foreground of the landscape, in the centre of an island or of some broad open space approached by stepping stones. This stone, together with No. 1, must, in some form or other, be introduced into all Japanese gardens; for, as the " Guardian Stone" represents the presiding genius of the garden, so does the " Worshipping Stone" indicate the oratory or position of worship. The former must be clearly seen from the latter; and the " Guardian Stone" occupying as it does the most important position in the background, it follows that, next to the dwelling itself, the best general view of the landscape is obtained from the " Worshipping Stone." Stone 4 is placed in the nearer foreground and to one side of the garden. It is of high elevation, with flattish faces and a broad base, and is called the " Perfect View Stone," being supposed to mark an important point in the landscape; two or more broad low stones are introduced to group with it. When placed in a " Guest's Isle" it is called the " Guest-saluting Stone"; in addition to which the names " Interviewing Stone," " Shoes-removing Stone," " Nightingale-dwelling Stone," and " Water-fowl Stone," are all occasionally applied to it. Stone 5 is used on the opposite side of the garden to No. 4, and is somewhat similar in shape, though more conical, and secondary in size. It is called the " Waiting Stone," and should be mated with a low flat boulder called the " Water Tray Stone," both being placed near the edge of the lake, and carefully arranged with regard to the highest level of the water. Placed on the " Master's Isle," this stone occasionally receives one of the following names, to indicate its imaginary functions :—" Stone of Easy Rest," " Stone of Amusement," and " Seat Stone." No. 6, called the " Moon Shadow Stone," occupies an important position in the distance, being placed in the hollow between the two principal hills, and in front of the distant peak. Its name implies an indistinctness and mystery attaching to it in common with the distant peak, in front of which it is placed. As is the case with all vertical stones, it is accompanied by one or more horizontal stones, but the addition of shrubs or other detail is not allowed, as thereby the idea of remoteness would be lost. No. 7, called the " Cave Stone," is a *standing* stone of similar character to the " Guardian Stone," which it occasionally replaces. In the present example it is erected a little to the right and rear of Stone 1, and beside the central group of trees; and a broad flat rock is paired with it. No. 8 generally goes by the name of the " Seat of Honour Stone," but is also called the " Stone of *Kwannon.*" It is a broad flat stone, and after the " Worshipping Stone" is the most important *reclining* stone of the garden. It is allied with a small vertical stone of secondary importance. Stone 9 is called the " Pedestal Stone," or the " Snail Stone;" it ranks first among the stepping stones arranged in the foreground, being higher than the others and of a double stepped form. Stone 10, called the " Idling Stone," actually consists of a pair of stones, broad, low, and slightly rounded, placed in a shady spot near the edge of the water, and in the mid-distance of the garden. Other stones shown in the Plate are secondary in importance and have no special names, but they are grouped in a manner similar to that adopted with those already described.

In enumerating the principal trees marked in the Plate, it must be observed that the singular term *tree* is often used to imply a group or clump of trees. No. 1 may be called the "Principal Tree," though the Japanese term, *Shojin-boku*, literally translated, means "Tree of Upright Spirit." In the present example it is represented by a group of trees placed in the central part of the background, behind the cascade. A fine large pine or oak of striking shape should be selected for this position, surrounded by a few other trees of different character of foliage. No. 2, called the "View-perfecting Tree" (*Keiyo-boku*), is secondary in rank only to No. 1, with which it should contrast in appearance. It occupies a position more in the foreground, and in lake scenery may be placed on an island, as in the present instance. Being generally a solitary tree, and in a very prominent situation, the exact forms of its trunk, branches, and foliage are carefully studied, with a view to harmonise with the adjacent objects, whether a stone lantern, well-frame, or water basin. The view of the principal features of the distance beyond it should not be obliterated, and on this account a rugged pine or some tree of light open foliage is preferred. No. 3, called the "Tree of Solitude" (*Sekizen-boku*), is a tree, or group of trees, of thick foliage placed on one side, in the background of the garden, the object being to give shade and to impart a solitary wooded aspect to this portion of the grounds. No. 4 is called the "Cascade-screening Tree" (*Takigakoi-ki*), and consists of a group of low leafy trees or bushes planted at the side of the waterfall in such a way as to conceal portions of it. No. 5 receives the name of "Tree of the Setting Sun" (*Sekiyo-boku*); it is planted in the background of the garden towards the west, with the purpose of intercepting the glare of the setting sun, which may be partially seen between the foliage. To add to the rich effect of the leafage in the evening glow, it is customary to employ maples or other trees of reddening foliage in this position. Blossoming trees, such as the cherry and plum, are occasionally introduced; and, even when evergreens are employed, maples or some other deciduous trees must be mixed with them. No. 6 is called the "Distancing-pine" (*Mikoshi-matsu*), the fancy being that it should suggest a far-off forest. It is therefore placed behind the further hills of the garden and partly hidden from view. The branches of this tree should not be too carefully trimmed, such artificial treatment detracting from the impression of distance aimed at. If the garden be a small one, the "Distancing Pine" may be a tree actually outside the boundary. The term *pine* is used in a general and not an absolute sense, and an oak tree may be substituted if desired. No. 7 goes by the name of the "Stretching Pine" (*Nagashi-matsu*), or "Monkey-pine" (*Enko-matsu*); the latter name is taken from the long-armed monkeys often depicted in Japanese art, and both terms refer to the straggling, sprawling character of the branches of this leaning tree, which is generally a single evergreen placed in the foreground, and bending over the lake or stream, from the bed of which it is supported by crutches. A kind of juniper is sometimes used instead of a pine.

Other features marked in the Plate are:—*A*, the Garden Well, with a weeping willow beside it; *B*, a Snow-view Lantern, placed on the island, close to tree No. 2, and in such a position that the light will be reflected in the water; *C*, the Back Gate of the garden; *D*, a Boarded Bridge leading to the lake islet; *E*, a Plank Bridge; *F*, an arched Stone Bridge with moulded stone parapet; *G*, a date-shaped stone Water Basin with its sink and drain; *H*, an ornamental Stone Lantern behind the basin. The stepping stones in the foreground mark the walks from the verandah of the house, the surrounding area consisting of beaten earth.

Plate XXVI., which illustrates a Hill Garden of the *intermediary* or semi-elaborated style, will next be explained. Only four hills are introduced into this design. By comparison, the Hills 1, 2, 3, and 5, in Plate XXV will be recognisable, but are merged into one hillock of varied undulations. The "Distant Peak," "Near Mountain," and "Mountain Spur" are just suggested by the outline, a resemblance which is aided by the grouping of the stones, trees, and cascade. Hill 4 occupies a position in the foreground corresponding to that in the *finished* style, but it is larger in size, on the principle of using rougher and bolder detail in the less elaborate model. Stones 1, 2, 3, 4, 5, 6, 7, 8, and 9, correspond in position, names, and functions to those of Plate XXV. It may be observed, however, that Stone 5—the "Waiting Stone"—has been merged into one with the Water Basin, which in the former Plate existed separately; also, that other stones have been enlarged in scale. In accordance with the same method of bolder and more sketchy treatment, the numerous auxiliary stones, having no special names or functions, but which are considered necessary to unite together the important rocks and add detail in the *finished* style, are here much reduced in number, and enlarged in proportionate size. In this way they occasionally attain sufficient importance to receive special names. For example, Stone 10, at the side of the wooden bridge, called the "Bridge-edging Stone," takes the place of four or five secondary stones in the more elaborate garden. Also, Stone 11, which is called the "Distance-screening

Stone 1.
Guardian
Stone.

Stone 2.
Cliff Stone.

Stone 3.
Worshipping
Stone.

Stone 4.
Perfect View
Stone.

Stone 5.
Waiting
Stone
(as Basin.)

Stone 6.
Moon Sha-
dow Stone.

Stone 7.
Cave Stone.

Stone 8.
Seat
of Honour
Stone.

Stone 9.
Pedestal
Stone.

Stone 10.
Bridge-
edge Stone.

Stone 11.
Distance
Stone.

Stone 12, 13.
Cascade
Stones.

Hill 1.
Near
Mountain.

Hill 2.
Companion
Mountain.

Hill 3.
Mountain
Spur.

Hill 4.
Near Hill.

Hill 5.
Distant
Peak.

Tree 1.
Principal
Tree.

Tree 2.
Tree of Set-
ting Sun.

Tree 3.
Tree
of Solitude.

Tree 4.
Cascade
Screening
Tree.

A.
Katsuga Lan-
tern.

B.
Snow-scene
Lantern.

C.
Wooden
Bridge.

PLATE XXVI. HILL GARDEN—INTERMEDIARY STYLE.

Tree 2.

Tree 1.

Tree 3.

Stone 7.

Stone 1.

Stone 5.

Stone 6.

Stone 4.

Stone 9.

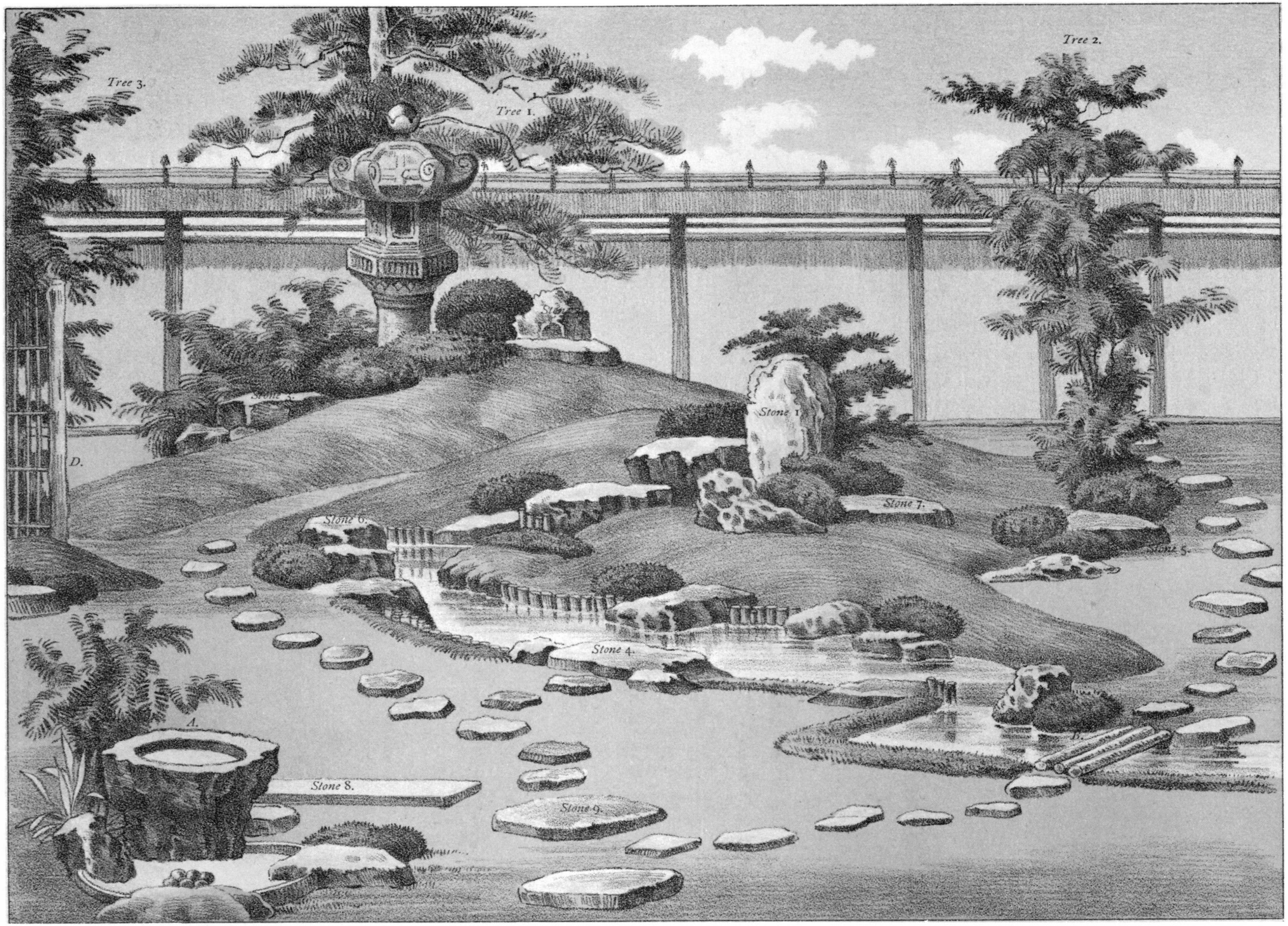

Stone 8.

D.

PLATE XXVII. HILL GARDEN—ROUGH STYLE.

Stone," has no counterpart in Plate XXV. Moreover, though there are numerous small rocks at the base of the cascade in the *finished* style, only one is specially named; but in the *intermediary* style may be observed two good-sized rocks, (Nos. 12 and 13), one vertical and the other horizontal in character, and each mated with another rock of opposite nature; but there are no other secondary stones.

With regard to trees, the groups or clumps of the *finished* style become, in the Plate before us, single trees, and some are entirely eliminated. No. 1, the "Principal Tree," is represented by a single pine tree with low bushes beneath. No. 2, the "Tree of the Setting Sun," is indicated by a group of leafy trees on the extreme west; and No. 3, the "Tree of Solitude," by a somewhat larger clump on the east. No. 4, the "Cascade-screening Tree," becomes a leaning pine tree, its branches partly screening the waterfall. The "View-perfecting Tree," "Distancing Pine," and "Stretching Pine" of Plate XXV are omitted. The lake in this garden is comparatively a small sheet of water, resembling an inlet, but having the indispensable waterfall at its head. A peninsula replaces the lake island, and one bridge only is introduced instead of three. The "Snow-view Lantern," which is placed on the island in a garden of the *finished* style, is, in the present case, introduced in the background to form a group with the western tree-clump, and has beside it a special stone, No. 11, called the "Distance Stone." The other stone lantern, in the centre of the view, is of larger scale than its counterpart in Plate XXV, and takes the place occupied by the "Cave Stone" in that illustration, the latter occupying the other side of the landscape in the present example. The shrine, water basin, lantern, and other details observable in the more elaborate garden are entirely omitted. The rougher style of design adopted also influences the character of the enclosing boundary, and instead of the plastered and roofed paling with covered gateway, a simple bamboo fence and plain gates are introduced.

In the *rough* style of Hill Garden illustrated in Plate XXVII., detail is further reduced in quantity and increased in proportionate size. At first sight very few of the features of the *finished* style are recognizable, but careful observation and comparison reveal certain similarities. Only two low mounds are introduced as garden hills, but their undulations are skilfully arranged so as to faintly suggest the near and distant mountain and the lower spur in front. The adorning stones assist in maintaining a faint resemblance to the original and more elaborate model. Stone 1, the "Guardian Stone," preserves its vertical character but no longer serves as a cascade-cliff. It is backed by a low tree or shrub, and companioned with flat stones and rounded bushes; it also still marks one of the principal points of the background.   No. 2 receives the name of the "Moon Shadow Stone," and occupies a position on the most distant prominence, paired with a flat stone; in other respects, however, the idea of distant solitude originally associated with it is no longer preserved, for it forms part of a clump composed of shrubs, bushes, a stone lantern of large scale, and a spreading pine tree.   No. 3, a flat stepped stone,—also belonging to the same group, and, on the opposite side of the mound to Stone 2,—serves to give a suggestion of Hill 2 in the *finished* style.

The comparatively large scale of rocks in this *rough* style enables them to be occasionally employed in place of hillocks, to assist in balancing elevated land con-tours.   In addition to a function of this kind, Stone 3 is said to take the place of the "Perfect View Stone," and should have some thick-leaved tree or shrub be-hind it.   No. 4 is the indispensable "Worshipping Stone,"—the principal *reclining* stone of all gardens.   Placed on the edge of the stream, it also serves in this abbreviated design as the "Idling Stone," referred to under No. 10, in Plate XXV. Stone 5, in the west, is the "Seat of Honour Stone," together with a com-panion stone and bushes, and backed with a clump of young trees occupying the position of the "Tree of the Evening Sun."   No. 6 is a stepped stone placed on the bank of the stream to the east, here fulfilling the function of the "Waiting Stone."   In this example of the *rough* style of Hill Garden the sheet of water becomes a mere stream, having its source behind the "Guardian Stone" with its accompanying rocks; by this means the idea of the cascade inlet is, to some extent, maintained.   The stream is crossed by a single bridge, constructed simply of round logs.   The water basin in the east foreground becomes very rough and primitive in form, and only one stone lantern is introduced, this being in the background of the garden.   The stepping stones attain comparatively great size and importance, No. 9— the "Pedestal Stone," and No. 10—the "Label Stone," being specially arranged.

FLAT GARDENS.

Next to be explained are different examples of the (*Hira-niwa*), or Flat Garden style.   Designs of this type are supposed to represent either a mountain valley, or an extensive moor; if the former, the surroundings should be steep and thickly planted; if the latter, the landscape should be bare and open.   *Hira-niwa* are mostly used for confined areas in crowded cities, or for laying out in front of buildings of

Tree 1.
Principal
(Central)
Tree.

Tree 2.
Tree of the
Evening Sun.

Tree 3.
Tree of
Solitude.

A.
Water Basin.

B.
Stone Lan-
tern.

C.
Well Frame.

D.
Distant Lan-
tern.

E.
Well Drain.

Stone 1.
Guardian
Stone.

Stone 2.
Cliff Stone.

Stone 3.
Hill Stone.

Stone 4.
Peak Stone.

Stone 5,
Worshipping
Stone.

Stone 6.
Perfect View
Stone.

Stone 7.
Island Stone.

Stone 8.
Moon Shadow
Stone.

Stone 9.
Evening Sun
Stone.

Stone 10.
Two Gods
Stone.

Stone 11.
Pedestal
Stone.

Stone 12.
Label Stone.

PLATE XXVIII. FLAT GARDEN—FINISHED STYLE.

secondary importance. Numerous examples may be seen in the back courts of merchants' houses in Kioto and Osaka, no interior space being apparently too small or circumscribed for converting into a fresh-looking and artistic garden of this kind. Three degrees of elaboration are, however, applied to this as to other classes of compositions; and Flat Gardens, if in the *finished* style, are not considered out of place as a portion of the more extensive grounds of the gentry and nobility. Whilst a Hill Garden will be used in front of the principal reception rooms, a Flat Garden may be employed facing rooms of less importance in the same estate.

The elaborate or *finished* style of Flat Garden is illustrated in Plate XXVIII., in which it will be observed that the greater part of the area consists of level beaten earth. Stone 1, the " Guardian Stone," occupies the central position of the background and together with Stone 2, the " Cliff Stone," and other nameless rocks of contrasting forms, make a group intended to suggest the mouth of a cascade. Though the garden is a dry one, the idea of the presence of water is kept up by an arrangement of piles forming a basin border, within which large white pebbles are placed, backed by Stones 3 and 4, which are intended to give a suggestion of Hills 2 and 5 of the Hill Garden style. It will therefore appear that, even in the type of gardening which permits of neither hills nor water, so essentially are these features considered a part of every landscape, that their existence is always suggested. Stone 4, in addition to the hill contour which it expresses, takes also the place of the " Cave Stone " of former arrangements. Stone 5 is the " Worshipping Stone," occupying an important position in the centre of the area of flat beaten earth. No. 7 is called the " Island Stone " because, regarding the central expanse of earth as a lake, it suggests the principal island or peninsula of the garden. The curious similarity in arrangement will be easily detected on careful comparison with Plate XXV. No. 6 is the " Perfect View Stone," placed near the well on the east, with shrubs and other companion stones. Stone 8 is the most prominent of a group of rocks arranged with intermediate bushes in the background, on the west; it is called the " Moon Shadow Stone," corresponding to that of the same name in the Hill Garden, in so far that it is kept in the distance and partly hidden. No. 9 is a group of stones combined with a bush or bushes of red-leaved foliage, placed in the west of the garden, and called the " Stone of the Evening Sun;" and behind it stands the only large tree shown in this garden, which receives the name of the " Tree of the Evening Sun." It should be a deciduous tree of reddening leaf. Tree 1, which from its position is called the " Principal Tree," and sometimes the " Cascade-screening Tree," is here merely a leafy evergreen placed between Stones 1 and 2. The " Tree of Solitude " is represented on the east by two small pine trees and other shrubs, forming a shady group, together with rocks, plants, and a stone lantern, marked *D*. Low rounded bushes and large-leaved plants are distributed between the other stones of the garden, the water plants being introduced near the well-drain, or the piled basin of the background, wherever the idea of water is called for. Another evergreen leans over the well, and a bent pine is trained behind a screen fence in the west foreground. This fence forms a group with the water basin *A*, and a stone lantern *B*, all adjoining the verandah of the house. The well border *C* becomes an important feature in the Flat Garden; in the present instance it is a rustic wooden frame, situated in the east foreground, with a pebbled draining-bed and stepping stones. In front is placed Stone 10, a rough boulder in several steps, called the "Stone of the Two Gods." No. 11, the "Pedestal Stone," and No. 12, the "Label Stone," are introduced among the stepping stones of the foreground. It must be observed, however, that in this example the idea of an open expanse is kept in the centre of the grounds, suggesting the lake of Hill Gardens, and the stepping stones are therefore grouped only near the well and water basin, and in the extreme foreground.

The *intermediary* style of Flat Garden, (see Plate XXIX.), though not differing so much in scale from the *finished* style as in the case of Hill Gardens, is somewhat bolder in treatment than the more elaborate example. The feeling of open expanse in the centre, as expressed in the previous example, is missing. In the middle of the composition is the "Guardian Stone" No. 1, and in front of it is No. 3, the "Seat of Honour Stone," the two forming part of a group with a stone pagoda, pine tree, and some low shrubs and plants, No. 3 is the "Moon Shadow Stone," placed in a remote part of the garden, and paired with a flat stone. No. 4 is the "Worshipping Stone," and No. 5, a pair of stones together called the "Stone of the Setting Sun," on account of their position in the west. Stone 6 is the "Stone of the Two Gods," in a similar position to that in the previous example. No. 7, the "Pedestal Stone," and No. 8, the "Label Stone," form the principal features of the arrangement of stepping stones which encircle the central part of the grounds, branching towards the garden gate in the west, and to the well in the east, their junction being marked by a large oblong step in front of the verandah of the house. The bare space in the centre of the garden suggests water, but of less extent than in Plate XXVIII., and the "Worshipping Stone" typifies an island. The well is more primitive in style, being made of roughly hewn stone, and adorned with an overhanging dwarf pine and neighbouring water plants. The arrangement of the water basin, fence, and lantern near the verandah is much as before, but a bolder scale and somewhat

Tree 1. Principal Tree.

Tree 2. Tree of the Evening Sun.

Tree 3. Tree of Solitude.

Tree 4. Stretching Pine.

A. Stone Pagoda.

B. Well.

C. Water Basin.

D. Stone Lantern.

E. Garden Gate.

Stone 1. Guardian Stone.

Stone 2. Seat of Honour Stone.

Stone 3. Moon Shadow Stone.

Stone 4. Worshipping Stone.

Stone 5. Stone of the Setting Sun.

Stone 6. Stone of the Two Gods.

Stone 7. Pedestal Stone.

Stone 8. Label Stone.

PLATE XXIX. FLAT GARDEN—INTERMEDIARY STYLE.

PLATE XXX. FLAT GARDEN—ROUGH STYLE.

A.
Snow-scene
Lantern.

B.
Water
Basin.

C.
Garden Gate.

D.
Well Frame.

Stone 1.
Guardian
Stone.

Stone 2.
Worshipping
Stone.

Stone 3.
Stone of
Evening Sun.

Stone 4.
Stone of
the
Two Gods.

rougher forms are employed. Two other stone lanterns are shown; one in the east background, grouped with some rocks and a small clump of trees—No. 3, representing the "Tree of Solitude;" and another near a clump of bamboos and shrubs on the west, indicating No. 2, the "Tree of the Evening Sun." The large pine tree No. 1, near the "Worshipping Stone," is the "Principal Tree," and No. 4, overspreading the well, is the "Stretching Pine."

In the *rough* style of Flat Garden, illustrated in Plate XXX., details become fewer and still larger in proportion, there being virtually but one cultivated group or oasis in the desert of flat beaten earth. Well, lantern, and the most important trees, stones, and bushes are all clumped together, the remaining area being ornamented with a few stepping stones, a water basin and drain, and two small groups of stones, east and west. Stone 1, in the central group, is the "Guardian Stone," No. 2 is the "Worshipping Stone" and "Seat of Honour Stone" merged into one, and these together are combined with a third stone of arching form, making one of the triple lithic combinations shown in Plate II., and described on page 46. Stone 3, a little removed to the west, is the "Stone of the Setting Sun," grouped with two other rocks, a bush, and a large-leaved plant. Stone 4, called the "Stone of the Two Gods," is the principal feature of a small group on the east foreground. The stepping stones in this model are less numerous, bolder, and rougher in shape than in the other styles, and no hewn stones are introduced. A pair of pine trees, with a tall shrub and low plants and bushes, form the only mass of vegetation in the garden, which serves at the same time to shade a rustic well-frame, with its pebbled bed, rocks, and water plants. A large "Snow-scene" stone lantern, the single feature of its kind, also forms part of this clump. In the corner of the foreground to the west is shown the water basin, drain, and screen fence, indicating the end of the room verandah. A bamboo enclosure of the simplest kind surrounds the garden.

TEA GARDENS.

The *Cha-niwa*, or gardens attached to Tea Rooms, next require notice. To understand the meaning of the designs and arrangements followed in such enclosures, some knowledge of the formulæ of the Tea Ceremonial is necessary. The practice of this cult is said to have developed largely under the patronage of the generalissimo, Yoshimasa, who constructed at his villa on Higashiyama a small Tea Room in which he commenced the study of the ceremonial, under the tutelage of a

Nara priest, called Shuko. Many names stand out prominently from amongst the host of Tea Professors following Shuko (see pages 18-19). Each noted master in turn introduced changes and modifications in the sizes and disposition of Tea Rooms, and the distribution of subsidiary buildings, gardens, and approaches. A volume might

fail to explain adequately all the intricacies of the diminutive structures required for the eso-teric practices of the *Cha-no-yu.* Supreme importance is bestowed upon the most trivial details, extending to such minutiæ as the fractional depth and thick-ness of a window bar, or the exact number and spacing of the nail-heads in a doorway. An indication only of the principal uses and requirements, must suffice to explain the customary arrangements of the gardens adjoining the rooms. (Figure 46 shows a little Tea Garden from Sakai.)

FIG. 46.

These Tea Gardens are generally divided into an outer and inner enclosure, separated by a rustic fence with a gateway. The outermost enclosure contains the main entrance gate, and beyond this is often a small building, in which it was originally the custom for the Samurai, or military class, to change their clothing before attending the ceremonial. Plate XXXI. illustrates the grounds of a small Tea Room, and the principal features there shown may be described as follows:—

The outer enclosure, *A,* contains a picturesque open shed or arbour, *D,*—having a raised bench, and called the *Koshikake-machiai* or "Waiting Shed,"—which plays an important part in the Tea Ceremonies. To this structure the guests adjourn at stated intervals to allow of fresh preparations being made for their entertainment in the tiny Tea Room. Sometimes the Waiting Shed adjoins the fence dividing the outer from the inner garden, and serves at the same time as an entrance-porch

Stone 1.
Front
Stone.

Stone 2.
Water Jug
Stone.

Stone 3.
Candle-stick
Stone.

Stone 4.
Ascending
Stone.

Stone 5.
Sword
Hanging
Stone.

A.
Outer
Enclosure.

B.
Inner
Enclosure.

C.
Outer
Entrance.

D.
Waiting
Shed.

E.
Lavatory.

F.
Stooping
Gate.

G.
Tea Room.

H.
Sword Rock.

I.
Well.

K.
Crouching
Water Basin.

PLATE XXXI. TEA GARDEN.

between the two. In such a case, the gate itself occupies a low opening in the wall of the Waiting Shed, and visitors are obliged to stoop in passing through. For this reason, the old name of " Diving-in Gate " (*Nakakuguri-mon*) has come to be applied, irrespective of its form, to the entrance between the inner and outer Tea Garden.

In the present example, it is merely a light wooden door fixed in a bamboo fence, as shown at *D*. A detached lavatory *E*, with its water basin, forms an important adjunct of the outer enclosure. Sometimes the inner area of a Tea Garden is provided with another similar convenience. Within this inner and principal enclosure is the Tea Room, *G*, a small building, vary-

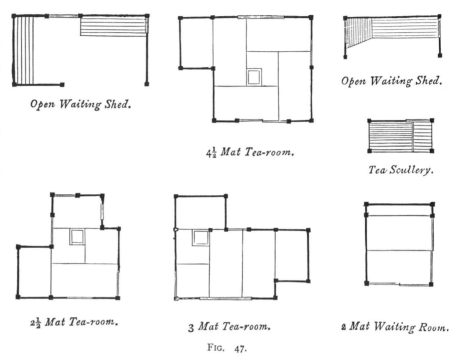

Open Waiting Shed.

4½ Mat Tea-room.

Open Waiting Shed.

Tea Scullery.

2½ Mat Tea-room.

3 Mat Tea-room.

2 Mat Waiting Room.

FIG. 47.

ing in size from two and a half to six mats in area, and provided somewhere at the back with a still-room or scullery, for cleaning and storing the tea utensils. It may be here explained that all Japanese buildings of the old style are measured according to the number of mats required to cover their floors. In ordinary rooms the size of these mats is 6 ft. by 3 ft., but for Tea Rooms they are often made as small as 4½ ft. by 2¼ ft. The smallest Tea Room—that of two and a half mats—therefore measures not much more than 30 square feet in area. Figure 47 illustrates the plans of different sized Tea Rooms, together with a Waiting Room, two Waiting Sheds, and a Tea Scullery.

The Tea Room is entered from the garden through a low door, about two and a half feet square, placed in the outer wall, and raised about two feet from the ground, the guests being obliged to pass through in a bending posture, indicative of humility and respect. The host uses another doorway which communicates with the Scullery. Before entering, the two-sworded gentry of former times were accustomed to rid themselves of their weapons, which were deposited on a hanging sword-rack fixed to the outer wall at *H*. The position of the sword-rack and the entrance

control to a great extent the arrangement of the stepping stones and other accessories of the Tea Garden. A rustic looking Well *I*, forms an important feature of
this inner garden, and the principal lanterns, water basin, trees, and plants occupy
this portion of the grounds. The Water Basin shown in *K* is of the low or
" Crouching Basin " class, peculiar to Tea Gardens ; it is situated near the further
corner of the garden, adjacent to the larger stone lantern. Stone 1, called the
" Front Stone," adjoins the Water Basin, and is stood upon when using the water ;

Tea Garden at Kitano.
FIG. 48.

it also here takes the place of the " Worshipping Stone " of more elaborate gardens.
Stone 2 is the " Water Jug Stone ; " Stone 3, the " Candle-stick Stone ; " Stone 4 is
termed the " Ascending Stone," and forms a step to the outer door of the Tea
Room ; and Stone 5 is the " Sword-hanging Stone."

The prevailing notion of a pathway leading to the different buildings is kept
up alike in the inner and outer garden, the skeleton of the whole design being formed
by the stepping stones, which make a meandering route connecting the Water Basin,
Waiting Shed, Lavatory, and Gateway with the Tea Room. The areas surrounding

PLATE XXXII. TEA GARDEN—OUTER AND INNER ENCLOSURE.

these foot-ways consist of beaten earth, purposely kept damp and moss-grown. The different clumps of trees, bushes, plants, and grasses are often arranged in an unkempt manner so as to impart a wild and gloomy effect to the garden. A characteristic example of the style is shown in Fig. 48, illustrating a Tea Garden at Kitano designed by Kanamori Sowa. Most Tea Gardens are remarkable for extreme simplicity combined with an affectation of natural wildness. They may be said to assume an air of respectable poverty and decay, accompanied by the most punctilious cleanliness.

Garden called " Niuwa-tei.
FIG. 49.

In the wooden and stone lanterns, water basins, rocks, and gateways, an appearance of antiquity is sought. The surrounding fences, though often of quaint and pleasing design, are of the flimsiest and most delicate description—like the tiny buildings they enclose, which are specially devoted to the exercise of a ceremonial meant for the cultivation of simplicity and gentleness of manners. Some masters of the Tea cult consider fences undesirable enclosures for Tea Gardens, because of their artificial character, and prefer high banks covered with leafy vegetation, or thick hedges, either of which produce a more natural effect.

There is a special style of composition, much in favour, called the "Tamagawa Tea garden." Of the six noted rivers in Japan bearing the name of *Tama-*

gawa (see page 100), some are specially distinguished for the flowers which bloom on their banks. The river at Toi in the province of Settsu is noted for its deutzias; that at Noji, in the province of Omi, for its lespedeza bushes; whilst the Tamagawa at Ide, in the province of Yamashiro, is famous for its kerria flowers. The application of the name to a class of Tea Gardens originated with Rosha, a famous *Chajin*, who built a Tea Room on the banks of the Tamagawa at Chofu, in the province of Musashi. A garden after this style always contains a narrow

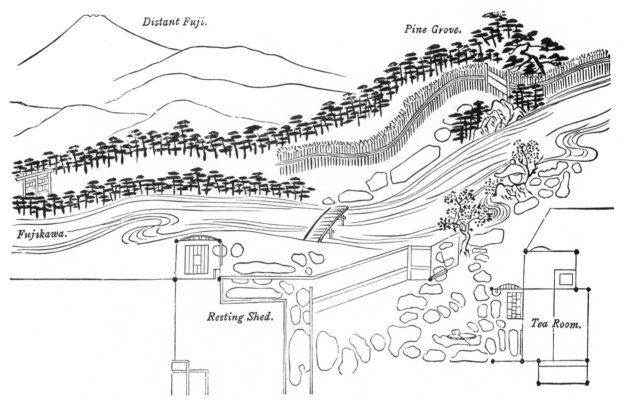

Tea Garden representing the scenery of Fujisan.
FIG. 50.

winding stream of clear running water, having a pebbly bed bordered with boulders, water plants, and water grasses. The stream may be either crossed by rude stepping stones, or spanned by a simple plank bridge as shown in Figure 49. At least one antique looking lantern, a water basin, a group of rocks,—including the indispensable "Guardian Stone,"—and a few trees and shrubs, constitute the principal features of such a garden. The level areas between these objects are traversed by the usual stepping stones arranged in a winding and irregular manner. Very often a Tea Garden of this type will be designed to resemble a mountain dell, with hills or banks surrounding it, the stream being constructed in imitation of a small torrent-bed, and the whole forming a romantic hollow a little below the level of the Tea Room. In

PLATE XXXIII. TAMAGAWA TEA GARDEN.

certain ancient designs the six noted rivers were represented together in one garden by means of tiny streams branching from a spring, which formed their common source.

Numerous other departures from the ordinary treatment of Tea Gardens seem to have been made from time to time, some of which are illustrated by Figures scattered through the text. These woodcuts are taken from old books, and no attempt has been made to alter the primitive method of delineation, which, in addition to its quaintness, possesses the merit of giving an idea of both plan and elevation in one.

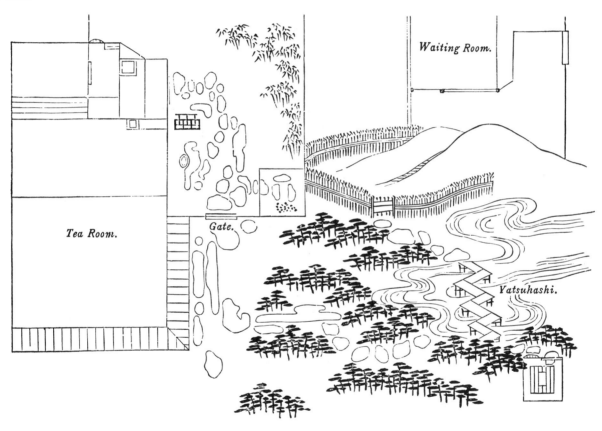

Fig. 51.

Figure 50 illustrates a Tea Garden attributed to Imagawa Yoshimoto Ko, and is suggestive of scenery near mount Fuji. Passing through the grounds is a flowing stream representing the Fujikawa, on the opposite side of which is a rustic fence with a small gateway. The further banks are planted with young pine trees to convey the idea of the Mio pine forest, through which a path leads along the stream to the main outer entrance, on the left. Crossing from the further bank by a plank bridge, the outer enclosure of the Tea Garden, with its Waiting Shed, Diving-in Gate, and

Lavatory, is reached. The dividing fence is carried to the edge of the stream, which from that point forms the natural boundary. The drawing shows the inner or Tea Garden proper, containing the Tea-Room, Sword-rack, low Water Basin, Lantern, a few trees, and numerous stepping stones. From this portion of the grounds may be seen to best advantage the imaginary distant mount Fuji, with its lower hills, pine forest, and rapid river.

Another Tea Garden, which suggests the scenery of Yatsuhashi, in Mikawa, is shown in Fig. 51 on page 149. The Waiting Room, in which the clothes are changed previous to the tea ceremony, is represented beyond the outer fence, and from it the approach leads by a stepped pathway between two hills. The outer enclosure of the Tea Garden contains a broad shallow pool of water, planted with irises and crossed by a winding bridge of single planks, in imitation of the Yatsuhashi landscape. The surrounding sandy flats are dotted with young pine trees, and a walk of stepping stones winds through them to the entrance of the inner enclosure. The "Diving-in Gate" is shown, but no Waiting Shed is indicated, the verandah of a large room adjoining the Tea Room itself, and opening on to the outer enclosure, apparently taking its place. Occupying the inner garden may be seen the Tea Room, with Sword-rack, Water Basin, and Lavatory, which, with a number of stepping stones, and a little group of bamboos, form the principal ornaments of this portion of the grounds.

Figure 42,—already referred to on page 124,—illustrates another example of a somewhat unusual kind of Tea Garden. The background consists of numerous small hills with wild cherry-trees planted between them, over which a climbing pathway extends to the outer passage and gateway. To this foot-path is connected a row of stepping stones, branching on the one hand to the outer Lavatory and a low Lantern, and, on the other, to a structure serving both as a Resting Shed and Entrance Gateway to the inner Tea Garden. A meandering row of similar stones leads from this entrance to a thatched Tea Room and a Lavatory. The Ascending Stone, Sword-hanging Stone, Sword-rack, Label Stone, and other familiar features of an orthodox Tea Garden, may be recognised in the illustration.

PASSAGE GARDENS.

The *Roji-niwa*, or Passage Gardens, are those laid out in the narrow courts or approaches to buildings. The same term is sometimes applied to the gardens in front of Tea Rooms, which, as previously explained, are often little more than narrow passages leading to the miniature structures required for the Tea Ceremonial. A distinction is, however, observed between what is purely and simply a Passage Garden, and one which fulfils at the same time the purposes of a Tea Garden. In both, walks of stepping stones arranged in a picturesque manner are the governing features, and likewise in both, an antiquated style is affected; but whereas it is held that a Tea Garden should be poor and humble in character, a Passage Garden, on the contrary, may betoken considerable richness and luxury. Again, the enclosing fences of the former should be dainty and even fragile in appearance, whilst those of the latter must appear strong and durable.

A Passage Garden forming the approach to the principal rooms of a large property often occurs as an accidental necessity of the site; but occasionally a narrow strip of land is purposely arranged in this manner, with the chief object of commanding a distant prospect. In the latter case, the enclosing fences are kept low, and the surface strewn with gravel and ornamented chiefly with flowering plants, avoiding the use of high shrubs or trees calculated to obstruct the view. The level area of a Passage Garden generally consists of beaten earth or clean sand, having a pathway formed of stepping stones of various shapes. Examples, however, are common in which these foot-stones are embedded in a concreted or cemented surface. Here and there, at the sides and in the corners of the enclosure, are introduced rocks, stone lanterns, and groups of trees or shrubs. The angle nearest the west should always be planted with leafy vegetation, to afford shade from the glare of the evening sun.

Even in narrow and sparsely furnished gardens like the above, it is usual to introduce rocks and slabs of stone which do duty for such features as the "Guardian Stone," "Worshipping Stone," "Stone of the Two Gods," and other lithic features of Japanese landscape gardening. The principal stone lantern is placed near the "Guardian Stone," which occupies the most important angle of the oblong passage. When a detached lavatory is introduced, it must have its screen-fence and water basin, and planted near it should be some of the following trees, shrubs, or plants :— *Pinus parviflora, Nandina domestica, Buxus japonica, Nuphar japonicum, Gardenia florida, Polypodium tricuspe, Ardisia japonica,* or different varieties of the Rhododendron. Flowering trees are often grown in Passage Gardens, the surrounding areas being then invariably covered with sand.

There is a special kind of Passage Garden in which Maple-trees alone are planted. Such a design should contain a narrow winding trench, lined with pebbles, and having water plants on the borders to suggest a rivulet,—a far-fetched hint of the maple scenery of Tatsuta, or Tsuten (see page 11; and Figure 39, page 114). When clear, running water can easily be obtained, a tiny shallow stream planted with irises, lespedezas, or kerria, may be introduced into a Passage Garden, to suggest the scenery of one of the Tamagawa landscapes. Still another garden of this class has a running stream the banks of which are planted with chrysanthemums. The rules laid down as to the artistic distribution of stepping stones are strictly

"Garden of Mountain Grass."
Fig. 52.

followed in all *Roji-niwa*, a larger proportion of hewn stones and a more formal and finished arrangement being employed than in the case of Tea Gardens.

FANCY GARDENS.

A few illustrations are appended of gardens designed by famous men, which belong, strictly speaking, to none of the styles previously described. Figure 52 shows what is called the "Garden of Mountain Grass," as laid out specially for the purpose of entertaining guests at the sport of hawking. A few rocks of interesting shape are scattered (apparently haphazard, but really with considerable art), in a sea of wavy mountain grass, resembling, in their manner of distribution, islands or sea-rocks dotted in the ocean. No plants, shrubs, or trees of any kind are permitted in a garden of this sort.

Figure 53 represents what is called a "Cherry-tree Garden," distinguished by a winding stream, a few quaint rocks, and a grove of flowering trees—consisting of

Cherry-tree Garden.

FIG. 53.

different rare garden varieties of the cherry, such as *Yaye-zakura*, *Senye-zakura*, *Ise-zakura*, and *Shiogama-zakura*. An interesting feature of this style of garden is a long and elevated wooden passage leading through the grounds from the adjoining residence, and ending in a broad pier constructed over the stream which supports a thatched arbour. From this rustic pavilion the spectator looks down upon the blossom-clad boughs of the surrounding trees. A design called the "Garden of Late Spring-time" is shown is Figure 54. It is suited for laying out in front of a villa near a river, intended to be visited during the flower season. A long and winding trellis, covered with wistaria creepers, borders the edge of the adjoining river, and a tuft of bamboos is planted near. The foreground consists of a flat sanded area crossed by stepping stones, which lead from the verandah of the residence; a few rocks of quaint and interesting shape are placed in the stream.

Under the head of Fancy Gardens, reference must be made to a curious conventional treatment applied to sanded areas—called *Sunagata-niwa*—facing reception

Garden of " Late Spring-time."
FIG. 54.

rooms in certain important gardens, and already illustrated in Figure 12, page 58. The example given is taken from a portion of the grounds of Hotta, the Daimio of Kaga, at Kanazawa, as specially prepared in ancient times for the honour of a visit from the Shogun. A row of oblong, round, and irregular shaped stones are arranged so as to form a rectangular walk in front of the sanded surface, which is raked into patterns to represent in a conventional manner water and waves, and on which no one but the gardener was allowed to walk. In this sea of sand are placed three rocks or rock-groups, two of which are broad and flattish in form, intended to represent tortoises, and one vertical in character, signifying a crane. The congratulatory symbolism conveyed by these representations has already been explained. A few plants and grasses are placed between the rocks, which are covered with moss and lichen. Complimentary gardens of this kind, called *Onari-niwa*, or "Gardens of the August Visit," were often temporarily constructed in former times to celebrate special occasions, the pine tree, bamboo, and sometimes the plum tree being among the emblems of felicitation introduced.

Figure 55 illustrates a characteristic garden composition executed from the design of the artist Sen-no-Rikiu, in imitation of the coast scenery of Matsushima, near Sendai, a place to which frequent re-ference has been made. The lake has a rocky island of volcanic char-acter contain-ing a large crater, the rug-ged edges of which are planted with one or two bent

Garden design by Sen-no-Rikiu.
FIG. 55.

and contorted pine trees. A bridge connects this island with the rocky shore. On the opposite side of the lake is a high rounded hill representing the aspect of a distant wooded mountain, planted with pine trees near the summit and having a grove of bamboos surrounding its base.

Many other favourite natural scenes, in addition to those of which special mention has been made, form the frequent subjects of common garden representa-tion. The river scenery at Uji, with its historical bridge and ancient temple of Koshoji; the view of *Otowa-no-taki*, a beautiful cascade near Kioto, and its pretty fane; the rare and picturesque sea-rocks of the Ise and Oshiu coasts; the wooded island of Miyajima, with its maple groves, and its fine old temple jutting out into the open sea; the lovely pine-clad peninsula and placid hill-encircled bay of *Ama-no-Hashidate*, or the "Floating Bridge of Heaven;" the weird willow-covered and reed-grown marsh and ancient battle ground of *Asaji-ga-hara*, near the river Sumida;—these, and numerous other familiar and picturesque sights, the landscape gardener is never tired of depicting in his choicest compositions. Seeking in this way inspiration from those natural sources which for countless generations have formed the theme of the poet and the motive of the painter, and around which time has cast a halo of romance, surely it is no idle boast to claim that he can adapt his beautiful art to the highest or lowliest station of life, or frame it in sympathy with whatever sentiment may stir the human soul.

PLATE XXXIV. LARGE LAKE GARDEN.

PLATE XXXV. SOTETSU (CYCAS REVOLUTA) GARDEN.

PLATE XXXVJ. GARDEN OF GINKAKUJI.

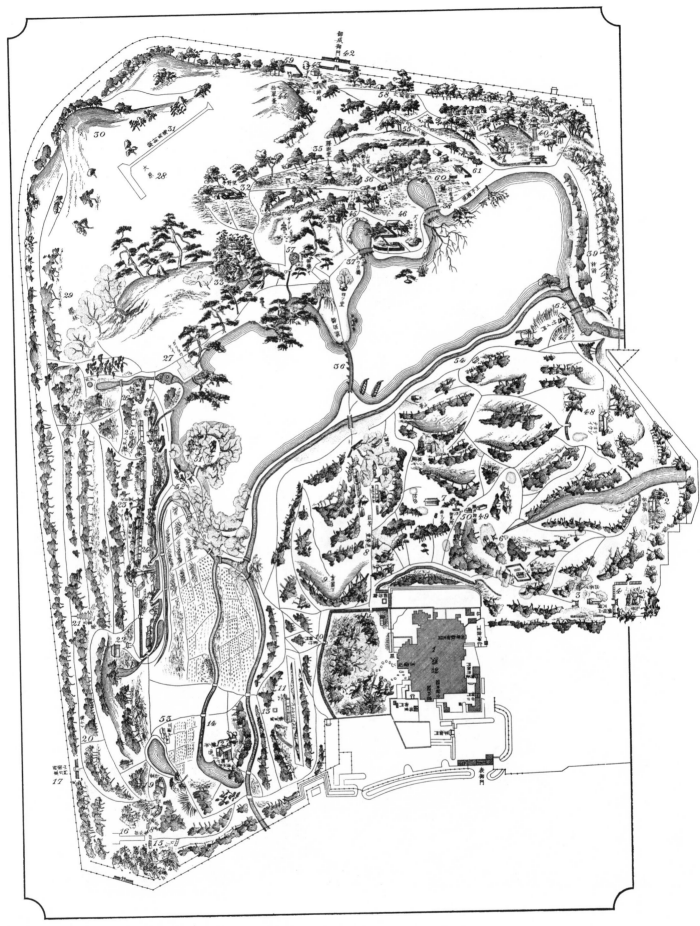

PLATE XXXVII. GARDEN PLAN

Supplement to

LANDSCAPE GARDENING IN JAPAN

Supplement to

LANDSCAPE GARDENING IN JAPAN

by Josiah Conder, F.R.I.B.A.

Dover Publications, Inc., New York

PREFACE.

In the preparation of this Album, which forms a Supplement to "Landscape Gardening in Japan," the writer has availed himself of the skillful collaboration of Mr. K. OGAWA, the well-known Japanese Photographic Artist. The original volume, being of a technical and historical character, has been fully illustrated from native works,—a method of illustration in many cases essential to the proper elucidation of the designs, and, at the same time, one which seemed to provide the best means of conveying the true spirit of the ancient art in all its aspects.

The introduction of modern heliographic plates, side by side with such quaint and idealistic draughtsmanship would have proved inappropriate and misleading, especially as the existing gardens reproduced by the camera are but imperfect and fragmentary examples of a craft comparatively neglected in recent days. At the same time, the illustration in a separate form of some of the best compositions remaining, by the most scientific means available, presented itself as a fitting and desirable addition to the analytical work.

The selection for the present Album has been made from many sources, and some of the photographs were specially prepared for the purpose by Mr. K. OGAWA, by whom all the Collotypes, without exception, have been executed.* The principal object in view has been, within a limited compass, to make the arrangement fairly comprehensive, by illustrating as much as possible the various types of Japanese Landscape Gardens. Descriptions of some examples given may be found at length in Chapter I. of the original work; references are also appended in the text of the present volume, which is therefore limited to a brief notice of the subject of each Plate. A few illustrations of typical natural views have been added in order to render clearer the faithfully representative character of these artificial landscapes.

Tokio, July, 1893.

*In this Dover edition, these plates are reproduced as black-and-white halftones.

CONTENTS.

Supplement to

LANDSCAPE GARDENING IN JAPAN

PLATE I.

SHINOBAZU-NO-IKE, UYENO.

This is a large lotus-lake situated just below the elevated ground now occupied by the Uyeno Park, and containing a prettily wooded peninsula, with a shrine amidst the trees dedicated to the goddess Benten. The conversion of the surrounding shores into a modern race-course within recent years has somewhat destroyed its wild and picturesque character, but, regarded from the neighbouring heights, it still presents a fair example of a particular type of Japanese scenery, often reproduced in the landscape gardens of the country. The lake is said to have been excavated under the direction of the priest Jigen Daishi, in 1625, when a temple was first founded at Uyeno, and with the intention of imitating· on a small scale the famous Lake Biwa, in the province of Omi. The little shrine to Benten,—a goddess specially associated with lakes and lotuses,—originally stood on an island, which was visited from the shore in boats. The causeway which now converts this island into a promontory or peninsula was added in the year 1660. Reed-covered marshes and a wavy sea of emerald lotus leaves,—sprinkled with pink and white at blossom time,—the whole set off by gnarled pine trees, and surrounding wooded bluffs, impart to it considerable natural beauty at certain seasons. The illustration here given has been selected partly to show in detail the mass of graceful undulating lotus leaves contrasted with the pine,— the monarch among the trees of Japan, the soul of nearly every landscape real or artificial, and the emblem in Japanese art of all that is virile and enduring.

Plate I

Shinobazu no Ike, Uyeno.

PLATE II.

SCENERY OF MATSUSHIMA.

The islands off the coast of Oshiu, collectively known as Matsushima, or the Pine Islands, are classed among the three most beautiful sights in Japan. Said to number 808 in all, they vary from imposing masses of considerable dimensions down to mere sea rocks, large and small alike being overgrown with pine trees of picturesque shapes. The neighbouring heights afford a commanding view of the entire archipelago stretching in an irregular line for over forty miles from the town of Shiogama to Kin-kwazan, the parent island of the group. The sheltered coves and bays formed by the innumerable peninsulas and islets impart a tranquil beauty to the scenery, an effect which is enhanced by a light wooden bridge spanning the narrowest channel and tending to convert the whole view into the semblance of a beautiful garden. These volcanic islands with their precipitous sides, rock-strewn beaches, and summits clad with wind-twisted pine trees form the favourite models for the islets of lakes in Japanese gardens. The grounds of the Daimio of Kuwana in Tsukiji, Tokio, formerly contained a number of pine-clad islands representing the scenery of Matsushima, and in numerous smaller gardens the same idea is conveyed by one or two tiny islets scattered in the lake.

Natural Scenery of Matsushima.

Plate II

PLATE III.

ISHIYAMA, LAKE BIWA.

As far back as the middle of the eighth century, a monastery was founded upon this beautiful wooded eminence. Its position on the banks of the Setagawa, just at the point where that river runs into Lake Biwa, gives it the advantage of a commanding view of the surrounding scenery. The spot has become famous as the retreat of the talented authoress Murasaki Shikibu, who, in monastic seclusion and inspired by the lovely prospect of Lake Biwa, here wrote her historical romance-*Genji Monogatari*. Ishiyama, or the Rocky Mountain, receives its name from the colossal natural rocks which project here and there from the rich surrounding soil on which maples and pine trees flourish in great profusion. Notwithstanding their elevation, these quaintly shaped monoliths bear the abrased and excoriated markings peculiar to stones long subjected to the wearing and decomposing action of water. Sea-rocks and river boulders of similar character are extensively used in the landscape gardens of the country, and the ancient rockeries of Ishiyama may be taken as one example amongst many in which this charming peculiarity of Japanese gardening finds its prototype and model in natural scenery. The priests of the temple have taken advantage of these picturesque rock masses to convert the surrounding hill-sides into a beautiful landscape garden on a gigantic scale.

Plate III

Scenery of Ishiyama, Lake Biwa.

PLATE IV.

NATURAL CASCADES, HAKONE.

An example is here shown of a group of cascades called Tamadare-no-taki, situated near Dogashima in the Hakone district, which may be taken as characteristic of different types of waterfalls introduced into landscape gardens. The large fall on the left of the picture pours over a rugged rock surface, and is broken into numerous streamlets curving in different directions. Such cascades are termed by the Japanese "Thread-falls" or "Vermicelli-falls," because thy suggest the tangled lines of floss silk or vermicelli. The Shiraito-no-taki and Somen-no-taki, at Nikko, are famous examples of this class. In the centre of the group is a high precipitous cascade partly veiled by foliage and characteristic of what is termed a "Leaping-fall," of which Kirifuri-no-taki and Kegon-no-taki, near Nikko, are good examples. On the right, is a thin dribbling fall, somewhat after the style called "Linen-fall" owing to the supposed resemblance to a strip of thin white cloth agitated by the wind. The low torrent forming the overflow of the pool below must not be left unnoticed; it is also a favourite feature in landscape gardening, used in combination with either of the higher falls. By a curious fancy it receives the name of the *Me-daki*, or Female Cascade, in contrast to the main waterfall, which, owing to its bolder character, is called the *O-daki*, or Male Cascade. The natural scene here illustrated has been given somewhat the appearance of a garden view, by the addition of a stone lantern and vertical rocks disposed according to the rules of landscape gardening.

Plate IV

Natural Cascades, Hakone.

PLATE V.

HAMA RIKIU GARDEN.

The Imperial garden parties held in the Spring, for viewing the cherry blossoms, have rendered this garden familiar to most residents and visitors. Prior to the Restoration, the site was occupied by the summer palace of the Shogun, called the Hama-goten, or "Palace of the Coast," and it formed a favourite resort during the hot season, situated on the shore of the Tokio Bay. The garden was designed with considerable imagination and skill to suggest famous views in Japan, such as,— Matsushima; the Eight views of Omi; and different coast scenery. "Swallow Tea-house," "Pine-tree Tea-house," "Thatched Tea-house," "Hut of the Salt-coast," "Ocean View Hill," "Fujisan-viewing Hill," "Azuma Arbour," and "Trellissed Arbour" were a few of the names given to particular features of the grounds, some of which remain still intact. The upper illustration of Plate V shows the garden-lake and surrounding hillocks overgrown with evergreens and clipped bushes. In the centre of the lake may be seen one of the pine-clad islets connected to the shores by bridges. The lower illustration exhibits the long double wooden bridge, with intermediate pavilion, which crosses the lake in two right angle lines. The further bridge is roofed with trellis-work, overgrown with wistarias which make a splendid show of flowers in the early summer. A large quantity of cherry trees of single and double blossom, planted on the lawns and hills surrounding the water, now form the chief attraction of this Imperial villa garden.

Hama Rikiu Garden, Lake View.

Plate V *Hama Rikiu Garden, View of Bridge and Trellis.*

PLATE VI.

FUKIAGE GARDEN.

The Kin-En, generally known as the Fukiage Garden, formed originally a part of the grounds of the old Yedo Castle. A historical description noting the various changes through which it has passed is given in "Landscape Gardening in Japan." At present this garden is included within the grounds of the central Palace of the Emperor, and is no longer accessible to the public. The upper illustration on Plate IV. shows a portion of the hill-garden as it existed some few years ago, the centre being occupied by a curious rockery and a cascade consisting of two falls. The upper waterfall leaps from the hill-side into a basin formed by a rocky cliff, and the overflow from this forms the second torrent. Flanking this lower cascade may be observed the "Statue Stone," or "Guardian Stone," fully described in the preceding treatise upon Japanese Gardening; and on the opposite side of the view are two stone lanterns of different designs, one on the hillock, and one on the level below. The foreground is occupied by large *recumbent* rocks and a row of stepping stones leading to the rocky pathway which crosses the hills of the background past another stone standard-lantern of what is called the *Kasuga* shape. The lower illustration shows a portion of the grass-covered moor, or park, of this garden, ornamented with rounded bushes, clumps of handsome trees, and an enormous stone lantern of the "Snow-scene" class. At the side may be seen the end of the Fukiage lake, a small sheet of water, with clipped bushes and a few rocks on its banks.

Fukiage Garden, Rockery and Cascade.

Plate VI *Fukiage Garden, Moor and Lake View.*

PLATE VII.

IKE-NO-NIWA, KIOTO PALACE.

The Ike-no-Niwa, or "Garden of the Lake," in the grounds of the Imperial Palace at Kioto, may be taken as a characteristic though somewhat imperfect example of a Japanese lake-garden. As the surrounding areas partake of the nature of broad gravelled approaches to the different detached buildings of the palace, the expanse of water lacks the charming and natural environment of verdant hills which distinguishes other gardens of this class. A few boulders, evergreen bushes, and trees fringe the stone-faced banks on the palace side, and prettily carved stone and wooden bridges connect the lake-islets with the shores. These islands abound in curious rocks, and dwarf pine trees trained out over the surface of the water: other handsome scoriated rock masses are scattered in the shallows of the lake. In the background of the view given in Plate VII. may be seen the handsome curved roof of one of the Imperial buildings, remarkable, like the gardens surrounding them, for their chaste simplicity as compared with the more elaborate and fantastic style which characterises the old castle palaces of the Daimios. This is but a small portion of the extensive grounds surrounding the ancient Palace at Kioto, which consists of several separate blocks, each having its independent garden in varied style.

Ike-no-Niwa, Imperial Palace, Kioto.

Plate VII

PLATE VIII.

KINKAKUJI GARDEN, KIOTO.

The garden of the Kinkakuji, or Golden Pavilion, is one of the most his-torically interesting spots of the ancient capital, Kioto.   It was laid out in the four-teenth century for the Regent Ashikaga Yoshimitsu as a landscape to surround a palace built for his seclusion.   From this place of retirement, in priestly garb, and ostensibly indifferent to the cares of State, he secretly directed the government of his successor.   A three-storied pavilion richly covered with gold formed the principal feature of the palace; this still remains, bearing traces of its former magnificence.   The lake which surrounds this garden pavilion, now thickly covered with the water-weeds of centuries, was called the "Mirror Ocean," and contained three pine-clad islets shaped to resemble in their outline the principal islands of the Japanese Empire.   Much artifice is said to have been bestowed upon the whole composition, in the grouping of rare trees and rocks, and in adapting the design to the surrounding prospects.   Perhaps the best proof of its original artistic perfection is to be found in the wildly natural aspect which it now bears, time having assisted art in that self-concealment which it is the latter's highest purpose to attain.   As now to be seen, the spot is no longer recognisable as an artificial garden, but resembles rather some romantic watered glen in which man has "built himself a lordly pleasure house."

Kinkakuji Garden, Kioto.

Plate VIII

PLATE IX.

GINKAKUJI GARDEN, KIOTO.

The Regent Yoshimasa, following the example of his predecessor Yoshimitsu, built himself a secluded retreat which he called Ginkakuji, or the Silver Pavilion, and which bore a striking resemblance to the Kinkakuji just described. The landscape-artist, Shoami, is said to have been the designer of the surrounding garden. It bears many traces of the Tea Garden style, which received a great impetus during the rule of Yoshimasa. A lake containing pine-clad islands and rare water-rocks is the principal feature of the grounds; it flows close up to the silver-plated pavilion,— a structure of two stories, and of more modest proportions than the gilded pavilion of Yoshimitsu. A view of the lake and dwelling, as they now remain, is given in the lower illustration of Plate IX., and the upper illustration represents a portion known as the lotus-lake, thickly overgrown with lotus leaves, and crossed by monolithic granite bridges, with an intervening island of rocks and pine trees. A thickly wooded hill in the background imparts a charming beauty to this view. Other interesting features of this old garden are referred to in the writer's previous volume on "Landscape Gardening in Japan."

Lotus Lake, Ginkakuji.

Plate IX

Lake and Pavilion, Ginkakuji.

PLATE X.

TOKUSUI-IN GARDEN, KIOTO.

The Abbot's palaces belonging to the Shinshu Monto sect of Buddhists have always been remarkable for their princely magnificence. That of the Eastern Hongwanji, in Kioto, presents a good example of the luxury displayed in the buildings and surroundings of these establishments. A suite of gorgeously decorated chambers, painted by some of the best artists of the time, and originally forming part of the Regent Hideyoshi's palace at Fushimi, serve as the Abbot's chief reception rooms. In the grounds adjoining may be seen a three-storied building, somewhat resembling in its outline that of the Kinkakuji, and called the Huin-kaku, or "Pavilion of Fleeting Clouds." This, like parts of the Momoyama Palace, was removed from Fushimi, having been presented to the Hongwanji Temple by the great Taiko-Sama. It is round this quaint villa that is constructed the small garden Tokusui-In, a portion of which is represented in Plate X. A narrow lake encircles two sides of the building, crossed in one place by a fantastic wooden bridge, the floor, parapet, and curved roof of which are all gracefully arched. The belt of water widens out in one place and contains a little island adorned with evergreen bushes and rocks, and connected with the opposite shore by bridges formed of granite monoliths. Portions of the banks are thickly planted with maples, pines, and blossoming trees, shading the water and its moss-covered rocks, and producing a delightfully cool effect. The foreground has garden lanterns, curious rocks, and other characteristics of a Japanese landscape garden.

Plate X

Tokusui-In Garden, Kioto.

KORAKU-EN, KOISHIKAWA.

This is the best preserved of the old gardens of Tokio. Its full description, as originally designed for Mitsukuni, the Daimio of Mito, in the seventeenth century, is given in the work "Landscape Gardening in Japan." Most of its original features remain intact, rendering it a very interesting and instructive example; it also has the advantage of being easily accessible to the public. Plate XI. shows an inlet which runs into the lake, representing one of the rivers of Japan, crossed by a bridge consisting of two slabs of granite supported in the centre on stone bearers: its banks are overgrown with grass and bushes, giving it the appearance of a natural stream. In the background may be seen the thickly wooded borders of the lake. Plate XII. illustrates a picturesque view of the lake with an island connected to a rocky islet by a stone bridge consisting of a single slab. Rounded bushes relieve the bareness of the bold rockeries, and other stones lie scattered on the beach of the promontory grouped with a lantern and a number of bushes. The foreground is marked by a handsome old tree of great age, and the island is thickly planted with evergreens. The opposite banks of the lake, planted with an orchard of blossoming fruit trees, may be faintly distinguished. The waterfall which supplies the lake of this garden is illustrated in Plate XIII.

Plate XI

River View, Koraku En, Koishikawa.

Lake View, Koraku En, Koishikawa.

Plate XII

PLATE XIII.

GARDEN CASCADES.

This Plate gives two examples of artificial cascades from noted landscape gardens. Ornamental grounds of any importance are considered incomplete without the introduction of this feature in some form or other. Sometimes no actual fall of water is obtained, but elevated mounds, rocks, and boulders are arranged to indicate the configuration of a cascade. Such a dried-up waterfall may be seen in the garden of the Akasaka Rikiu, as represented in the upper illustration of Plate XIII. In this particular case the resemblance is to a mountain torrent, consisting of a long series of steps, parts being covered with boulders and portions strewn with sand and pebbles. A tall rock, somewhat conical in shape, placed on the right of the principal declivity, represents the "Guardian Stone"—an important accessory of all garden cascades. The "Cliff Stone," also frequently referred to in the technical volume on "Landscape Gardening in Japan," may be easily recognised. The lower illustration represents the cascade of the Koraku-En at Koishikawa, displaying a single broad sheet of water flanked by the "Guardian Stone." The background is thickly wooded, branches of the surrounding trees being arranged so as to partially veil the fall, in accordance with rule. A number of fine rocks are disposed in a natural and interesting manner in the pool below.

Cascade, Akasaka Rikiu.

Cascade, Koraku En, Koishikawa.

PLATE XIV.

DAIMIO OF MITO'S GARDEN, HONJO.

Among the numerous Tokio gardens belonging to the former territorial nobles, that of the Daimio of Mito, at Honjo, illustrated in Plate XIV., is a good example on a small scale. The view given shows a paucity of large trees,—a peculiarity of most Japanese gardens, and especially of those occupying city sites. The greenery consists of dwarf pine-trees, and evergreen shrubs and bushes, with a large quantity of artificial detail in the form of granite lanterns, pagodas, and rocks. In the foreground is a monolithic block of granite, forming a bridge across the stream, and near this is a handsome stone lantern, of what is called the *Snow-scene* class, carried on four stone legs, and with a cap of wide diameter. On the hillock behind may be observed another gigantic lantern of the *Standard* class flanked by several rocks of interesting outline, and surrounded by clipped bushes and dwarf pine trees. A small pagoda, just visible from between the trees, occupies the background, and a rugged flight of stone steps, flanked by rocks and bushes, passes over the brow of the hill. Other small rocks line the banks of the garden stream in the foreground.

Plate XIV

Daimio of Mito's Garden, Honjo.

SATAKE-NO-NIWA, HONJO.

The Satake-no-Niwa is a characteristic example of the more artificial kind of Hill Garden, and is at present easily accessible to the public. It abounds in rare rocks, pagodas, and lanterns, collected by its original owner Mizuno Dewa no Kami. An extensive lake occupies the centre of the grounds, surrounded by hills which are thickly planted with evergreen trees and bushes cut into rounded forms, presenting a great variety of vivid colouring. During the spring and summer, the bright greens of the foliage are set off by red maples, azaleas, and other flowering shrubs. The shores of the lake are spread out at places into sanded and pebbly beaches, crowded with river boulders, rocks, and picturesque stone lanterns. Plate XV. gives a general view of this garden, showing the lake and opposite hillocks, and in the lower illustration of Plate XVI. is shown a corner of the lake, thickly shaded with handsome trees, and over-grown with irises and other water-plants. A rustic looking temple-shrine, with a *Torii*, occupies the background. The upper illustration of Plate XVI. represents a portion of a garden of a similar class at Shinjiku. Here may be seen to perfection the typical Japanese arrangement of garden hills with rounded bushes and lanterns.

Plate XV

Satake no Niwa, Honjo.

Daimio's Garden at Shinjiku.

Plate XVI

Satake no Niwa, Honjo.

PLATE XVII.

HOTTA-NO-NIWA, FUKAGAWA.

Until recent years the Hotta-no-Niwa,—a Tokio garden belonging to the Daimio of Sakura, in the province of Shimosa,—was one of the most elaborate city gardens. Unfortunately it no longer exists, having been broken up and the material conveyed elsewhere. As in almost all first class gardens, an extensive lake formed the central feature. Around this were winding walks and intercepting mounds and hillocks sloping down to the water's edge to terminate in sandy beaches adorned with enormous stone slabs, rocks, and graceful lanterns. The garden hills were covered with a number of evergreen bushes clipped into spherical and trailing shapes, and interspersed with curious rocks and granite standard-lanterns. In the lower illustration on Plate XVII. may be observed the principal vertical rock of the garden, situated in front of the main hillock, in the background. The steps and stones below it are arranged in such a way as to suggest, to those acquainted with the rules of Japanese landscape gardening, the cascade-inlet of the lake. At one point a trellis of wistaria creepers overhangs the water, and on the opposite side a raised gallery forms a cool summer retreat. In the foreground of the upper illustration may be noticed a characteristic leaning pine-tree with an attenuated branch trained over a stone lantern of the *Snow-scene* class. The distance displays a curious stone bridge consisting of long granite slabs supported upon wooden piles driven into the bed of the stream. This garden may be taken as a very good example of the style of Hill Garden formerly very common in the thickly populated districts near the river and canals of Tokio. The water of the neighbouring river is utilised to form the lake, and the noise and unsightliness of the crowded streets outside are excluded by a boundary of high hillocks giving the garden the appearance of a secluded country spot.

Hotta no Niwa, Fukagawa.

Plate XVII

Hotta no Niwa, Fukagawa.

PLATES XVIII. AND XIX.

BOTANICAL GARDEN, KOISHIKAWA.

These grounds, which belong to the Imperial Educational Department, are partially devoted to the cultivation of exotic plants and trees, and are called the Shokubutsu-En, or Botanical Gardens, of Tokio. In consequence of their miscellaneous character, certain portions exhibit the stiff formality of European gardens, but other parts still preserve the purely Japanese style of the original design, as executed a century and a half ago for the Daimio of Sagara,—the original owner of the site. The full page illustration of Plate XVIII. shows a portion of the lake and surrounding hills of the garden, the former covered with water-weed and fringed with rocks and bushes, and the latter clad with coniferous evergreens and rounded bushes. Occasional ornamental rocks, a lantern, and a group of dwarf palms constitute other interesting features of the surrounding areas. Set back amid the shadow of some pine-trees may be seen the *vertical* rocks marking the head of the lake, which near this point is crossed by a granite bridge. Plate XIX. presents another view of the lake, and the grassy mounds surrounding it which carry quite a number of neat rounded bushes. Below, on the same Plate, may be seen a group of lotuses, and other detail in the form of bushes, a stone lantern, and a leaning pine-tree. The illustrations of this garden are produced from photographs taken by Mr. K. Ogawa, and are remarkable as showing with great clearness the delicate detail of the different kinds of foliage in which Japanese gardens abound.

Botanical Garden, Koishikawa.

Plate XVIII

Botanical Garden—View of Lake and Hills.

Plate XIX

Botanical Garden—Bushes and Lotuses.

TSUYAMA GARDEN, TOKIO.

The spot occupied by this garden is of some historical interest, having been presented by Iyeyasu, the first of the Tokugawa Shoguns, to one of his Ministers of State. It afterwards passed into the hands of the Daimio Tsuyama Matsudaira. The present owner is a wealthy silk merchant named Sugimura, but the garden is still known as the Tsuyama Garden. Three views of these grounds are given; the first being taken from across the narrower end of the lake, showing the outlet at the side of the residence, crossed by a wooden bridge. On the further side is a conical hillock shaped to represent Fuji-san, having its slopes adorned with rounded bushes and artificially trimmed pine-trees. This hill has a spur and the intermediate depression is crowded with stones and low bushes, high evergreens occupying the background. The lower view on Plate XX. is taken from in front of the building, looking across the whole length of the lake. Two important features may be observed in the form of peninsulas or promontories jutting out into the water, one in the right foreground, and the other in the distance on the left. Both are provided with a pebble-strewn beach, ornamented with low shrubs, numerous rocks, and a stone lantern. The distant promontory carries in addition a little arbour partly hidden amid trees. This may be considered the principal view of the garden, the further banks of the lake having a large rockery indicating the imaginary source of water. Plate XXI. presents another aspect of this composition, as seen from the opposite end looking towards the residence. It shows more clearly the further promontory with its sea-beach, lantern, and pine-tree stretching out over the water. The lower illustration on this Plate is taken from a public garden at Mukojima, called the Komatsushima Garden, receiving its name from the island of small pine-trees in the centre of the lake. It is somewhat bare and uninteresting in the details, but is given as an example of the more common kind of public garden frequented by holiday-makers.

Garden of the Daimio Tsuyama, Hill View.

Plate XX

Garden of the Daimio Tsuyama, Lake View.

Garden of the Daimio Tsuyama, Lake View.

Plate XXI
Public Garden, Mukojima.

PLATE XXII.

GARDEN AT KOMAGOME.

This beautiful modern park covers the site once occupied by the garden called *Mukusa-no-Sono*, belonging to Yanagisawa, a favourite of the Shogun Tsuna-yoshi Ko. This noble was famous as having risen from the rank of a petty court chamberlain to that of the wealthiest territorial Daimio. The grounds, as extended by their present owner, cover nearly a hundred acres, and comprise,—the lake-garden immediately facing the residence; a winding stream, the banks of which are thickly wooded; numerous plantations of pines, cedars, and other evergreens; groves of blossoming trees; orchards of fruit trees; a duck pond; a vegetable garden; and a model farm. The lake view shown in Plate XXII. is remarkable for its serene and unassuming grandeur. In other gardens of this class a multiplicity of detail, in the form of hillocks, spherical bushes, rocks, and lanterns, creates a restless finical effect which is here altogether absent, being replaced by a dignified repose and stately simplicity. The lawns surrounding the ornamental water are adorned with some magnificent old pine-trees of picturesque shape, and of a size rarely found in such numbers in a single garden; and these, together with a colossal stone lantern, a few shrubs, and rocks judiciously and sparingly arranged, impart a noble scale to the foreground of the composition. In the background may be observed a high *Standing* stone constituting the central feature of the view, but not in this case connected in any way with the water-supply of the lake. The cascade is at the eastern extremity of the lake, tastefully designed to suggest a mountain torrent. In the middle of the wide expanse of water may be seen a group of rocks arranged to form an open archway, in imitation of the hollowed sea-rocks which are seen at various places near the Japanese coast. The lake is also furnished with a pretty wooded island connected to the shore by a simple curved bridge of timber and wattling covered with earth. A single garden hill of considerable height, thickly planted with camellias, azaleas, pines, and oaks, forms an important feature of the background, and commands a fine view of the surrounding garden.

Plate XXII

Garden at Komagome.

GENTLEMAN'S GARDEN, FUKAGAWA.

Fukagawa, one of the busiest and most crowded parts of Tokio, possesses a fine garden, constructed within recent years with all the taste and skill that wealth can command. As in the case of nearly all important grounds, especially those laid out as this is near a river or canal, the controlling feature of the design is a large and irregular lake. Plate XXIII. illustrates what is intended as the principal or central view of the garden from a point immediately in front of the main Japanese residence. In the background is a high garden hill, somewhat conical in form but with an irregular summit, near the base of which the semblance of a stream is produced by a winding bed of broken stones tending to a group of precipitous rocks which indicate the position of a supposed cascade. Here may be recognized the "Guardian Stone," "Cliff Stone," and other essential rocks which always distinguish a garden waterfall. The hill and artificial stream may be taken to express the idea of Mount Fuji and the Fuji-kawa, though the representation is remarkable for great freedom of treatment. In the foreground, on the right, is discovered the beach of one of the peninsulas of the lake, with a magnificent granite lantern, fine scoriated rocks, and a characteristic example of the leaning pine-trees which the gardeners of the country train over the water, and with which these grounds are crowded. The whole perimeter of the lake is ornamented with stones and rocks of great rarity and variety. Plate XXIV. presents another vista of the lake at a point where two of its wooded islets nearly meet, leaving a connecting sand-bank planted with water reeds and rushes. Beyond this beach may be seen a peep of the head of the lake, with the distant Fuji-san and cascade-mouth. This is by far the most picturesque view of the garden, though the effect is said to have been to some extent accidentally produced. In this illustration may be seen a number of the carefully selected rocks which have been collected from various parts of the country.

Gentleman's Garden, Fukagawa, Central View.

Plate XXIII

Plate XXIV

Gentleman's Garden Fukagawa, Lake View.

PLATE XXV.

FUKAGAWA GARDEN.—DETAILS.

The garden just referred to offers several fine examples of the interesting details which characterise designs of the best style. The upper illustration of Plate XXV. shows a peculiar kind of garden bridge which the Japanese call *Rankan-bashi*, or "Bracket Bridge." Such constructions are used over deep streams the beds and banks of which will not admit of piles being driven in. A series of logs is projected from the stone abutments, forming bracket-like arrangements which carry the ends of the principal cross-beams, thereby diminishing the span between the supports. The flooring consists of small chamfered logs laid crossways and fitted close together with their ends projecting. The balustrade is of neat and elegant proportions with end newels of simple design. The lower illustration shows some important features close to the dwelling, including the projecting gallery, called *Nure-En*, and a large date-shaped water-basin of granite which is used with a ladle from this gallery. The water-basin necessitates the sink or drain below, which is rendered artistic by an arrangement of fine boulders and rocks. Close by is placed a magnificent stone standard-lantern, sheltered by a handsome pine-tree trained so that some of its branches cross in front of the fire-box or head of the lantern. The skillful blending of architectural formality with the natural wildness of the garden is well displayed in this illustration.

Bracket Bridge, Fukagawa Garden.

Plate XXV

Lantern and Water Basin, Fukagawa Garden.

PLATE XXVI.

TEA GARDEN, FUKAGAWA.

The lake-garden at Fukagawa, illustrated in Plates XXIII. and XXIV., occupies the principal area of the grounds to the south and west of the Japanese residence. Connected by corridors with the main block of living and reception rooms is a set of Tea Rooms for the practice of the Tea Ceremonial, designed in the frail and delicate style which characterises such *bijou* constructions. The front Tea Room looks out upon a little garden—illustrated in Plate XXV.,—remarkable for its natural loveliness. It has in every respect the semblance of a wild mountain dell deeply shaded with maple trees and evergreens, in the centre of which is a rocky bed resembling the parched channel of a valley rivulet. Among the boulders of this watercourse is a naturally hollowed stone which serves as a water-basin. To the right and left may be seen stone lanterns partly hidden amidst the foliage. The windows of the Tea Room open on a level with the bottom of this hollow, which is enclosed by hills and banks thickly planted and ornamented with occasional rocks and a miniature stone pagoda. Ascending the slopes, a small upper garden is reached, with winding walks of stepping stones, an enormous natural rock, bush-clad hillocks, and surrounding escarps quaintly faced with stone. This area is divided from the lake-garden by a low rustic fence constructed of wood, bamboo, and broom; it is entered by a tiny gateway picturesquely roofed with thatch. This Tea Garden exemplifies to perfection the wild sequestered character which is often given to such garden designs.

Plate XXVI

Tea Garden at Fukagawa.

PLATE XXVII.

GENTLEMAN'S GARDEN, BANCHO.

The garden illustrated in this Plate is that of a gentleman's suburban villa in the district called Bancho. The residence, which is partly one-storied and partly two-storied, is an ordinary middle class dwelling. The grounds are partly turfed, with an earthen walk immediately in front of the building; and, across the turf and beaten earth alike, pathways are formed of large irregular slabs of Nebukawa stone—a kind of schist produced in the neighbourhood of Odawara. In the background may be seen a sunken gravelled basin, representing a stream, crossed by a curved wooden bridge which is connected with the principal line of stepping stones. On the opposite side of this bridge is a low hillock thickly planted with small trees and adorned with a large stone lantern and quaintly shaped rocks. Still further in the background may be seen three other granite lanterns of different shapes, and a stone well-border with a frame made out of a tree-trunk, with a cross-piece, and tiny roof to protect the well-pully. Azalea and olea bushes occupy the foreground, which is simple and somewhat bare in character.

Gentleman's Garden, Bancho.

Plate XXVII
Gentleman's Garden, Bancho.

PLATE XXVIII.

MERCHANT'S GARDEN, FUKAGAWA.

This is a garden attached to one of the numerous villas situated near the Sumida River, in Tokio. The lower illustration shows the garden lake, over which is constructed a trellis for wistarias, carried on props rising from the water. On the opposite banks may be seen the usual dwarf pine-trees and spherical bushes, a number of ornamental rocks, a picturesque lantern, and a little summer-house. Here and there, blossoming trees are planted amid the evergreens. The foreground is occupied by an old bent pine-tree leaning over the water and supported on poles. The upper illustration exhibits some characteristic garden detail, consisting of a stone standard-lantern of the shape called *Kasuga*, an old plum-tree, and a rare specimen of the *Sophora japonica*, entirely hollowed out from age and decay. The common kind of bamboo fence, called *Kenninji*, after a temple of that name, is also shown. The lantern and plum-tree mark the approach to a little shrine reached through a Shinto archway by means of a row of stepping stones.

Merchant's Villa Garden, Fukagawa.

Plate XXVIII

Merchant's Villa Garden, Fukagawa.

PLATE XXIX.

PUBLIC GARDENS.

None of the important towns of Japan are without several public gardens. In many cases the grounds surrounding Shinto shrines or Buddhist temples serve the purpose of a peoples' park. Such healthy holiday resorts, which in Western countries have often been secured by means of public sacrifice and State expenditure, or through private munificence, have, in Japan, been preserved for the people by the necessary *entourage* of religious establishments. The ordinary devotee worships from outside the sacred edifice, and the long paved approaches, the hundred steps, the archways, water sheds, and lanterns are as much a part of the holy accessories as are the painted aisles and chapels of a cathedral interior. The upper illustration of Plate XXIX. shows the grounds surrounding the shrine of Shuzenji, which serve as a public garden at Kumamoto. In the background is the Shinto shrine from which the park receives its name, preceded by its raised ante-court and archway. The lake, of irregular shape, has two islets, one connected with the banks by stepping stones, and one reached from either side by a curved and balustraded stone bridge. Another row of stepping stones crosses the widest portion of the lake. A few pine-trees, rocks, clipped bushes, and stone lanterns add ornament to the grounds. The lower illustration represents a part of the grove surrounding the Shinto-Buddhist shrine of Sanno-sama in Tokio. This is one of the oldest fanes of the city and was in past times specially patronised by the Tokugawa Regents. The triennial festival of Sanno is next to that of Kanda Miojin in splendour and popularity. The spot occupied by this religious establishment consists partly of a high and thickly wooded bluff overlooking the Akasaka district. It is ascended from either side by high flights of steps, is well shaded by fine old trees, and forms a cool and attractive summer resort. The view taken shows a tea-house in the lower part of the grounds, and gives some idea of the rural character of the surroundings.

Public Garden of Shuzenji, Kumamoto.

Plate XXIX

Public Garden of Sanno, Tokio.

PLATE XXX.

TEA-HOUSE GARDENS, OJI.

The suburban tea-houses of the capital possess, in many cases, attractive gardens. At Meguro, a village to the south-west of Tokio, several very good examples may be seen, which are specially visited when the pœonies are in blossom. The Ogi-ya and Ebi-ya, two tea-houses situated on the banks of the Taki-no-gawa,—a stream running through the suburb of Oji,—are much frequented in the spring and autumn. In Japan, buildings for recreation and amusement are by preference placed close to running water, and in many cases are constructed so as actually to overhang a stream, the fondness for water being carried so far that sometimes unhealthy creeks are built over in this manner. The narrow and rapid stream at Oji, shown in Plate XXX., is crossed from the tea-houses by light wooden bridges, and on the opposite bank a strip of land has been laid out as a Hill-garden, in the characteristic native style. Rounded bushes, quaintly trimmed pine-trees, and other evergreens, in addition to rocks, lanterns, and rugged stone steps, combine to produce a very picturesque effect.

Teahouse Garden, Oji.

Plate XXX

Teahouse Garden, Oji.

PLATE XXXI.

OKANO-NO-NIWA, NEGISHI.

This illustration has been given to show the style of a common city tea-house garden, of the poorest class, in which a few simple features, artistically arranged, have been made to do duty as ornament. The upper view shows a rivulet crossed by a bridge constructed of two fine slabs of granite which overlap and are supported in the middle on a wooden trestle built from the bed of the stream. A stone lantern of the *Standard* class, another of the *Legged* class, and a few large rocks and dwarf pine-trees, constitute the chief features of this portion of the grounds. The lower illustration shows the rusticated stone well and pebbled drain-bed, with the forked trunk of a tree to carry the well-pully; also rows of stepping stones leading to the different rooms, a screen fence, and a few old trees. This garden belongs to the class called " Tea-gardens," which have been specially described in " Landscape Gardening in Japan."

Small Teahouse Garden, Negishi.

Plate XXXI

Small Teahouse Garden, Negishi.

MONASTERY GARDENS, NIKKO.

Plate XXXII. is illustrative of the well-known garden of a monastery called the Dainichi-Do, at Nikko. It is situated in a little depression and prettily arranged so as to take advantage of the view of the surrounding hills and woods. A few flowering trees, willows, and pines, are introduced into the grounds, which are for the most part ornamented with formally clipped box, azalea and juniper bushes, here and there trained into the shape of long hedges. The centre is occupied by a miniature lake supplied by an underground spring of the purest water; its deep bubbling pools are surrounded by rocks thickly coated with moss. A red lacquered shrine, dedicated to the god Dainichi, flanks the lake, and several stone lanterns of unusual shape, a miniature stone pagoda, and numerous garden rocks, are grouped together on the banks of the pool. Plate XXXIII. shows the grounds of another monastery at Nikko, known as the Mangwanji. A large lake in front of the main building contains islands representing the crane and tortoise—felicitous emblems in Japanese art. Fine rocks and evergreens adorn the level areas of the garden, which is bordered by clumps of old trees and thick hedges. The lower view given in Plate XXXIII. exhibits the narrow inlet of the lake crossed by a curved wooden bridge, at the side of which are large rounded bushes and a leaning pine-tree. One or two stone lanterns and a detached summer-house may be seen in the background. The lower illustration shows the waterfall, arranged in two low torrents flanked by rocks, and, a life-sized stone statue of Fudo,—the deity to whom all waterfalls in Japan are dedicated,—at the head of the cascade. Two stone pagodas of different shapes may be observed on the surrounding banks, and also a shed from which the view of the cascade can be enjoyed.

Monastery Garden, Dainichi Do, Nikko.

Plate XXXII

Monastery Garden, Dainichi Do, Nikko.

Cascade in Garden of Mangwanji, Nikko.

Plate XXXIII

Monastery Garden, Mangwanji, Nikko.

PLATE XXXIV.

DAIMIO'S GARDEN, KANAZAWA.

Among the numerous provincial gardens of Japan, that originally belonging to Mayeda, Daimio of Kashiu, at Kanazawa, is of considerable importance. Like many of the nobles' gardens in the old castle towns, it has now been converted into a public pleasure resort. The view presented shows the garden waterfall issuing from rocks buried in a wealth of shady foliage. From its base a torrent runs into the lake; and in front of the cascade is a fine marble pagoda of unusual shape and proportions. It is square on plan and consists of three high stories with a small mezzanine between the intermediate roofs. Below the main waterfall may be observed the lower or *female* cascade, an invariable accessory of such features in gardening. A bridge composed of one enormous block of granite spans the neck of the lake, just below the torrent. The thickly planted trees surrounding the cascade impart to the composition a highly natural and rural effect.

Daimio's Garden at Kanazawa.

Plate XXXIV

KORAKU-EN, OKAYAMA.

The town of Okayama, in the province of Bizen, boasts a very handsome garden known as the Koraku-En, which at one time formed a part of the grounds surrounding the military palace of the lords of Bizen. It contains a large lake adorned with two islands and terminating in a stream which winds in a serpentine manner through the garden. Plates XXXV. and XXXVI. exhibit different views of the lake and central island, the latter adorned with a small quantity of effective detail, comprising a handsome granite lantern, a few bold rocks, clipped bushes, and picturesque dwarf pine-trees. The other island is connected by a bridge with the shore of the lake and carries a pavilion, or garden arbour, built overhanging the water's edge. The work "Landscape Gardening in Japan" contains a full description of the principal features of this garden, in which reference is made to its two islands, principal hillocks, iris-pool, enormous rocks, and other interesting features. The wide extent of this composition, combined with the large scale imparted to it by the sparing introduction of bold detail, gives it a park-like simplicity and grandeur somewhat similar to that displayed in the large garden at Komagome, described in the text to Plate XXII. The design is however more formal and artificial than that of the latter, and on this account better illustrates the rules of orthodox landscape gardening. The colossal and grandly proportioned keep of the old castle may be seen towering above the large trees of the garden.

Plate XXXV

Koraku En Garden, Okayama.

Koraku En Garden, Okayama.

Plate XXXVI

Koraku En Garden, Okayama.

PLATE XXXVII.

GARDENS, KIOTO AND AWOMORI.

This Plate has been introduced to show different treatments of vegetation in Japanese gardens. The upper illustration is taken from the garden of the Eastern Hongwanji, a Monastery in Kioto, which is planted with dwarf palms of the *Cycas revoluta* species, called by the Japanese *Sotetsu*. These, together with junipers, azaleas, and other clipped bushes, and fine rocks and boulders, are grouped on either side of a sunken sanded channel constructed to represent a river bed. In one place this bed is crossed by a granite bridge consisting of a single slab. A background is formed of thickly planted trees and rocks, from behind which the imaginary stream appears to issue. This garden is a fine example of the *Kare Sansui*, or "Dried-up Water Scenery," frequently introduced into Japanese gardens, and described at length in "Landscape Gardening in Japan." The lower illustration represents the garden of a merchant at Awomori, and displays a fine example of a Japanese pine-tree of magnificent size, trimmed in the *tama-tsukuri* style. The garden is simple in character, having a small lake edged with rocks, bushes, and water-plants; rows of stepping stones lead from the residence, and a few lanterns and interesting rocks are introduced.

Sotetsu Garden, Hongwanji, Kioto.

Plate XXXVII
Merchant's Garden, Awomori.

PLATE XXXVIII.

GARDEN AT KAGOSHIMA.

A glance at the accompanying illustrations will reveal a special character belonging to this garden, somewhat different from that of other examples. It is one of the gardens of Shimazu, the Daimio of Satsuma, at Kagoshima, and is rather more severe in treatment than the landscape gardens of Tokio. The almost complete absence of large trees and the important part played by high rockeries and artificially clipped bushes impart a quality to the composition, which, though highly refined and artistic, is, at the same time, somewhat austere. The lake, beginning in a wide pool at the base of the highest bush-covered cliffs, assumes a serpentine form and terminates in a narrow stream crossed by a wrought granite slab. The borders of the lake in front of the residence are neatly finished with rocks and stone slabs of a variety of shapes, separated by low spherical bushes and occasional evergreens. At one point, an important group of rocks forms the support to a stone lantern-head. In the background of the lower illustration on Plate XXXVIII. may be observed an elevated rock-basin, backed by a bush-covered rockery and hills, and containing overflowing water. This is the garden cascade, detached in the present instance from the lake, and having its own lower pool or basin with surrounding boulders. In one place, a clump of palms assists in imparting a distinctly tropical appearance to the garden.

Daimio of Satsuma's Garden, Kagoshima.

Plate XXXVIII
Daimio of Satsuma's Garden, Kagoshima.

PLATE XXXIX.

SHIRASE-NO-NIWA, NIIGATA.

This illustration represents a lake-garden which is remarkable for its extreme artificiality and for a preponderance of redundant detail. Nearly all the trees in this design consist of a particular kind of pine, trimmed in the *tama-tsukuri* style,— a method by which each tuft of foliage is cut into a disc-like form. The borders of the irregular lake are crowded with numerous stones and boulders, with shrubs, water-plants, and grasses, planted between them. Though there is constant repetition of similar detail in this design, the arrangement is distinguished by considerable variety. The level walk in front of the residence has a row of stepping stones and a granite lantern; a few turfed hillocks, planted with the ever-recurring pine, and a summer-house, may be seen in the background. A bamboo fence and roofed gateway mark the position of the garden entrance. It is said that the extremely artificial treatment displayed in the trees and rockeries of this example is particularly characteristic of the style of landscape gardening as developed on the Western coast of Japan.

Plate XXXIX

Shirase no Niwa, Niigata.

PLATE XL.

GARDEN ROCKERY, NEDZU.

This Plate is illustrative of an artificial rockery, constructed in the small quadrangle of a suburban tea-house, and designed in imitation of the natural hollowed rocks which abound in different parts of the scenery of the country. Beneath the arch formed by the rock-work winds a little stream leading from the well-drain and supplying a pool provided with a small fountain. Moss, lichen, grasses, small plants, and dwarf evergreens are grown on the rockery, and a miniature stone pagoda decorates the top of the arch. Such artificially constructed rockeries are not very common in Japanese gardening, the preference being always given to single natural stones of interesting shape; but, when occasionally introduced, they are designed in imitation of some object in natural scenery, and in this respect they differ from the meaningless and shapeless conglomerations of stone and slag employed under the name of rockeries in European gardens.

Teahouse Court Garden, Nedzu.

Plate XL

INDEX.